YITSCHAK BEN GAD

The ROADMAP to NOWHERE

Balfour Books

First printing: October 2004

ISBN: 0-89221-578-X
Library of Congress Number: 2003117178

Printed in the United States of America

Please visit our website for other great titles:
www.newleafpress.net

For information regarding author interviews,
please contact the publicity department at (870) 438-5288.

I would like to thank the people who helped make this book a reality. Special thanks go to my wife, Judith Ann, for her good advice, her patience, and her unlimited encouragement. My sincerest appreciation and thanks go to Mr. Dan Abraham, a man of vision and peace, for his generosity; to Esther Levens (Kansas), Patti May (Virginia), and Dr. Maurice Roumani for their dedication, advice, and help. Last, but not least, special thanks to Jim Fletcher, editor-in-chief of Balfour Books. All these distinguished friends have made this book a reality.

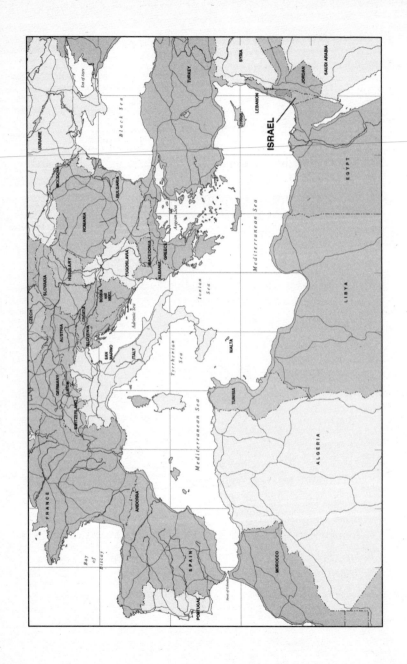

CONTENTS

PART IV — Arafat and the Palestinian Authority: Policy of Lies, Hatred, and Fanaticism

PART V — Arafat's History of Terror against Non-Jews

PART VI — Palestinian State: Strategic and Military Dangers

INTRODUCTION

> *What we have found in Afghanistan confirms that, far from ending there, our war against terror is only beginning. . . . Thousands of dangerous killers, schooled in the methods of murder, often supported by outlaw regimes, are now spread throughout the world like ticking time bombs — set to go off without warning. . . . I will not wait on events while dangers gather. . . . The United States of America will not permit the world's most dangerous regimes to threaten us with the world's most destructive weapons. . . . Our war on terror is well begun. . . . We will win this war, we will protect our homeland, and we will revive our economy.*
>
> U.S. President George W. Bush
> State of the Union address
> January 29, 2002

To many Americans, the terror attacks on the World Trade Center and the Pentagon on September 11, 2001, were unexpected, horrifying nightmares. Some liken the attacks to the atomic bombing of Hiroshima in 1945. Others are reminded of the outset of World War II. To some American Jews, the attacks parallel the destruction of the Jewish temple in Jerusalem about 2,000 years ago.

Many say that the face of the world was irrevocably changed on September 11, 2001. It is clear now to many people the world over that terror can be extremely destructive. Israel, who for years has suffered the consequences of Yassir Arafat's terror and that of the radical Islamic groups, fully sympathizes with the victims of the September 11, 2001, attacks and the American people. Like the Americans, Israel is convinced that the time has come for the world to wake up and to unite in the common goal to fight terror.

This book is the continuation of my previous book, *Politics, Lies and Videotape*. Over the last decade and more — 1991–2003 — sundry different and dramatic events have occurred in the world in general and in the Middle East in particular. In the beginning of 1991, Saddam Hussein of Iraq was defeated and expelled from Kuwait. October 1991 marked the convening of the Madrid Peace Conference. The goal was to achieve peace between Israel and her neighbors. On September 13, 1993, the late Prime Minister of Israel, Yitzhak Rabin, and PLO Chairman Yassir Arafat met at the White House with President Bill Clinton and they signed the Oslo Agreement. Israel recognized the PLO in exchange for the PLO's promise to recognize the State of Israel and to cease using terrorist acts as a means to achieve political gains.

In 1994, Israel and Jordan signed a peace treaty. The years 1996–2000 were marked by innumerable gestures made by Israel, aimed at building confidence among the Palestinians. Israel withdrew from eight Palestinian cities and towns, and over 90 percent of the Palestinian people in the West Bank and Gaza live today under the jurisdiction of the Palestinian Authority. Moreover, Israel has helped the Palestinian Authority economically by permitting thousands of Palestinians to enter into Israel and work. Israel has appealed, time and again, to the world's leaders seeking financial help for the Palestinian economy. Israeli investors have been encouraged to invest in Palestinian projects and joint ventures.

Most significant is the fact that Israel's recognition of Yassir Arafat opened the doors of the White House to the Palestinian leader. He became accepted almost everywhere, the world over.

Despite all his achievements over the last decade, Arafat has proven again and again that his behavior was not that of a statesman, but rather like a gang leader. His promises, whether oral or written, have not been honored. He repeatedly violated signed agreements and he has made the method of double talk a profession. To his people and the Arab world, he would say one thing (in Arabic) and to foreigners he would say something quite different (in English).

Yassir Arafat spoke about peace yet allowed Palestinian terrorists to murder Israelis. The direct result of this has been the indiscriminate killing and maiming of thousands of innocent men, women, and children. In direct violation of the Oslo Agreement, the official Palestinian media has continued to incite the masses against Israel. The official Palestinian Authority media has used anti-Semitism and Islam to sway the Palestinian people, including children, to hate and to kill Israelis and Jews.

Other members of the Palestinian Authority compete with one another with their radical declarations against Israel. These so-called Palestinian leaders are politically blind. They prove, time and again, that they are not true leaders capable of making historical decisions for the betterment of their people. Almost all of them refuse to face reality and to find a compromise with Israel.

Between the years 1993 and 2003, thousands of Israelis have been murdered, or wounded and maimed by Palestinian terrorists in buses, coffee shops, in passenger cars, shopping malls, and on the streets of numerous cities: Jerusalem, Tel Aviv, Netanya, Hadera, Haifa, etc. Throughout these trying years, Israel has asked Yassir Arafat and other Palestinian leaders over and over to put an end to terror and incitement. Israel asked them to honor the agreements Arafat had signed, but to no avail.

In the summer of 2000, the Labor government, under Prime Minister Ehud Barak, met with Yassir Arafat at Camp David. Barak offered unprecedented and far-reaching concessions. He agreed to discussion on the partition of Jerusalem and withdrawal almost to the June 4, 1967, lines — the lines prior to the Six Day War of 1967.

Arafat's answer to these offers on Israel's part was an all-out rejection. Instead, he opened fire and began what he called the "Al-Aksa Intifada" (uprising) in October 2000. As a result, once again, thousands of Israelis and Palestinians were either killed or wounded. Monetary damages have reached billions of dollars to both the Israeli and Palestinian economies.

The "Roadmap" peace plan, endorsed by the United States and others and which was published in 2003, is another attempt to try to bring the Palestinian Authority to face reality, to relinquish terror, and to seek and achieve peace. Judging from the sad past, one cannot be very optimistic about the outcome of these efforts. The Palestinian Authority has not relinquished its illusions about the annihilation of Israel and the establishment of a Palestinian state over all the land from the Mediterranean Sea to the Jordan River.

This book deals with the basics of the Arab-Israeli conflict. It includes some of the developments over the last decade with emphasis on the Palestinian Authority, Bin-Laden's terror, the power and influence of Islam and its attitude towards Christians and Jews, and related issues. Included in this text is some new and original thinking with regard to possible solutions to the Palestinian-Israeli dilemma, the settlements, the Golan Heights, Iraq, Iran, Saudi Arabia, and other topics.

This book is based on a great collection of material from different sources in a number of languages, and especially from the material of the Arab media, newspapers, television, radio, the leading U.S. networks, the Israeli media, the Israeli Foreign Office, and PLO publications (see detailed list in the bibliography at the end of the book). The approach of the book is unique in that it is composed of thousands of short questions, answers, comments, and quotations from various sources dealing with subjects concerning the Middle East.

The goal is to enable the average reader, who may show some interest in our troubled area, to get an idea about most of the subjects without having to strive or to read at great length. The questions and subjects are based upon my selective and subjective discretion. I have no intention of dealing with all aspects of the conflict. The idea is to deal with either forgotten issues or with subjects that may demonstrate the severe dangers posed by terror and which the world in general and Israel in particular are facing today and will be facing in the future. The quotations are meant to strengthen the points dealt with in each chapter.

The future historian who will write the history of the Arab-Israeli conflict will be amazed at his final, sad conclusion: the Jewish state won all the wars imposed upon her by her Arab neighbors, yet, at the same time, Israel lost all the wars of public relations.

Bear in mind that Israel, in territory, is a mere one-sixth of one percent of the huge territory of the 21 Arab states. Despite this fact, Israel is the only country in the world whose natural right to exist is questioned by the majority of her Arab neighbors.

Yitschak Ben-Gad
Netanya, Israel
Fall 2004

PART I:

THE WEST
VIS-À-VIS
ISLAM

CHAPTER I

RADICAL ISLAM — DANGER TO THE WORLD

THE WRITING WAS ON THE WALL

Islamists hate America for what it is, not for the policies it pursues. . . . To all totalitarians, including the Islamic variant, America represents an ineluctable challenge that they must fight. — Daniel Pipes, Mideast expert, *Commentary*, April 2002

On September 11, 2001, the United States was taken by complete surprise. The American people never imagined that terrorists would challenge and provoke the United States and cause such massive destruction on American soil with thousands of casualties.

After the collapse of the Soviet Union, it was clear that the only remaining superpower to lead the world was the United States. America, with its huge economic influence, its great military power, and its political influence around the globe, was believed to be very safe. America's "splendid isolation," set securely between the Atlantic and Pacific oceans, ensured its borders within a buffer zone.

America's "concept" of safety is the main reason behind the United States's passive reaction to the many apparent threats that were to be forthcoming. The enemies of the West in general and the United States in particular were for years preparing their infrastructure and weapons for war. The attack came, yet the United States was unprepared.

> *We must find ways in which to prevent the collection of funds for terrorist organizations which are disguised as charitable organizations.* — Ehud Barak, former Israeli Prime Minister, excerpt of his speech in New York, 1995

Q: Did the enemies of the United States hide their evil intentions?
A: Not at all. The enemies of the United States have overtly and publicly declared their enmity for the West. Time and again, they announced their despise of America. Some proclaimed it a religious duty, as in the *fatwa* (Islamic religious edict) of Osama Bin-Laden, publicized worldwide in February 1998: "To kill the Americans and their allies, civilians, and military is an individual duty for every Muslim who can do it in any country in which it is possible to do it."

Israel has monitored such sentiments in the mosques of Gaza and which were broadcast live by the Palestian Authority: "Wherever you are, kill those Jews and those Americans who are like them — and those who stand by them. They are all in one trench against the Arabs and the Muslims." Radical Islamic countries and organizations such as Hizbullah, Hamas, Islamic Jihad, Iraq, Iran, and others have said again and again that the United States, the Big Satan, and Israel, the Little Satan, are the bitter enemies of the Islamic world.

Q: What has been Iran's position?
A: The Iranians have made anti-American sentiments a national crusade.

In 1994, Hashemi Rafsanjani, the speaker of the Iranian parliament exhorted Islamic militants to "hijack planes . . . or blow up factories in Western countries" and "declare open war on American interests throughout the world."

Q: What has been the attitude of the Islamic fundamentalists to the United States?
A: The *Boston Globe* of September 13, 2001, has the answer: "How often have we seen them burning American flags? How often have

we been demonized as 'the Great Satan'? How often have they attacked U.S. citizens, U.S. embassies, U.S. assets? For at least a decade it has been apparent that the most intense hatred of the United States and its values could be found in the world of Islamist fundamentalism. But too many Americans — and too many of their leaders — preferred not to notice."

Q: Are there examples of Islamic attacks against America?
A: Yes. In the fall of 2000, the USS *Cole*, docked in Yemen, was bombed. Seventeen soldiers were murdered. American embassies were bombed in Kenya and Tanzania in 1998. A total of 224 people were murdered. The barracks of American soldiers in the Khobar Towers in Saudi Arabia were bombed in 1996, with 19 U.S. troops murdered. There was the incident of the car bomb at the U.S. military center in Riyadh, Saudi Arabia. Five people died in that attack. The first bombing of the World Trade Center was in 1993. Six people were murdered.

Q: Is the Palestinian Authority involved in this incitement?
A: Yes. "The Palestinian suicide bombers of today are the noble successors of the Lebanese suicide bombers, who taught the U.S. Marines a tough lesson in [Beirut]. . . . These suicide bombers are the salt of the earth, the engines of history. . . . They are the most honorable among us."[1]

> *When you think about the price you may pay, imagine the resources, energy, determination that you will be forced to pay after a successful terror attack like the fall of one of the twins of the World Trade Center. . . . If we invest only ten percent from this amount before this disaster happens, perhaps this disaster will never happen.* — Ehud Barak, former Israeli Prime Minister, excerpt of his speech in New York, 1995

> *We in Israel have fought against terror for a long time. . . . From my experience I can tell that the challenge of terror is going to be harder in the future. We need a lot of energy, many resources, a determined leadership, and a lot of public support.* — Ehud Barak, former Israeli Prime Minister, excerpt from his speech in New York, 1995

Translated from Arabic, the cartoon reads: "Islam is the solution." The cartoon depicts a knife tearing through three flags of the infidels: the United States, Israel, and Russia. This cartoon was published in a pamphlet of the Palestinian Authority and reprinted by the Israeli Foreign Office in a pamphlet entitled: "The PLO Non-Compliance: Record of Bad Faith," November 2000.

Q: Were there any American experts warning about the forthcoming danger?
A: Yes. Steven Emerson, America's leading expert on Islamic terror, gave a very clear warning which was published in 1997 in the *Middle East Quarterly*. He wrote, "If anything, the threat is greater now than before. . . . The infrastructure now exists to carry off 20 simultaneous World Trade Center-type bombings across the United States."

In May 2000, the *Wall Street Journal* carried an article written by Daniel Pipes and Steven Emerson in which they warned that Al-Qaeda, Osama Bin-Laden's terror network, was "planning new attacks on the US." They also wrote that Iranian officials "helped arrange advanced weapons and explosives training for Al-Qaeda personnel in Lebanon where they learned, for example, how to destroy large buildings."

To Learn from the Tragedies of Others

On October 6, 1973, Israel was attacked by over half a million Egyptian and Syrian soldiers in Sinai and on the Golan Heights, respectively. The results of that war were very severe for Israel. Israel ultimately won the war, but had to pay a very high price for that victory. Approximately 3,000 Israeli soldiers were dead and over 10,000 others were wounded. The monetary damage amounted to billions of dollars. What happened and what led to that surprise attack?

After the smashing victory of the Six Day War in June 1967, many Israeli politicians, and especially military personnel, concluded that the Arabs would not begin another war against Israel. The concept was that, after their harsh defeat, it would take the Arabs many years to rebuild their military power to a level in which they could challenge Israel.

Many sundry reports from Israeli intelligence indicated that the Arabs were indeed preparing their military machines for an attack on Israel.

However, the Israeli leaders, relying on their misconception, refused to believe the intelligence findings. The "concept" was much stronger than reality. The surprise attack of the Arab armies on Yom Kippur Day (Day of Atonement) 1973 shook the Israeli people and their self-confidence.

The painful price of that horrible war is still being paid by the Israelis to this very day.

> *What bears no doubt in this fierce Judeo-Christian campaign against the Muslim world, the likes of which has never been seen before, is that the Muslims must prepare all the possible might to repel the enemy on the military, economic, missionary, and all other areas. It is crucial for us to be patient and to cooperate in righteousness and piety and to raise awareness to the fact that the highest priority, after faith, is to repel the incursive enemy which corrupts the religion and the world.* — Osama Bin-Laden interview, prior to September 11, 2001

Daniel Pipes, the well-known analyst of Islamic terror, wrote the following:

Many indications point to the development of a large Islamic terror network within the U.S., one visible to anyone who cared to see it. Already in early 1997, Steven Emerson told the Middle East Quarterly that the threat of terrorism is greater now than before the World Trade Center bombing [the first bombing in 1993] as the numbers of these groups and their members expand. In fact, I would say that the infrastructure now exists to carry off twenty simultaneous World Trade Center type bombings across the U.S.[2]

In a different article, Daniel Pipes wrote:

Visit an American university . . . and you'll often enter a topsy-turvy world in which professors consider the United States (not Iraq) the problem and oil (not nukes) the issue.[3]

Dr. Serge Trikovic wrote the following in the *Jewish Political Review:*

Radical Moslems dominate the Islamic life in the United States, to the point that moderates, even if they exist, hardly have a voice. They control every major Moslem organization, including the Islamic Association for Palestine, the Islamic Circle of North America, the Islamic Committee for Palestine, the Islamic Society for North America, the Moslem Arab Youth Association, the Moslem Public Affairs Council, and the Moslem Students Association. They also control a growing majority of groups in the U.S. but whose real purpose is to recruit new members, raise funds, coordinate strategies with other militant leaders, indoctrinate new "foot soldiers" and even participate in training sessions. . . .

When the leader of the nation of Islam visited Iran on the anniversary of the fundamentalist revolution, he declared that, "God will destroy America by the hand of the Moslems. God will not give this honor to Japan or to Europe. It is an honor that He will reserve for the Moslems."[4]

One year later in Harlem, Louis Farrakhan declared:

A decree of death has been passed on America. The judgment of God has been rendered and she must be destroyed.

Arab historian Ameen Paris Rihani said the following:

> *The people of Yemen and Asir are still savage, not one of them would trust his brother. They live in perpetual fear and anxiety. . . . They are like wild beasts which fear everything and everybody that may come near them. As to the Yemen . . . all our people are armed, all fight, and all kill for the least thing. We are very jealous of our rights. . . . If in this village two houses would suddenly engage in a fight, the entire population would split into two parties and join in the fight. War could break out in the village. When it subsides, and only then, would the people ask what the cause of the fighting was. They fight first, and then inquire as to the cause of the fight. This is our way of life in Yemen. We fight our own relatives. The brother would fight his own brother, the son his own father.*[5]

INSTRUCTIONS TO A SUICIDE BOMBER: PRAY AND KILL

> *As Bernard Lewis and other scholars have long noted, Arab cultures despise weakness in an adversary above all. They attacked us on September 11 not because we were strong but precisely because we had failed to strike at earlier terror attacks.* — Review & Outlook, *Wall Street Journal*, March 30, 2003

After the destruction of the World Trade Center in New York on September 11, 2001, the FBI found and published a shocking document translated from Arabic. It was found in the suitcase of Muhammed Atta, one of the suicide bombers. The following is the translated document.

First Stage

The night before: take a shower. On the last night swear to die and refreshen your intentions to do so. You must shave yourself and put perfume on your body. Take a shower and make it clear that you know all the aspects of the "operation."

A. Read the following chapters from the Koran: *Al-taubah* ("the repentant") and *Anfal*.

B. Pray that God will grant you victory over the infidels.

C. Pray that God will give you self-control and that He will make your mission easier and that you will not be exposed before the mission is completed.

D. Purify your soul. Do not think about this world or this life — the time has come to do serious things in life.

E. You should feel complete tranquility because the time that separates you and your marriage in heaven is very short.

F. After your mission is complete, the happy life starts. Then God is satisfied with you and pleasure is permanent.

G. Remember how the few have defeated the many. Bless your body with reading some chapters from the Koran.

H. Check your weapons before you go on your mission. Sharpen . . . your knife. Don't torture the animal before slaughtering it.

Second Stage

On your way to the airport, when the cab brings you there, do not be nervous. Remember your God at all times. All their equipment such as magnetic gates and technology will not stop you because of God's will.

Beware that no one will see or hear your blessing "No God except God."

Do not be confused and do not show any signs of tension or nervousness.

Be happy, relaxed, and optimistic because you are going to fulfill what God wants of you.

God willing, you will spend beautiful time with virgins in Paradise.

God will protect you. He will make your mission easier and will grant you success and self-control.

Third Stage

When on the plane, pray to your God.

On the plane, you should remember that your mission is close to completion.

A. Before boarding, pray to your God again and again and remember that this is a struggle for God's sake.

B. When the plane starts moving down the runway repeat your prayers again and again.

C. When the plane takes off remember your God and the words of his prophet Mohammed.

D. When the confrontation starts, you should behave like champions who refuse to return to this world.

E. When the confrontation starts, scream *"Allahu akbar"* [God is great] because this plants fear in the hearts of the infidels. Remember that Paradise is open for you.

F. Slaughter, but do not torture the people you kill. Do not have mercy on the infidels. If you do, you will be considered a traitor.

G. If there is no alternative, take prisoners. Take them and then kill them.

H. Encourage your partners in the mission again and again. Remind them of God and tell them that this mission is for God's sake.

Seconds before your death, repeat again and again the prayer *"La ilahah illa Allah Umahammadu Rasuluallah"* [There is no other God except God and Mohammed is the messenger of God]. After you complete your mission, we will meet in Paradise.

. . . the roots of Muslim rage . . . go beyond hostility to specific interests or actions or policies or even countries and become a rejection of Western civilization as such, not only what it does but what it is, and the principles and values that it practices and professes. . . . [America the Big Satan is conceived] as innately evil, and those who promote or accept [its values] as the enemies of God [that must be destroyed].
— Professor Bernard Lewis, "Roots of Muslim Rage" essay, 1990

MOTIVES BEHIND THE KILLINGS

Muslims must fight until their opponents submit to Islam. — Koran, Sura 9, verse 5

The letter, hand-written in Arabic and found by investigators after the September 11, 2001, tragedies, includes very detailed instructions for the suicide hijackers. The letter was inclusive, and detailed their behavior from the night before the operation up until their last moments. Regardless of the author, the letter serves as a revealing and penetrating glimpse into the minds of the attackers and the mental state of the suicide hijackers.

It also reveals the thought processes amongst the radical Islamic elements. These are the same elements presently waging war on Western culture in the name of "global *jihad*" (global holy war).

I. Religious Elements

The motives behind the terrorists' killing of the innocent are:

A. to be close to the *sahabah* — companions of the prophet Mohammed in the seventh century C.E. During the preparations for the attacks and during the operation itself, they were to visualize themselves as fighting alongside their ancestors.

B. to further the success of the mission and the acceptance of death in the fighters and to prove the cowardice of their enemies who prefer the present world to the world to come. The idea of heroism is an important element in most of the writings and preachings of these Islamic groups. The suicide hijackers intentionally embraced death and forfeited the things of this world.

C. to liken death in battle — martyrdom — to marriage. This is a recurring concept found frequently in the wills left by Palestinian suicide bombers. It is most likely an element of self-persuasion before the operation along with the idea of 72 beautiful virgins awaiting them in paradise. This is the belief of the *shahid* (martyr).

II. How to Operate

Total obedience was demanded of the hijackers. They were instructed to operate as a team. They were indoctrinated with the belief that they were going to face critical situations which "require strict abiding and obeying 100 percent." The term "obedience" is mentioned several times in the letter. There is a strict warning against being involved in any dispute or desire for personal revenge. First priority was to be given to the communal interest and success of the mission.

The letter also contains a number of operational instructions which cover each stage of the mission and almost every moment of their lives from the night before the attack until the very last seconds.

In the last seconds before zero hour, while facing their targets, they were instructed to pray if possible and to end their prayers with the *shahadah:* "There is no God but Allah and Mohammed is his messenger." This most likely proves that they knew that meeting the target meant their death. The text was obviously phrased for those entering upon a mission from which they would not return: "When the attack comes, hit firmly and strongly as the heroes do, those who do not wish to come back to the worldly life."

III. Indoctrination

These hijackers are different from other devoted radical Islamists who fought in Afghanistan, Chechenya, and Kashmir. The motives for such an operation against the United States is notably vague compared to the local conflicts in secular Moslem regimes in which some of them may have fought. Therefore, it can be assumed that there was a need for constant indoctrination, especially in the days leading up to the attacks. It can be assumed as well that the success of such complicated operations depended on at least a number of the hijackers being told the details of the mission only at the last moment. This is one explanation why there were little if no information leaks to American and European intelligence authorities prior to the attacks.

Most of the hijackers led a life of complete assimilation into Western society. This increased the difficulty in maintaining a high level of readiness to carry out the suicide attacks, even with the known high degree of religious devotion of the Islamic radicals. Among the Palestinians today there are those who are totally devoted to the radical doctrine and fanatic Islamic interpretations of the Hamas and the Islamic Jihad. These groups have carried out over a hundred suicide operations. However, the Palestinians live under a continual regime of conflict, in difficult conditions and under the influence of a large and consistent media and public indoctrination. In a kindergarten run by the Hamas, you can read slogans on the wall that say: "The children of the kindergarten are the *shuhada* [holy martyrs] of tomorrow." Classroom signs in

Gaza's Islamic University and in the *Al-Najah* University in Nablus read: "Israel has nuclear bombs, we have human bombs." Suicide attacks are considered prestigious and acts of heroism, which are given legitimacy and support by Islamic scholars and spiritual leaders. The profile of a potential suicide bomber has changed. Now we find more and more well-educated youngsters volunteering and participating in these suicide missions.

Professor Ariel Merari, expert on Middle East suicide bombings, said the following: "Suicide candidates, when they are chosen by an organization, enter into one end of a production process and in the other end they come out as complete, ready suicides. There is a psychological process of preparation that consists of boosting motivation, pep talks, and the creation of points of no return."

Q: What is the concept of 72 beautiful virgins awaiting suicide bombers in Paradise?
A: In the literature of groups such as Hamas, Hizballah, the Palestinian Islamic Jihad, etc., the concept of 72 "black-eyed virgins" is widely disseminated. The suicide mission is seen as a kind of marriage, *ars al-shahada* (marriage of martyrdom). Since many of the suicide bombers are young and unmarried, and in a traditional society, unmarried men may not even have had sexual relations, the reward of 72 virgins is a significant incentive.

Q: Is this issue mentioned in the instruction letter?
A: Yes. It is mentioned twice in the letter: "Hence, it will be a day with God's permission you will spend it with the most beautiful women in Paradise" and "know that Paradise has been decorated for you with the best of its decorations and ornaments and the most beautiful women are calling upon you come, oh you commander, with the order of God and they have dressed in the best of their attire."

> *I refused and said: my only mother my wedding in this world is the day of martyrdom the day I meet the black-eyed and the blood on my face is my decoration.* — Hizballah poem, cir. 1980s

In 1991, before the onslaught of suicide operations, Hamas published an article concerning the "wedding of martyrdom." It was published in its main official journal, *Filastin al-Muslimah*

(Muslim Palestine). The article serves as an introduction to the doctrine of global jihad. It reads:

> *The whole world is persecuting you and the Satanic powers ambush you. The whole world is your front, and do not exclude yourself from the confrontation. . . . The life of misery prevent you from the meaning of life and turn your life into death. You live as a dead man. . . . We stand today in a crossroad: life or death, but life without martyrdom are death. Look for death and you are given life.*

Q: Why is total discipline among the hijackers of major importance?
A: Total discipline and allegiance were of major importance to the success of the September 11, 2001, attacks since the hijackers were not well informed in Islam. In one part of the instruction letter it is written: "Mention God many times and be learned that the best of mentioning God is reciting or reading the Holy Koran."

Q: Is America mentioned in the letter?
A: Interestingly enough, America is not mentioned by name even once in the letter. This is indeed very odd, especially when the letter is an instruction document for people who are about to sacrifice their lives in a mission aimed at killing Americans. In one paragraph the author refers to the future victims as being part of a "civilization of disbelievers."

IV. True Believers — Never Afraid

Q: What does the letter say about the civilization of the disbelievers?
A: With regard to the civilization of the disbelievers, the author wrote: ". . . for their devices and doors and technology all of it has no benefit in slaughter except with the permission of God. And the believers do not get afraid of it but those who get afraid of it are the agents of the devil . . . those who admire the civilization of the West, those who drink their love and their worship with cold water and were afraid of their equipment which are weak and trivial."

Q: What do the hijackers think of the potential victims?
A: The author uses phrases as if the hijackers are people who are going to slaughter animals. This was most likely chosen so as to preclude any feelings of mercy that the hijackers might feel. The

letter reads: "Check your weapons, before departure, and before you leave. . . . Let everyone of you sharpen his knife and kill his animal." These phrases also indicate the kind of blind hatred that is suited to anyone fighting the devil rather than human beings.

Q: Is there any clue as to the identity of the author of the letter or to which organization he belongs?
A: None whatsoever. It is understandable that the author would wish to cover all tracks leading to the identification of the planners of the attack. It is a fact that no group or individuals claimed responsibility for the attacks. In similar writings in the past there would be at least some hints as to the Islamic trend of the group. However, this was not the case this time.

Careful analysis of the instruction letter of the September 11, 2001, attacks reveals that it intended to give the terrorists a sense of an historic mission, to turn the clock back to the seventh century A.D. and to convince the attackers that they were companions of the Prophet Mohammed fighting those same battles.

The conclusion is very grim. The September 11, 2001, tragedies may prove to be a mere hint of things to come. As the American administration has publicly warned several times since those attacks, there may be future Islamic terrorist attacks planned and carried out on Western soil. Most likely these will be carried out by an infrastructure of "programmed terrorists" located within some of the Muslim communities in the West, rather than by those from foreign terrorist camps.

> *The main target of Islamic fundamentalists is the Great Satan, the United States. Israel is just the mini-Satan. The only differences between Bin-Laden and Arafat is we know where Arafat is, and he has better PR.* — Benjamin Netanyahu, former prime minister of Israel, interview on CNN

Premier Ariel Sharon:

> *A little over a decade ago, the American victory in the Persian Gulf War established the necessary conditions for convening the Madrid Peace Conference. It was proved then that security is the prerequisite of peace. Similarly, a victory in the war on terrorism today will provide a new diplomatic basis for a stable Middle East peace.*[6]

They Meant What They Said — The West Refused to Believe It — Kill Americans, Christians, and Jews

Allah send [against] them soldiers they cannot see . . . Allah bring victory to Islam and the Muslims . . . guard the believing leader of Iraq, the symbol of belief and jihad, the leader Saddam Hussein.

We call on Muslims everywhere, and Arabs. We say to them: This is the day of jihad. The jihad has become a personal duty of every Muslim. To refrain from jihad today would constitute a violation of Allah's commands. It is a sin. Long live jihad. — Sheik Abed al-Ghafour al-Qays in his sermon in Abed al-Qadr al-Gaylani Mosque, Baghdad, March 27, 2003[7]

The following document is part of the mounting evidence that links the Bin-Laden network to the September 11, 2001, terrorist attacks on New York and Washington. In this document, Osama Bin-Laden and his associates state that the statement is a *fatwa* (religious ruling) requiring the killing of Americans, both civilian and military. The statement is dated February 23, 1998, and was co-signed by Sheikh Osama Bin-Muhammad Bin-Laden; Ayman al-Zawahiri, amir of the jihad group in Egypt; Abu-Yasir Rifa'i Ahmad Taha, Egyptian Islamic group; Sheikh Mir Hamzah, secretary of the Jamiat-ul-ulema, Pakistan; and Fazlur Rahman, amir of the jihad movement in Bangladesh.

Praise be to God, who revealed the Book, controls the clouds, defeats factionalism, and says in His Book: "But when the forbidden months are past, then fight and slay the pagans wherever ye find them, seize them, beleaguer them, and lie in wait for them in every stratagem (of war); and peace be upon our Prophet, Muhammad Bin-Abdallah, who said: I have been sent with the sword between my hands to ensure that no one but God is worshiped, God who put my livelihood under the shadow of my spear and who inflicts humiliation and scorn on those who disobey my orders."

The Arabian peninsula has never — since God made it flat, created its desert, and encircled it with seas — been stormed by any forces like the crusader armies spreading in it like locusts, eating its riches and wiping out its plantations. All this is happening at a time in which nations are attacking Muslims like people fighting over a plate of food. In the light of the grave situation and the lack of support, we and you are obliged to discuss current events, and we should all agree on how to settle the matter.

No one argues today about three facts that are known to everyone, we will list them, in order to remind everyone:

First, for over seven years the United States has been occupying the lands of Islam in the holiest of places, the Arabian Peninsula, plundering its riches, dictating to its rulers, humiliating its people, terrorizing its neighbors, and turning its bases in the peninsula into a spearhead. If some people have in the past argued about the fact of the occupation, all the people of the peninsula have now acknowledged it. The best proof of this is the Americans' continuing aggression against the Iraqi people using the peninsula as a staging post, even though all its rulers are against their territories being used to that end, but they are helpless.

Second, despite the great devastation inflicted on the Iraqi people by the crusader-Zionist alliance, and despite the huge number of those killed, which has exceeded one million . . . despite all this, the Americans are once again trying to repeat the horrific massacres, as though they are not content with the protracted blockade imposed after the ferocious war or the fragmentation and devastation.

So here they come to annihilate what is left of this people and to humiliate their Muslim neighbors.

Third, if the Americans' aims behind these wars are religious and economic, the aim is also to serve the Jews' petty state and divert attention from its occupation of Jerusalem and murder of Muslims there. The best proof of this is their eagerness to destroy Iraq, the strongest neighboring Arab state, and their endeavor to fragment all the states of the region such as Iraq, Saudi Arabia, Egypt, and Sudan into paper statelets and through their disunion and weakness to guarantee Israel's survival and the continuation of the brutal crusade occupation of the Peninsula.

All these crimes and sins committed by the Americans are a clear declaration of war on God, his messenger, and Muslims. And ulema have throughout Islamic history unanimously agreed that the jihad is an individual duty if the enemy destroys the Muslim countries. . . . Nothing is more sacred than belief except repulsing an enemy who is attacking religion and life.

On that basis, and in compliance with God's order, we issue the following fatwa to all Muslims: the ruling to kill the Americans and their allies — civilians and military — is an individual duty for every Muslim who can do it in any country in which it is possible to do it, in order to liberate the al-Aksa mosque and the holy mosque (Mecca) from their grip, and in order for their armies to move out of all the lands of Islam, defeated and unable to threaten any Muslim. This is in accordance with the words of Almighty God, "and fight the pagans all together as they fight you all together," and "fight them until there is no more tumult or oppression, and their prevails justice and faith in God."

This is in addition to the words of Almighty God: "And why should ye not fight in the cause of God and of those who, being weak, are ill-treated (and oppressed)? — women and children, whose cry is: 'Our Lord, rescue us from this town, whose people are oppressors; and raise for us from thee one who will help!' "

We — with God's help — call on every Muslim who believes in God and wishes to be rewarded to comply with God's order to kill the Americans and plunder their money wherever and whenever they find it. We also call on Muslim ulema, leaders, youths, and soldiers to launch the raid on Satan's U.S. troops and the devil's supporters allying with them, and to displace those who are behind them so that they may learn a lesson. . . . Almighty God also says: "O ye who believe, what is the matter with you, that when ye are asked to go forth in the cause of God, ye cling so heavily to the earth! Do ye prefer the life of this world to the hereafter? But little is the comfort of this life, as compared with the hereafter. Unless ye go forth, He will punish you with a grievous penalty, and

---

put others in your place." Almighty God also says: "So lose no heart, nor fall into despair. For ye must gain mastery if ye are true in faith."

Senator Tom McClintock is quoted:

> *The issue before us is not about vengeance for our murdered countrymen. It is not about bringing anybody to justice. It is not about teaching anybody a lesson. It is about destroying an enemy that has the will — and will soon have the means — to destroy civilization unless we stop them. —* Senator Tom McClintock, *Outpost*, November 2001

The Moslems never hid their intentions to kill Americans. Osama Bin-Laden said the following in an interview prior to the September 11, 2001, tragedy: "Similar is our history with respect to our differences with the Saudi regime; all that has been proved is our joy at the killing of the American soldiers in Riyadh and Khobar, and these are the sentiments of every Muslim. Our encouragement and call to Muslims to enter jihad against the American and the Israeli occupiers are actions which we are engaging in as religious obligations. Allah Most High has commanded us in many verses of the Koran to fight in His path and to urge the believers to do so. Of these are His words: 'Fight in the path of Allah, you are not charged with the responsibility except for yourself, and urge the believers, lest Allah restrain the might of the rejectors, and Allah is stronger in might and stronger in inflicting punishment.' "

The famous Arab historian Ibn Khaldun (1332–1406), in his book *The Muqaddamah (Introduction to History)* described the nature of the Arab nation — the nation of Bin-Laden and his colleagues. He said the following:

> *[The Arabs] are a savage nation, fully accustomed to savagery and the things that cause it. Savagery has become their character and nature . . . it is their nature to plunder whatever other people possess . . . [they] are not concerned with laws, [not concerned] to deter people from misdeeds or to protect some against the others. They care only for the property that they might take away from people through looting and imposts. . . . Under the rule of [the Arabs] the subjects live as in a state of anarchy, without law. Anarchy destroys mankind*

and ruins civilization. . . . It is noteworthy how civilization always collapsed in places the Arabs took over and conquered, and how such settlements were depopulated and the [very] earth there turned into something that was no longer earth. The Yemen where [the Arabs] live is in ruins. . . . The same applies to contemporary Syria. . . .

A Moslem must not take a Jew or a Christian for a Friend. — Koran, Sura 5, verse 54

"Fatwa" — A License to Kill

. . . death as a martyr brings assurance of paradise, rewarded in heaven with 70 virgins, guaranteed by Islamic belief in Allah. To become a martyr is to win the highest approval of family members. A mother says that the death of her son as a martyr was "the happiest day of her life." A father says: "What more could a father ask than to have his son sacrificed to kill the infidels." Both quotes are taken word for word from a video from PA (Palestinian Authority) sponsored TV: "The Story of Child Self-Sacrifice," by Itamar Marcus of Palestinian Media Watch.[8]

The infamous videotape depicting Osama Bin-Laden speaking before a group of unknown participants was released to the public by the Pentagon shortly after its interception in Afghanistan. In that tape, one of the unknown participants is heard saying that the mass killings in the United States on September 11, 2001, were justified. He said that according to Sheick Salman Al-Alwan's view, the attacks against America were proper in the *Shariah* (Islamic Holy Law). Another Islamic religious leader, Abu Hamza, expressed his opinion about Pakistan's nuclear capacity. He said, "If a nuclear bomb is needed to defend the Moslems, we should have it."

In his book, *Terrorist Organizations in the Islamic World*, the author, Abdullah Amami, expresses his opinion about the Tunisian terrorist group called *Alnahda* (the Awakening). This is the organization that toppled the regime of the former Tunisian president Habib Burgiba. The members of this organization acted only once they received a fatwa —a religious edict — instructing them to kill even their own comrades-in-arms if needed in order to overthrow Burgiba's regime. The fatwa given by sheick Zalah Karkar, who included in his edict the assassination of Burgiba himself, if needed.

> *This is a religious war. Make no mistake — their aim is to take over Saudi Arabia and to supplant Israel, turning it into a Palestinian state. The word supplant is particularly important.* — President Bill Clinton, speaking at the Kennedy Center, October 9, 2001

A fatwa is, in reality, a license to kill for a Moslem. It serves to free him from any hesitations he might harbor and frees him from any guilt. In the past, fatwas were given in secret and the organizations that received them were mostly underground organizations. Nowadays, the fatwas are published openly by well-known sheicks. They are published in the mass media: on television, radio, newspapers, the Internet, etc.

These days there is a kind of competition between religious Islamic leaders who will authorize and publish more fatwas calling on Moslems to kill individuals, members of rival groups, and people of different nationalities — men, women, children, and other innocents alike. Any religious leader taking an opposing stand to these edicts to kill would appear weak and frightened to his followers.

In the past, most fatwas were given retroactively. The purpose of this was not to give the victims the chance to defend themselves. The assassination of the former president of Egypt, Anwar Al-Sadat on October 6, 1981, was later justified by some Islamic sheicks. He was murdered before he knew that he was a target. There are some Islamic leaders who think that the late Iranian leader Ayatollah Homeini was mistaken to have publicly published a fatwa calling on Moslems to kill Salman Rushdi.

Homeini claimed that Rushdi, in his book entitled *The Verses of Satan*, mocked Islam. As a result, the "infidel and hostile" West defended and protected Rushdi, who is still alive today. There are many in the Moslem world who believe that Rushdi should have been killed first and then the fatwa released justifying his murder.

> *My prayer is that Saed's brothers, friends, and fellow Palestinians will sacrifice their lives, too. There is no better*

way to show God you love him. — Father of Saed Hotari, suicide bomber who murdered 21 teenagers and wounded 100 others at the Dolphin Disco Club, Tel Aviv, June 1, 2001

The well-known Saudi sheick, Abd Al-Rahman Alhawali, expressed his opinion publicly about Afghanistan's Northern Alliance troops. He declared that they are infidels because they cooperate with the United States in order to topple an Islamic regime — the Taliban. Moreover, he said that a true Moslem can never support non-Moslems in their war against other Moslems. In his opinion, the September 11, 2001, attack on the World Trade Center was a legitimate reaction to U.S. President Clinton's attacks against Al-Qaeda in Afghanistan following the explosion in the U.S. Embassy in Nairobi, Liberia. He also justifies the attack on the Pentagon thusly:

> *The enemy [the United States] conducted against us psychological warfare and found those among us who would listen and spread its [the U.S.'s] values among us. . . . Since when is the Pentagon innocent? The famous American intellectual Gur Widal nicknamed the Pentagon "Hell and Satan's nest," while the World Trade Center is the center of money interests and black money.*[9]

> *The unbelievers [non-Moslems] are your sworn enemies.* — Koran I, Al-Nisa 4:96

> *Kill them wherever you find them. Thus shall the unbelievers be rewarded.* — Koran, Al-Baqara 2:90

Sheick Ali Bin Hudair Al-Hudair publishes his fatwas on the Internet. The following is his published opinion about the September 11, 2001, tragedy. He wrote this for his followers in Yemen:

> *The cry, sorrow and pain for the American victims from the midst of what is described as "innocent people" is very strange. These victims are infidels . . . and you should not feel sorry for them. The American infidel is considered a fighter because of his connection to his government and because he supports his government by money, advice, and opinion as is*

the case in their political regime. . . . It is a duty to kill their
fighters and their non-fighters such as the old man, the blind,
and the foreigners.

These words of Hudair Al-Hudair were later adopted by sheick Yossuf Al-Kardawi. He, in turn, demanded that the Hamas and the Islamic Jihad terrorist groups kill Israelis. Israel believes that at any given time, the Hamas organization has between 5 and 20 young men aged 18 to 23 ready to carry out suicide attacks on Israeli targets. Hamas has publicly claimed to have "tens of thousands" of youths ready to follow the footsteps of these suicide bombers. Hamas representatives have publicly boasted the following: "We like to grow them from kindergarten through college. Israel has nuclear bombs. We have human bombs."

In a poll conducted by the Palestinian Center for Public Opinion, 76 percent of the respondents supported suicide bombings against the Israelis. This same sentiment is widely shared throughout the Arab world. Opinions to the contrary are pathetically few and far between and fall on deaf ears. In mosques, in sermon after sermon and speech after speech, as well as in the Arabic language media, continual praise for the sacrifice of Palestinian children and youths to the national cause is the main theme. "We must educate our children on the love of jihad" (PA official on a sermon broadcast from Gaza).

The results of this indoctrination and suicide training have been felt in the United States as well. The suicide pilots that attacked on September 11, 2001, had similar terrorist training and indoctrination as those terrorists that continually attack Israel. They are one and the same. Across the globe, free nations are experiencing this jihad which intends establishing Islam as the dominant world religion. The "infidels" — Jews and Christians alike the world over — are the targets of this well-planned takeover. Israel, situated amidst 22 totalitarian Arab states, represents Western standards and, therefore, must be eradicated, according to this Islamic doctrine.

. . . terrorizing the American occupiers is a religious and
logical obligation. We are grateful to allah most exalted in
that He has facilitated jihad and His cause for us, against the
Americo-Israeli attacks on the Islamic sanctities. As for their
accusations of terrorizing the innocent, the children, and

*the women, these are in the category "accusing others with
their own affliction in order to fool the masses." The evidence
overwhelmingly shows America and Israel killing the weaker
men, women, and children.* — Osama Bin-Laden in an
interview prior to September 11, 2001

Sheikh Ekrima Sabri, the Palestinian spiritual leader put it
thusly: "Allah will paint the White House black." On another oc-
casion he said, "The Muslims say to Britain, to France, and to all
the infidel nations, that Jerusalem is Arab. We shall not respect
anyone else's wishes regarding her. In another sermon he said, "Allah shall take revenge on behalf of his prophet against the colonialist settlers who are sons of monkeys and pigs."[10]

Osama Bin-Laden: Arch-Terrorist and Murderer of Thousands

*Strike terror into the hearts of the enemies of God and
your enemies.* — Koran, Sura 8, verse 60

On December 13, 2001, the Pentagon released the transcript
of the infamous videotape of Osama Bin-Laden. United States officials say that the contents of the videotape provide additional
evidence that the Al-Qaeda leader is responsible for the September
11, 2001, terror attacks.

The videotape was filmed sometime in mid-November 2001,
and most likely in a location in or around Kandahar, Afghanistan.
The videotape depicts Osama Bin-Laden speaking before a room
of supporters. All those present were aware that the comments
were being videotaped. The conversation centered on their views
about the September 11, 2001, terror attacks in the United States.
The following quotations are excerpts from that videotape:

An unknown sheikh [Moslem religious official]: *You
have given us weapons, you have given us hope and we thank
Allah for you. . . . People now are supporting us more, even
those ones who did not support us in the past, support us more
now. . . . We came from Kabul . . . everybody praises what
you did, the great action you did, which was first and fore-
most by the grace of Allah. This is the guidance of Allah and
the blessed fruit of jihad.*

[Another person's voice can be heard recounting his dream about two planes hitting a big building.]

Osama Bin-Laden: *The difference between the first and the second plane hitting the towers was 20 minutes. And the difference between the first plane and the plane that hit the Pentagon was one hour.*

Sheikh: *They [the Americans] were terrified thinking there was a coup.*

[Note: Ayman Al-Zawahiri (Bin-Laden's deputy) says first he commended Osama Bin-Laden's awareness of what the media is saying. Then he says it was the first time for them (Americans) to feel danger coming at them.]

Unidentified man off camera: *Abd Al-Rahman Al-Ghamri said he saw a vision, before the operation, a plane crashed into a tall building. He knew nothing about it.*

Sulayman (Abu Guaith): *I was sitting with the sheikh in a room, then I left to go to another room where there was a TV set. The TV broadcasted the big event. The scene was showing an Egyptian family sitting in their living room; they exploded with joy. Do you know when there is a soccer game and your team wins, it was the same expression of joy. There was a subtitle that read: "In revenge for the children of al-aqsa, Osama Bin-Laden executes an operation against America." So I went back to the sheikh (meaning Bin-Laden) who was sitting in a room with 50 to 60 people. I tried to tell him about what I saw, but he made gesture with his hands, meaning: "I know, I know. . . ."*

Osama Bin-Laden: *He did not know about the operation. Not everybody knew [. . . inaudible . . .]. Muhammad [Atta] from the Egyptian family [meaning the Al-Qaeda Egyptian group] was in charge of the group.*

Sheikh: *A plane crashing into a tall building was out of anyone's imagination. This was a great job. He was one of the pious men in the organization. He became a martyr. Allah bless his soul.*

Bin-Laden: *The brothers, who conducted the operation, all they knew was that they have a martyrdom operation and we asked each of them to go to America but they didn't know anything about the operation, not even one letter. But they* *were trained and we did not reveal the operation to them until they are there and just before they boarded the planes. . . . Those who were trained to fly didn't know the others. One group of people did not know the other group.*

Bin-Laden (sometime later): *[inaudible] . . . we calculated in advance the number of casualties from the enemy, who would be killed based on the position of the tower. We calculated that the floors that would be hit would be three or four floors. I was the most optimistic of them all. . . . [inaudible] . . . due to my experience in this field, I was thinking that the fire from the gas in the plane would melt the iron structure of the building and collapse the area where the plane hit and all the floors above it only. This is all that we had hoped for.*

Sheikh: *Allah be praised.*

Bin-Laden: *We were at . . . [inaudible] . . . when the event took place. We had notification since the previous Thursday that the event would take place that day. We had finished our work that day and had the radio on. It was 5:30 p.m., our time. I was sitting with Dr. Ahmad Abu-al-Khair. Immediately, we heard the news that a plane had hit the World Trade Center. We turned the radio station to the news from Washington. The news continued and no mention of the attack until the end. At the end of the newscast, they reported that a plane just hit the World Trade Center.*

Sheikh: *Allah be praised.*

Bin-Laden: *After a little while, they announced that another plane had hit the World Trade Center. The brothers who heard the news were overjoyed by it.*

Sheikh: *I listened to the news and I was sitting. We didn't . . . we were not thinking about anything, and all of a sudden, Allah willing, we were talking about how come we didn't have anything, and all of a sudden the news came and everyone was overjoyed and everyone until the next day.*

Bin-Laden (sometime later in the videotape): *. . . [inaudible] . . . when people see a strong horse and a weak horse, by nature, they will like the strong horse. This is only one goal; those who want people to worship the lord of the* *people, without following that doctrine, will be following the doctrine of Mohammed, peace be upon him.*

(Bin-Laden quotes several short and incomplete *hadith* verses, as follows): *"I was ordered to fight the people until they say there is no god but Allah, and his prophet Mohammed."*

"Some people may ask: Why do you want to fight us?"

To sum up, Osama Bin-Laden believed that Islam commands him to kill the innocent. Thousands of Americans paid their lives because of Bin-Laden's wicked and twisted way of thinking.

But politics here was much more than patronage and debate. The major tool of persuasion was the gun, according to those who lived through it. — David Shipler, *New York Times,* July 25, 1982

It is public knowledge now that Osama Bin-Laden was not alone. He had the financial backing which enabled the establishment of the infrastructure of his international network. He has a good number of advisors, assistants, and fanatic Moslems who believe in him and who support him. Some of them are wanted by the United States.

Q: Who is Imad Mugniyah?
A: He is the master of many skills and is very close to Bin-Laden. He built the terrorist infrastructure Al-Qaeda (see the chapter about Mugniyah).

Q: Who is Ayman Alzawahiri?
A: Alzawahiri is considered to be Bin-Laden's second in charge. He is very close to Bin-Laden and was the commander of the military arm of the Islamic Jihad terrorist group in Egypt. His name is affiliated with the assassination of the late Egyptian President Anwar Sadat on October 6, 1981. He was caught and incarcerated for three years. After his release from prison, he went to Afghanistan and fought against the Russians in their war in Afghanistan. Later on, he met Bin-Laden and became his very close friend and advisor.

Q: Who is Ramzi Yossuf?
A: Ramzi Yossuf was brought to trial in the United States and sentenced to life imprisonment for his part in the futile attempt to destroy the World Trade Center in 1993. It is known that Bin-Laden met with Ramzi Yossuf and had connections with him.

Q: Who is Sheikh Abd Al-Rahman?
A: Abd Al-Rahman is the blind Egyptian Moslem spiritual leader who was caught and tried in America as well for his part in the 1993 attack on the World Trade Center. He is a very influential spiritual leader among the Moslems.

Q: What is known about the power of the Al-Qaeda terrorist organization?
A: According to American intelligence sources, the terrorists of Al-Qaeda are spread out in over 50 states and countries across the globe. Thousands of terrorists and splinter groups are affiliated with Al-Qaeda, the majority of which are fanatic and radical Islamic groups.

Q: Who were the terrorists that carried out the destruction of the World Trade Center on September 11, 2001?
A: Most of the terrorists involved in the attack were Saudi citizens. Some were citizens of other Arab countries such as Lebanon, Syria, and Egypt. Bin-Laden himself was born in Yemen, but held Saudi Arabian citizenship until that was revoked by the Saudi authorities.

Q: What were Bin-Laden's claims against the royal Saudi regime?
A: Bin-Laden publicly opposed the Saudi regime because:

1. He considered the U.S. foothold and influence in the kingdom as catastrophic. He considers the Americans to be infidels and whose presence in Saudi Arabia desecrates the holiness of Islamic lands.

2. During the time he held Saudi citizenship, he was a man of great influence in the kingdom. He knew quite well that the regime is corrupted and he felt such corruption was intolerable.

3. He was fully aware that the dictatorship of the Saudi regime repressed any opposition. People were not

permitted to voice any democratic views or to express wishes for change in the Saudi system.

Q: When did the United States attack the Taliban regime in Afghanistan?
A: The World Trade Center and the Pentagon were attacked on September 11, 2001, and the U.S. attack on Afghanistan commenced on October 7, 2001.

> *The prophet Mohammed advises his believers to beware of the Jews: "O true believers, contract not an intimate friendship with any besides yourselves: they will not fail to corrupt you. They wish for that which may cause you to perish: their hatred hath already appeared from out of their mouths; but what their breasts conceal is yet more inveterate. We have already shown you signs of their ill will towards you, if ye understand."* — Covenant of the Islamic Movement, Koran, Family of Imran, verse 118

Islam against Western Civilization

> *Kill them! Allah will answer them through your means! I hope that there are those among you who will kill and be killed!* — Dr. Mahmud Alzahar, a Hamas spokesman[11]

Thousands of innocent people have paid their lives as a result of radical Islamic religious indoctrination and hatred. Many Moslems have become the means by which to spread hatred and in order to kill others.

The tragedies of September 11, 2001, dramatically changed the views of those in the West with regards to the ill-understood "suicide bombers." In the past, such attacks were limited to Jews or Israelis and to the Middle East or Arab-Israeli conflict. The attacks proved to be a well thought-out form of all-out war against the West. Considered the "Great Satan," the West was to be punished for its corrupting effect on the youths of the Moslem world. The glamour of American culture, marred by its materialism, were thought to be leading Moslem youths astray. Moreover, the September 11, 2001, attacks proved a new reality. Suicide bombers are no longer individuals but rather a group of determined terrorists acting in unison to carry out a simultaneous series of hijackings. The hijackers had been groomed for years for the attacks.

In their struggle against Israel, suicide bombings have become the preferred means of Islamic terrorist organizations. Suicide bombers receive encouragement from the well-oiled incitement machines of religious officials as well as from political leaders in the Arab world and leaders of the terrorists groups.

> *Israeli society is a military society, and every person is either a soldier in the Israeli Army or a reserve soldier. This society must be intimidated, until they return to the countries from which they came. When they feel afraid and fearful, they will not feel secure in the country, and we must intimidate and frighten them.* — Sheikh Youssuf Kardawi, top spiritual leader of Moslem Brotherhood and authoritative doctor of Holy Law in Sunni Islam[12]

Incitement to continue terrorist attacks is carried out through a number of channels. There are public pronouncements and calls from religious figures and leaders as well as through the hateful propaganda which reaches the Palestinian society via the educational system and the mass media. The aim is twofold: as an effort to recruit additional volunteers for suicide attacks and as an attempt to establish support and public backing for the suicide bombers and their families from among the Palestinians and others in the Arab world.

The following are just a few examples of leaders inciting suicide bombers:

> *The suicide bombings are a legitimate means through which the Palestinians fight the enemy. Their aim is to serve Allah, and through them, they fight for Allah and for the Islamic faith and homeland. The attacks are the command of Allah.* — Youssef Jamah, Palestinian Minister of Holy Sites, in an interview on Egyptian Television, April 29, 2001

> *They [suicide bombers] embody the salvation from the occupiers of the pure and holy land, the accomplishment of freedom and the return of the dispersed Palestinians to their homeland. The Zionist entity is a cancerous entity and,*

therefore, there is no room for compromise with it. — Sheikh Hassan Nasrallah, the Secretary General of the Hizbullah on Radio Nur, Lebanon, March 31, 2001, calling upon the Palestinians to sacrifice more people and to carry out jihad missions

You [Israelis] have no place here, on the holy land of Palestine. You will never have security in this place, not even on a single centimeter of this land. This is a call for every Palestinian to turn into a time bomb — to fight them with every means at your disposal. — Khalad Mashal, Hamas leader, Reuters, February 16, 2001

The fighters for Allah kill and get killed. Can there be bravery which is superior to that shown by a person who sacrifices himself for his homeland, in order to sow fear, defeatism, death, division, and destruction amongst enemy ranks? — Sheikh Ahmad Yassin, Hamas leader, on Egyptian Television, April 29, 2001

The suicide missions are a legitimate act, and are included within the framework of the jihad in accordance with Allah, if the intention of the person perpetrating it is pure. These actions are one of the most effective means of the jihad. One of the most effective means against the enemies of the faith is to bring about disasters and attacks in their midst . . . in other words, to cause killing and mutilation, and to sow panic in their midst. These actions strengthen the Muslims and their spirit, and breaks the morale of the enemies. — Sheikh Alshaibi, Chairman of the Faculty of Religious Studies, University Bin Saud, Saudi Arabia, from the Lebanese paper *Alhayat*, April 30, 2001

Despite the overwhelming support of suicide attacks amongst Islamic leaders across the globe, there are a few religious figures who reject the religious legitimacy of such attacks. One example is Mufti Alsheikh of Saudi Arabia, who has maintained that suicide attacks have no basis in Islamic law. Sheikh Alzahar of Egypt claims that "if a person blows himself up between people who are fighting him, he is a *shaheed* (martyr), but if he blows himself up between young children, women, or the elderly that take no part in the fighting, he is not a shaheed." In their public responses to Mufti Alsheikh's ruling, the consensus has been to claim that his ruling was incorrect and that it was intended only to serve political ends.

Q: How significant is the support of these Moslem preachers and their hatred for the West among the local populace?
A: Although we hear time and again that these terrorist acts are "un-Islamic" deeds that are performed by "un-Islamic" zealots, there is an overwhelming popularity of these attacks and public support for their perpetrators among the Moslem populace.

Q: How did the masses in the Arab and Moslem world react to the September 11, 2001, attacks on America?
A: Much of the populace in most Moslem countries reacted with great jubilation to the September 11, 2001, tragedies. This is, of course, not necessarily indicative of the Islamic doctrine as such, but it does reflect the depth of the hostilities felt for the West, its wealth, and its values.

Q: Can this be assumed the "across-the-board" sentiment of the Moslem masses?
A: Obviously, there is no way to gauge the predominant sentiment among the masses throughout the entire Islamic and Arab world. However, according to the subsequent press write-ups, the massive public demonstrations, in which pictures of Bin-Laden were displayed with pride, slogans were shouted, and the American (and Israeli) flags and effigies were mutilated and then burned by frenzied crowds, there could be no mistaking the intensity of these feelings of animosity and hatred.

Q: How do these Moslems view the suffering and destruction of non-Moslems?
A: We have witnessed time and again the death and destruction of others being jubilantly celebrated with dancing in the street, with the distribution of candies and expressions of outright delight. It is as if someone's happiness and glory must come at the expense of others' misfortune, and that any success of the West is considered a Moslem failure and vice versa.

Q: Is reciprocity tolerated between Islam and the West?
A: No. Whereas mosques can be and are erected throughout the Christian and Jewish worlds, no churches can be built in Saudi Arabia or Afghanistan. Buddhist symbols were torn down by the Kabul government under the Taliban rule and churches are torched or blown up in Indonesia, Egypt, the Sudan, Kosovo, and elsewhere in the Moslem world. No doubt, there is a world of difference between Western values and Moslem values which are enhanced by the fundamentalists among the Moslems.

> *We do not possess the military hardware our enemy possesses. We do not have planes, missiles, or even a cannon with which we can fight injustice. The most effective tool to inflict damage and harm with the least possible losses is operations of this nature. This is a legitimate method based on martyrdom. The martyr gets the privilege of entering Paradise and frees himself from pain and misery.* — Abdallah Shami, head of the Islamic Jihad group, Gaza, 1994, interviewed by Israeli journalists about suicide bombers.

Q: Is there any criticism in Moslem countries with regards to religious fanaticism?
A: Such criticism is almost non-existent. Just the opposite is true. The following is a quote of the chairman of the Arab Writers Association, a group of intellectuals and politicians who set the tone of discourse in the Arab world. He said the following in the *Literary Weekly*, published in Damascus, Syria: "When the Twin Towers collapsed. . . . My lungs filled with pure air, and I breathed deeper than ever before. . . . Something has collapsed in America, and this is the beginning of America's collapse as the sole superpower. . . . This collapse will be followed by the building of a new base for the victory of the oppressed and miserable people. . . ."

> *When America searched for allies in its worldwide endeavor, the staunchest among them can only be counted among democracies whose committed leaders have a staying power based on their legitimacy in government. Tyrants, monarchs, military juntas not only cannot pledge a long-standing and unrelenting support to America, but their very collaboration with the West arouses opposition to both their participation*

in the war effort and to their personal hold on government.
— Raphael Israeli, *Outpost*, February 2002

Q: What is the common denominator of most of the terror organizations in the world?
A: Almost all the terrorist groups in the world are Moslems. All the universal organizations and networks among them are the product of Islamic fundamentalist doctrine.

Q: How is the world divided, according to Islam?
A: Islam divides the world into two: *Dar-al-harb* (the Abode of War) and *Dar-al-Islam* (the Abode of Islam). Islamic fundamentalists use this division to justify their jihad against non-Moslems.

Q: Who were the terrorists involved in the September 11, 2001, attacks in the United States?
A: The great majority of the hijackers were Saudi citizens and the rest were Egyptians. In the aftermath of the attacks, most of the suspects arrested by the FBI were Egyptians and Saudis. These are the very countries that are supposed to be the closest allies of the United States in the Moslem world.

In light of all this, can any objective analyst characterize Islam as a religion of peace? I doubt it.

Of Ishmael, whom the Arabs claim to be their forefather, the Bible reads:

> *And the angel of the Lord said to her, Behold thou art with child and should bear a son and shalt call his name Ishmael because the Lord has heard thy affliction. And he will be a wild man, his hands will be against every man and every man's hand against him.* — Genesis 16:11–12

WAHHABISM: SAUDI ARABIA'S RADICAL AND DANGEROUS FORM OF ISLAM

> *The Saudi-supplied textbooks . . . [in the U.S.] schools state that Muslims are obliged to consider all infidels the enemy. Certain enemies are not even acknowledged in geography class. Wahhabi schools in America are notorious for doctoring maps of the Middle East, and hanging them in classrooms*

— with Israel blotted out. — Susan Katz Keating, Front-PageMagazine.com, December 30, 2002

One of God's names is *Wahhab*, namely, the Plentiful. Other names for God are *Alrahaman* (the Merciful), *Alqadir* (the Powerful), *Alnasser* (the Victorious), *Alchakin* (the Wise), etc. In Islam, there are a total of 99 names for God. All the names are mentioned in the Koran.

It is common among religious Moslems to hold a string of beads in their hand called *masbahah*. It is customary to move the beads around the string one by one while mumbling the names of God. If the Moslem is a religious figure, he would repeat all 99 names of God in their proper order.

Collectively, the 99 names of God are referred to as *alasmah alhusnah*, meaning the good names.

Another custom among Moslems is to use the name *abd* (servant) before the name of God: *abd Alrahman* (the servant of the Merciful), *abd Alqadir* (the servant of the Powerful), *abd Alnasser* (the servant of the Victorious), etc. All these names are family names.

There is no other nation that uses the name of God as often as the Arabs. It is part of their venacular. *Wallah* (to swear by God), *inshallah* (God willing), *mashallah* (how wonderful), *yallah* (hurry up), *bismallah* (by the name of God) generally used at the opening of a speech, *hashallah* (God forbid), etc.

Wahhabism was founded by Muhammad Ibn Abd-Al-Wahhab in the 18th century. The movement started in the central area of Arabia. Wahhabism is an extremist, puritanical, and very violent movement that began under the pretense of "reforming" Islam.

Q: What is the connection between al-Wahhab and the house of Saud?
A: An alliance was formed between the house of Saud and al-Wahhab. The religious authority was to be maintained by the descendants of al-Wahhab while the political power would be held by the descendants of al-Saud. This is called the Wahhabi-Saudi axis, which continues to rule to this day.

Q: What is the attitude of Wahhabism to other trends in Islam?
A: From the outset, Wahhabism declared all existing trends In Islam to be unbelief. Traditional Moslems were considered unbelievers subject to robbery, murder, and sexual violation.

Wahhabism has always considered Shia Moslems in a genocidal context — as non-Moslems deserving annihilation. It has continually attacked the traditional, spiritual Islam.

Q: What has been the traditional policies of Wahhabism?
A: Wahhabism has always held steadfast to a two-faced policy with regard to the West. On the one hand, it has always depended on the armed forces of the Christian nations (England, France, and the United States) to help secure its domination in the Arabian peninsula. On the other hand, it would violently attack the Jews, Christians, Hindus, Sikhs, and Buddhists, as well as traditional Moslems, like the Sunnis, the Sufis and Shias throughout the rest of the world.

> *In time, in the Muslim view, all mankind will accept Islam or submit to Islamic rule.* — Bernard Lewis, quoted in FrontPageMagazine.com, December 30, 2002

Q: When did the presence of Western forces begin in Saudi Arabia?
A: The presence of Western troops in Saudi Arabia did not begin with the Gulf War of 1991. The British assisted the Wahhabi-Saudi axis against the Ottomans. Between the years 1946 and 1962, the Americans maintained an air base in Saudi Arabia. Then, in 1979, French paratroopers were deployed to kill Moslems protesting and holed up in the Grand Mosque in Mecca, thereby assisting the Saudis.

Q: How popular is Wahhabism outside the Arab peninsula?
A: Wahhabism is, on the whole, unpopular outside the Arab peninsula. However, wherever there is unrest or trouble, Wahhabism may flourish. For example, the Hamas terrorist group in Israel represents Wahhabism in its purist form. Sundry forms of neo-Wahhabi or ideology that has been Wahhabized have been formidable in Egypt (the Moslem Brotherhood) and in Pakistan. Neo-Wahhabis in both countries are known to have led attacks on other Moslems and other faiths.

> *Wahhabi Islamist extremism today is the soil in which Al-Qaeda and its sister terrorist organizations are growing.* — James Woolsey, former CIA director, quoted in the *Jewish Political Chronicle*, February 2003

Q: How popular is Wahhabism in the United States?
A: A little known fact is that the United States is the only country outside of Saudi Arabia where the Islamic establishment is controlled by Wahhabis. Eighty percent of American mosques are Wahhabi-influenced, even though this does not imply that 80 percent of the worshipers in these mosques are Wahhabis.

> *The Saudis have poured an astonishing sum of money into this effort. Reza F. Safa, author of* Inside Islam, *estimated that, since 1973, the Saudi government has spent some $87 billion to promote Wahhabism in the United States and the Western Hemisphere.* — Susan Katz Keating, FrontPageMagazine.com , December 30, 2002

Q: Why were 15 out of the 19 terrorists who attacked the United States on September 11, 2001, from Saudi Arabia?
A: There are three reasons:

1. Even though no more than 40 percent of the Saudi people consider themselves Wahhabis, the Wahhabi religious leaders have controlled the education system in the kingdom. As a result, all the Saudis have been raised in an atmosphere of violent hatred for other Islamic trends and for other faiths.

2. The Saudi regime has been undergoing deep social upheaval. The movements of protest have been diverted by the ultra-Wahhabi faction of the royal family, toward support of Bin-Laden and his terrorists.

3. There is a polarization in the Saudi kingdom marked by the flagrant hypocrisy between the decadence of the royalty and Wahhabi puritanism. The majority of the young generation wants to be free of Wahhabism altogether. However, there is always a segment of the population that reacts to Saudi hypocrisy, as it has always reacted, by a flight into ultra-radicalism found in Wahhabism.

This explains why 15 out of the 19 hijackers on September 11, 2001, were Saudis. It is the inevitable outcome of the Wahhabi ideology, not, as is commonly assumed, a special tactic by Osama Bin-Laden.

> *The Islamic Saudi Academy (ISA) in northern Virginia forthrightly states that even though it exists on U.S. soil, it is* "subject to the government of the Kingdom of Saudi Arabia."

Students at ISA are not required to study U.S. history or government. They do, however, receive instruction in Wahhabism. — Susan Katz Keating, FrontPageMagazine.com, December 30, 2002

Q: What was the attitude toward Wahhabism in the American media in the United States?
A: For years, the Wahhabis have been granted status by the American media as the main Islamic spokesmen. Interestingly enough, the majority of Moslem immigrants came to the United States to escape extremism. Most are horrified to find that their religion is in the hands of extremists. Before coming to America, they were convinced that the U.S. government would never permit this to happen. Their children are often indoctrinated and radicalized by extremists operating in Moslem schools. This includes Islamic Sunday schools and radical campus groups.

One event on that formidable day (Judgment Day) will be that Muslims will fight and kill Jews. The cowardly Jews will seek refuge behind trees. Much like the trees in the forest scene from The Wizard of Oz, *these trees will become animated and aggressive. They will call out to the righteous: "Oh Muslim, Oh servant of God, here is a Jew hiding behind me. Come here and kill him."* — A student at Islamic Saudi Academy in Virginia, quoted in the *Washington Post*, Susan Katz Keating, FrontPageMagazine.com, December 30, 2002

THE KORAN ON HOLY WAR

There is a legitimate debate if Islam is a religion of peace or one of war. Moslem spiritual leaders across the globe are having great disputes over this issue. Unfortunately, the radical elements in the Islamic world have the upper hand. Most of the Islamic leaders, and especially in the Middle East, support jihad and *shahada* (death for the sake of Allah). The massive destruction caused by Moslem terrorists over the last decade, and which resulted in thousands of innocent victims, were stimulated by these fanatic leaders in the Moslem world.

The following quotations from the Koran are just a few samples of the many verses that encourage Moslems to use force in order to kill and to be killed:

Prescribed for you is fighting, though it be hateful to you. Yet it may happen that you will hate a thing which is better for you; and it may happen that you will love a thing which is worse for you; God knows, and you know not.

They will question thee concerning the holy month, and fighting in it. Say: "Fighting in it is a heinous thing, but to bar from God's way, and disbelief in Him, and the Holy Mosque, and to expel its people from it — that is more heinous in God's sight; and persecution is more heinous than slaying." — Sura 2, The Cow, verse 212

So let them fight in the way of God who sell the present life for the world to come; and whosoever fights in the way of God and is slain, or conquers, We shall bring him a mighty wage. How is it with you, that you do not fight in the way of God, and for the men, women, and children who, being abased, say, "Our Lord, bring us forth from this city whose people are evildoers, and appoint to us a protector from Thee, and appoint to us from Thee a helper"? The believers fight in the way of God and the unbelievers fight in the idols' way. Fight you therefore against the friends of Satan; surely the guile of Satan is ever feeble. — Sura 4, Women, verses 76–77

So do thou fight in the way of God; thou art charged only with thyself. And urge on the believers; haply God will restrain the unbelievers' might; God is stronger in might, more terrible in punishing. — Sura 4, Women, verse 86

Fight and slay the pagans (non-Moslems) wherever you find them. — Sura 9, verse 5

TRACKING TERROR: TERROR NETWORKS IN THE UNITED STATES

The idea that one person's "terrorist" is another's "freedom fighter" cannot be sanctioned. Freedom fighters or revolutionaries don't blow up buses containing non-combatants; terrorist murderers do. Freedom fighters don't set out to capture and slaughter school children; terrorist murderers do. Freedom fighters don't assassinate innocent businessmen, or hijack and hold hostage innocent men, women, and children; terrorist murderers do. It is a disgrace that democracies would allow the treasured word "freedom" to be associated with the acts of the terrorists. — Senator Henry M. Jackson, Jonathan Institute conference on terrorism, Jerusalem, July 1979

Steven Emerson, world-renowned expert on militant Islamic groups and counter-terror investigator has published a new book after having researched these groups over an eight-year period. The book, entitled *American Jihad: The Terrorists Living Among Us* (Free Press), is a detailed account of the origins and activities of militant Islamic groups in America.

In his book, Emerson details the ways in which almost every radical Islamic group in the world has successfully implanted itself in the United States. It is nothing less than paradoxical that while calling for the defeat of Western civilization, especially America and Israel, these same groups and organizations were able to grow and flourish in the West because of its freedom and democracy.

Emerson begins his book by quoting Abdullah Azzam, whose organization is linked with Osama Bin-Laden's Al-Qaeda, in a statement he made in 1988 in Oklahoma City. Azzam said the following: "The jihad, the fighting, is obligatory on you wherever you can perform it. And just as when you are in America you must fast — unless you are ill or on a voyage — so, too, you must wage jihad. The word jihad means fighting only. Fighting with the sword." The September 11, 2001, attacks should not have been so surprising since, in the eight-year period prior to those fateful attacks, there were four murderous assaults by Islamic groups in America. Three more attempts were thwarted in the last minute.

In his book, Emerson details how he managed to investigate the terrorists' monetary sources. He monitored their attacks, and plans exposed their ties to so-called charitable Islamic foundations. He also aided a variety of government agencies in their battle against them.

After years of exhaustive investigation Emerson came to a clear conclusion:

> *The extremists have drowned out the opinions, influence, and voices of moderate Muslims by taking over most of the "mainstream" Islamic organizations in the West. While these*

*extremists claim to speak for all of Islam, in fact, they do not.
. . . The United States has become what I call occupied fundamentalist territory.*[13]

Q: What happened in 1992?
A: In 1992, Steven Emerson worked for CNN and was in Oklahoma City on Christmas. He drove downtown to the city's convention center and happened on a gathering of the Moslem Arab
Youth Association. At first, he was denied entrance into the meeting hall until he posed as a "recent convert" to Islam. Once inside,
he found ". . . a bazaar of vendors hawking all kinds of radical
material. There were books preaching Islamic jihad, books calling
for the extermination of Jews and Christians, even coloring books
instructing children 'How to Kill the Infidel.' "

Q: Once inside, what did Emerson hear?
A: Once inside, Khalid Misha'al, head of Hamas was feverishly
preaching violence. He urged the audience to use jihad against
the Jews and the West. Spontaneous cries of "Kill the Jews" and
"Destroy the West" were distinctly heard from among the audience. Emerson said, "I had heard such declamatory speakers many
times in the Middle East, but it was astonishing to hear it all being
preached here in a Middle American capital such as Oklahoma
City."

Q: Were the Americans aware of this incitement?
A: No. No one was reporting anything about this incitement in
the middle of America's heartland. U.S. law enforcement knew
nothing about the convention.

Q: What happened two months later?
A: Tragically, the World Trade Center underwent its first bombing two months after the notorious convention. Later, it would
be revealed that the conspirators in the attack had attended the
Oklahoma City conference.

Q: What did Emerson decide to do?
A: Steven Emerson was intrigued by the unfolding events and ap-
proached CNN with the idea of composing a one-hour special on
Islamic militants in America. The network rejected the idea. The
Public Broadcasting Service, on the other hand, accepted the idea

and Emerson immediately started to work on the documentary. It was aired in 1994 as "Jihad in America." The film revealed how little was known to American citizens about the terror that was fomenting under their very noses. More disturbing though was the fact that very little was known to the FBI.

Q: What happened in Detroit in 1993?
A: In 1993, a Moslem conference was held in Detroit in which representatives of the Hamas terrorist organization, Palestinian Islamic Jihad and other terrorist groups participated. Oddly enough, a senior FBI agent was asked to address the group. When asked by a participant in the audience on ways to ship weapons overseas, the FBI agent answered that he ". . . hoped any such efforts would be done in conformance with the Bureau of Alcohol, Tobacco, and Firearms guidance." Steven Emerson later revealed that the FBI agent mistakenly believed he was speaking to "some kind of Rotary club."

Q: What was the reaction of American Arabs and Moslems to the film "Jihad in America" which was aired on PBS?
A: The reaction from extremist Islamist groups was harsh and immediate. Those groups were the Council on American-Islamic Relations (CAIR) the American Muslim Council, the American Arab Institute, and the Holy Land Foundation. These groups claimed that the film was an attack on Islam and that its producer was a "Muslim-basher" and an "Islamaphobe."

Q: Did anything change in America as a result of this film?
A: No. Leaders of these groups continued to find their way to the highest echelons of the media and government in America. They were regularly invited to the Clinton White House. They were asked to consult at the State Department and their leaders were featured on the front pages of the country's major dailies. Sadly, as Mr. Emerson put it, "There were many people who just could not see the threat from militant Islam."

Q: What was the direct consequence for Steven Emerson's courageous stance?
A: Soon after the airing of "Jihad in America," federal officials informed Mr. Emerson that a foreign-based Islamic death squad had been dispatched after him. They requested that he immediately

leave his home. The FBI offered to place him in its witness protection program, but Mr. Emerson refused the offer, since that would have marked the end of his project. Instead, he has been living and working under cover while he continues to write and testify before Congress under his own name.

Q: Were others scared off by Moslem militants?
A: Yes. Many reporters and networks, out of fear, have followed the dictates of the Islamic groups. After receiving warnings from an Islamic group, National Public Radio (NPR) banned Mr. Emerson from its microphones. The NPR continues to deny this despite documents from its offices to Islamic groups explaining its "policy" not to allow Mr. Emerson on the air.

Once again, the writing was on the wall. Unfortunately, the American authorities didn't heed the signs that were flashing long before the tragedy of September 11, 2001.

Endnotes

1 *Al-Hayat al-Jadida*, Palestinian Authority official daily.
2 *Jewish Political Chronicle*, September 2001.
3 *New York Post*, November 12, 2002.
4 *Jewish Political Review* February 2003.
5 Ameen Faris Rihani, *Muluk Al-Arab [Kings of the Arabs]*, 3rd edition (Beirut, 1953).
6 *New York Times*, June 9, 2002.
7 *Jerusalem Post*, March 30, 2003.
8 Esther Levens, *Christian Jerusalem Post*, February 2002.
9 *Al Hayat*, London, April 2002.
10 *Jewish Voice*, October 2001.
11 Internet site "Albouaba," April 23, 2001.
12 Al-Jazira Cable TV, Dubai, April 11, 2001.
13 Steven Emerson, *American Jihad: The Terrorists Living Among Us* (New York: Free Press, 2002).

Chapter 2

Fanatic and Radical Islamic Terrorist Organizations and Terrorists

The Islamic Brotherhood: The Source of Fanatic Moslem Organizations

Fanatic Islam is a great threat to the civilized world. Millions of Moslems the world over in general and in the Middle East in particular believe that Western civilization should be liquidated and Islam should control the world. The Western world is witnessing today the gain of power of fanatic Moslem elements — power that was achieved partially in the Western democracies these fanatics wish to destroy. The civilized world did almost nothing to defend itself. Slowly but surely the powers of evil gained power and momentum, part of which was used against the United States on September 11, 2001.

The Islamic Brotherhood was established in 1928 in Cairo, Egypt.

Q: Who was the founder of the Islamic Brotherhood?
A: Hassan Albannah, a fanatic and young Moslem leader was its founder.

Q: What was the platform of this group?
A: To establish a huge Islamic empire, to uproot the Western crusaders and the secular Western culture from the Moslem world, to convert the non-Moslem masses through education and indocrination, and to destroy the Western states whom they consider to be the enemies of Islam.

Q; Does fanatic Islam differentiate between the United States and Israel?
A: The only difference between the United States and Israel, according to fanatic Islam, is in size. America is the "Big Satan" and Israel is the "Small Satan."

Q: Did Albannah have a large following?
A: Yes. At the very beginning, tens of thousands of poor Egyptians accepted Albannah's ideology. He established mosques, schools, sports clubs, and welfare services. Within a ten-year period, over one million Moslems were registered members in the Brotherhood in more than 2,000 branches across Egypt.

Q: Did Albannah act outside of Egypt?
A: Yes. Clergymen, who received their fanatic education in Egypt, were sent to other Arab states with the new ideology. Branches were established in Syria, Sudan, Jordan, and Palestine. Before 1948, when Israel was established, there were 38 branches of the Islamic Brotherhood in Palestine.

Q: How did the Islamic Brotherhood act in Egypt and in other Arab states?
A: In time, the focus was changed from religious and social reform, and the Islamic Brotherhood began establishing terrorist cells. They began purchasing weapons and they became a serious threat to the Arab regimes which they considered to be secular and corrupt.

Q: How are new members accepted into the Brotherhood?
A: New recruits place one hand on the Koran and the other hand on a gun and they swear their allegiance to the organization.

Q: What are some of the slogans of the Islamic Brotherhood?
A: Allah is our God; Mohammed is our leader; the Koran is our constitution; jihad is our way; death for the sake of Allah is our good deed.

At the outset of World War II, Hassan Albannah attempted to contact Germany's dictator, Adolph Hitler, and Italy's dictator, Mussolini. The intention was to topple the Egyptian regime. King Farouk's regime was infamous for its rampant corruption. The Islamic Brotherhood also sought to expel the British forces from Egypt. Followers of the Brotherhood succeeded in murdering some of the key figures in Farouk's regime and a number of politicians all hostile to the Islamic Brotherhood.

The Islamic Brotherhood then established a union. One of its members in the early 1950s was Yassir Arafat.

Hassan Albannah was murdered in 1949 by agents of the Egyptian regime. He was 43 years old.

Q: Who was Albannah's successor?
A: Sayyad Kutub Ibrahim succeeded Albannah in the organization. He had written a number of Islamic books on methods to indoctrinate the masses into joining the ranks of the Brotherhood. His texts became guidance books to members of the Islamic Brotherhood.

The terrorist organization called the Islamic Jihad is a splinter group of the Islamic Brotherhood. The first leader of this organization was Abd Alsalam Faraj, an Egyptian Moslem who was very influenced by writings and texts of Sayyed Kutub Ibrahim.

It is a fact and a point interesting to note that most of the hijackers who hit the World Trade Center and the Pentagon on September 11, 2001, were members of the Islamic Jihad. Members of this same organization assassinated Egyptian President Anwar Sadat on October 6, 1981.

In addition to the Islamic Jihad, the Islamic Brotherhood mothered hundreds of Islamic organizations and movements all over the world. Some of these groups are highly militant and use terrorism against all those whom they consider to be enemies of Islam. Others attempt to achieve the same goals through education or through politics. The latter groups use democratic means by which to achieve the same goals as their militant brethren.

Q: Why was Kutub so effective?
A: Kutub, in addition to his writings, was a very influential spiritual leader. He served as an inspiration to the suicide bombers. He was arrested by the Egyptian authorities.

Q: What were some of his goals?
A: His ultimate goal was to topple the secular Arab regimes. He regarded such regimes as enemies of Islam.

Q: How many books did Kutub write?
A: Kutub wrote 24 books, and the common message in all of the texts was the same and extremely violent. He preached that a true Moslem must struggle, at all cost, to fulfill his mission, even if that means suicide.

Q: What caused Kutub to turn so radical in his views?
A: Kutub spent the years 1948–1950 in the United States. He formed his radical philosophy during that period. He despised the American way of life which he claimed was very materialistic and greedy. He believed that the way of life in the States was a direct threat to Islam. The Egyptian regime of President Gamal Abd Al-Nasser sentenced Sayyed Kutub to death and he was executed on August 29, 1966.

In September 1970, Nasser died and his successor was Anwar Sadat. As a devout Moslem, Sadat was very patient and lenient with the Islamic Brotherhood.

As a splinter group of the Islamic Brotherhood, the Islamic Jihad, led by Abd Alsalam Faraj in Egypt, became a model and inspiration for many other organizations. For example, Fathi Shikaki established the Palestinian Islamic Jihad.

Q: What was Faraj's ideology?
A: He believed that the prophet Mohammed ordered the Moslems to set up the Islamic Kingdom and to restore the Khalifate as in the glory days of the eighth century and the Golden Age of Islam.

Q: What were some of his goals?
A: Like Kutub before him, Faraj believed that the Moslems should first topple secular Arab regimes. Only then could they turn their fight to Western civilization.

Q: What steps did Faraj take to implement his beliefs?
A: He put together a group of radical members and ordered them to topple the Egyptian regime. One of the young leaders who followed Faraj's ideology was Ubud Alzumur. In 1980, Alzumur became the head of the military arm of the Islamic Jihad.

Q: Who are some leading members of the Islamic Jihad?
A: One of them is Ayman Al-Zawahiri. He is the deputy of Osama Bin-Laden and one of those suspected of planning the terrorist attacks at the World Trade Center and the Pentagon on September 11, 2001.

Q: What other organization appeared in the late seventies?
A: The organization called "Algiamia Alislamiah," once again, a group that originated in Egypt.

Q: Who was the leader of this organization?
A: His name was Karm Zahdi. Both men — Faraj as leader of the Islamic Jihad and Zahdi as leader of Algiamia Alislamiah — planned and carried out the assassination of Sadat on October 6, 1981.

Q: Who else was part of the assassination conspiracy?
A: A co-conspirator to the assassination of Sadat was the blind leader, Sheikh Omar Bin Abd Alrahman. He became the spiritual leader and inspiration to many radical fanatic Islamic organizations.

Q: Where is Omar Bin Abd Alrahman today?
A: He is incarcerated in prison in the United States. He was found guilty for his involvement in the futile attempt to destroy the World Trade Center in 1993.

Q: What happened to the murderers of Sadat?
A: Faraj was found guilty and executed. Ayman Al Zawahiri was released from jail after having served a three-year sentence. Twenty years later, Iman Zawahiri is wanted by the FBI for his crucial part in the terror attacks on September 11, 2001. Zawahiri carried many passports: Egyptian, French, Swiss, and others. He is the undisputed leader of the Egyptian Islamic Jihad.

Q: How is Zawahiri connected to Bin-Laden?
A: Zawahiri and his colleagues, who murdered Sadat in 1981, are tough supporters of Bin-Laden's organization, Al-Qaeda (the base). Moreover, they play a major role in Bin-Laden's new organization, the "Islamic Front to Fight the Jews and the Crusaders." Zawahiri's son married Bin-Laden's daughter.

There are hundreds of Moslem organizations all over the world. They are located in Saudi Arabia, Afghanistan, Pakistan, Bosnia, Somalia, Sudan, Yemen, Algeria, Syria, Lebanon, and many other Moslem and Arab countries.

According to U.S. President George W. Bush, there are over 60 branches of Bin-Laden's organization alone, Al-Qaeda, all over the world, including Europe.

THE HAMAS ISLAMIC MOVEMENT

Allah is the target, the prophet is its model, the Koran its constitution, jihad is the path and death for the sake of Allah is the loftiest of its wishes. — slogan of the Islamic Resistance Movement Hamas

I swear by the holder of Mohammed's soul that I would like to invade and be killed for the sake of Allah, then invade and be killed, and then invade again and be killed. — as related by Al-Bukhari and Moslem Article 15, the Covenant of the Islamic Resistance Movement, August 18, 1988

The Hamas movement in Judea, Samaria, the Gaza Strip, and East Jerusalem is a highly fanatic and violent movement. In August 1988, Hamas published the *Covenant of the Islamic Opposition Movement*, in which it elaborated its thoughts and methods on different subjects. In the covenant, it described itself as one of the sections of the Islamic Brotherhood in Palestine.

A slogan of the Hamas Islamic Movement was found on a wall of a school in Taybeh (within Israel proper) on June 5, 1967. Taybeh is known to have a strong group of Hamas followers. The slogan read, "We will make Palestine a cemetery for the Zionist occupiers. God willing."

Q: What are the main concepts of Hamas?
A: The main ideological concepts of the movement are equal to the central trends of the Islamic Brotherhood. They include:

1. The liberation of all of Palestine and its return to the Moslems.

2. The resistance to the "Zionist enemy" and the jihad against the Jews as compulsory for every Moslem.

The aftermath of a suicide bombing in Israel.

3. Complete opposition to any peace initiative, since this may cause Arab-Israeli compromise that would enable the Jews to keep a part of Palestine.

Q: When was Hamas declared illegal?
A: At the end of August 1989, the Hamas movement was declared illegal by the Israeli military authorities. The meaning of this Israeli step was simple. It was illegal to be a member of Hamas, to help it, and to be present at its gatherings. More recently, the Hamas movement was declared a terrorist organization by the George W. Bush administration in early 2002.

Q: When was Hamas established?
A: Hamas was established at the outset of the uprising in December 1987. The movement gained momentum during the uprising in Judea and Samaria, but especially in the Gaza Strip. The leaflets of Hamas call upon the Palestinians to initiate clashes with the soldiers and to cause general disorder.

Q: *Who is the leader of Hamas?*
A: The famous leader of this new movement is Ahmad Yasin, a crippled religious leader who resides in the Gaza Strip. He has been arrested and then freed a number of times. In the spring of 2004, he was killed in Gaza by an Israeli air attack.

Q: *Why is Ahmad Yasin considered to be fanatic?*
A: The supporters of the Islamic Brotherhood conducted a severe struggle against the PLO in the

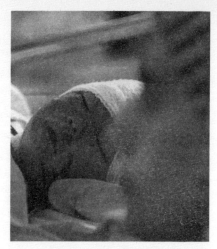

The human toll resulting from the Palestinian terrorism war.

Gaza Strip prior to the uprising. A short time before the uprising, Ahmad Yasin, the Hamas leader and a member of the Islamic Brotherhood, called upon every Moslem to fight Israel. He advocated that the territories be transferred to the United Nations. He established the Hamas military section known as Al-Mujahudoon (the fighters). Sheikh Salach Shahada of Beth Hanoon became the commander of this military arm. A special unit called *MAJD* was set up with one task to do: punish and even murder collaborators.

Q: *When did Israel discover the Hamas was involved in terrorist activities?*
A: At the end of March 1988, Israel discovered that the Hamas organization was involved in terrorist activities. In the Gaza Strip, explosivies, Molotov cocktails, and axes were found in some mosques. At that time, Yasin was arrested.

Q: *What are the differences between the PLO and Hamas?*
A: A deep ideological gap separates Hamas and the PLO. Hamas holds that a Palestinian state must be Islamic with a constitution based on the Koran. Some PLO factions advocate a secular state

for Palestinians that might include factions that are Marxist and atheist. Hamas does not intend to challenge the PLO until the Palestinians are free of the Israelis, but its leaders express no doubt that an armed clash will ultimately come about between Hamas and the PLO.

The Hizballah Terrorist Movement

The terrorist states — Libya, Syria, Iran, and others — offer protection to terrorist organizations, which in turn advance the interests of those states. Would Hizballah's terrorists be so confident in their actions if their bases did not lie in the perimeter of aggressive occupation of Lebanaon? Would Hizballah be able to operate at all without the support of Iran and Syria? — Alexander M. Haig Sr., former U.S. Secretary of State, *New York Times,* August 15, 1989

The Hizballah is one of the most radical Islamic movements in the Middle East. The organization's ideology is based on the rejection of any compromise whatsoever with Israel. According to Hizballah, the only viable solution is military, not political.

The founders of this terrorist group claim that the most important historical event for them was in the year 1982. It was when Israeli forces reached Beirut, the Lebanese capital, in order to expel the PLO terrorists from Lebanon. The Israeli operation was named "Operation Peace for the Galilee," and marked the defeat and humiliation of terrorist groups in Lebanon. Immediately following the operation, the Hizballah was formally established.

Q: What are the goals of the Hizballah?
A: The main goal of the Hizballah is to free Palestine, all of Palestine, including Israel itself, from the Israeli army.

Q: What other factors influenced the establishment of Hizballah?
A: Another factor of major importance to the establishment of Hizballah was the influence of the Islamic Revolution in Iran that was led by the Ayatollah Khomeini of Iran. The revolution occurred in 1979.

Q: Why is Hizballah close to Iran?
A: The Hizballah is an Islamic Shiite movement (Shia is one of the branches of Islam). Almost all Moslems in Iran are Shiite. As

a result, it is only natural for religious ideological indoctrination from Iran to take root in Lebanon amongst Hizballah members.

Q: Are there concrete expressions of Iran's closeness to Hizballah?
A: The Islamic ideological doctrine was very soon translated into direct financial support from the Islamic Republic of Iran, first through its revolutionary guards and then to Hizballah terrorists in Lebanon who were resisting the Israeli occupation militarily.

Q: How does Hizballah view the state of Israel?
A: Hizballah believes Israel to be an arch enemy which has no right to exist. Israel must be destroyed and replaced by an Islamic government in a Palestinian state. Jerusalem is to be the capital of this Palestinian state.

Q: How does the Hizballah regard Israel's withdrawal from South Lebanon in the summer of 2000?
A: Hizballah believes that Israel's withdrawal from South Lebanon marked Israel's defeat at the hands of the Hizballah. They believe that they are the victors and that they forced Israel's withdrawal.

Q: What are the facts concerning Israel's withdrawal from Lebanon?
A: In his 1999 campaign for prime minister of Israel, Ehud Barak promised the Israeli people that if elected he would withdraw from southern Lebanon within a year of his election to premier. His promise was clear and public, and he simply carried out his promise.

Q: What type of terror does the Hizballah use against Israel?
A: The Hizballah has bombed Israeli settlements in northern Israel time and again, as well as attacking Israeli military positions in southern Lebanon until Israel's summer of 2000 withdrawal. Since then, they continue to attack Israeli towns in the north and military installations in Israel proper in the north.

Q: What is Hizballah today?
A: The Hizballah today is one of the smallest political parties in Lebanon with only eight members in the Lebanese parliament.

Hizballah is the direct result of the overall strategy of the late Iranian leader Ayatollah Khomeini, and his successor, Iranian President Rafsanjani. The goal was to export the Islamic Shiite Revolution. War-torn Lebanon, with its lack of public order, coupled with the relatively large number of Lebanese Shiites, provided Iran with the ideal opportunity, which has been fully exploited.

The underlying strategy of the Hizballah is to eventually establish a radical Shiite Islamic republic in Lebanon. Its original political platform in 1985 called for the defeat of "western imperialism" in Lebanon. This was represented by America and France. It also called for the withdrawal of Israeli troops from Lebanon, the complete eradication of the state of Israel, and the ultimate establishment of Islamic rule over Jerusalem.

Q: By withdrawing from Lebanon in 2000 did Israel fulfill United Nations resolutions?
A: Yes. According to U.N. Security Council Resolution 425, Israel was to withdraw from southern Lebanon in its entirety. Israel completed a full withdrawal, checked out and confirmed by the United Nations. The Hizballah continues to insist that the withdrawal was not complete.

Q: What has Hizballah been doing since the Israeli withdrawal?
A: The Hizballah leader in Lebanon, Hassan Nasrallah, has continued to provoke Israel in attempts to cause an Israeli reaction. Following Israel's withdrawal, the Hizballah attacked, kidnapped, and then murdered three Israeli soldiers who were on patrol on Israel's northern border. They then kidnapped an Israeli businessman.

The Hizballah refused any information on the welfare of the soldiers and the businessman and refused to return the soldier's bodies for burial in Israel. Instead, Nasrallah continues to brag in his public appearances about the Israeli "defeat" at the hands of Hizballah in the summer of 2000. This is in addition to the continual attacks and bombings of Israel's northern cities and towns.

Q: What has been Israel's reaction to Hizballah provocation?
A: Israel considers Syria the patron state of Hizballah in Lebanon. Therefore, Israel holds Syria responsible for any attacks or provocations along her northern border. In the past, whenever Hizballah terrorists opened fire on Israel or provoked her, Israel retaliated by attacking Syrian forces in Lebanon.

The meaning of the term "Hizballah" is the "Party of God," and the name is taken from the Koran.

The emblem of the Hizballah depicts an arm raised and holding a machine gun with a quote from the Koran: "And here the party of God's people is winning." The sentence at the base of the emblem reads: "The Islamic revolution in Lebanon."

The middle section reads, "Hizballah," and to the right of the outstretched arm there is a globe, which means that the Islamic revolution is not limited to Lebanon.

Q: What did Iran do to strengthen its influence?
A: The Iranians continue to support Hizballah provocations against Israel from southern Lebanon and along Israel's northern border. Iran's goal is simple: to support the Islamic revolution which Iran exports, and to maintain a foothold in Lebanon. Iran had sent an estimated 5,000 military personnel: soldiers, advisers, trainers, and religious leaders. These Iranians work to indoctrinate the Shiite Moslems residing in southern Lebanon. Most of the Iranians left after having achieved their set goals.

Q: Who is the leader of the Hizballah?
A: The leader is Hassan Nasrallah, born in 1953, and who has been in power since 1992. He is the chairman of Majlas al-Shura (Council of Leadership).

Q: How does the triangle — Syria-Iran-Hizballah — work?
A: Iran and Syria have a special relationship. Iran cannot maneuver in Lebanon without the consent of Syria. Syria maintains troops in Lebanon, and the puppet government of Lebanon can do nothing without the consent of Syria. Syria does not maintain an embassy in Lebanon since Syria considers Lebanon to be an integral part of Syria.

Q: Why do Iran and Syria share such close ties?
A: In the aftermath of the collapse of the Soviet Union in the eighties, Syria lost its main supporter. She then turned toward strengthening her relationship with Iran. This policy has become the main component in Syria's defense program.

Q: What is unique about the Hizballah?
A: Unlike other organizations, Hizballah has established welfare institutions that help the poor Shiite Moslem community in southern Lebanon.

Q: Has the Hizballah had successes in its war against Israel and the United States?
A: Yes. Hizballah, as an agent for Syria, has caused the death and injury of hundreds of Israelis and Americans. They bombed the U.S. Marine headquarters in Beirut, destroying installations and causing the death or injury of hundreds. (This is one of many such attacks. For more details refer to the chapter on Syria and terrorism.)

Q: What are the communications organs of the Hizballah?
A: The Hizballah maintains a newspaper, *Al-Ahd*, a radio station, Al-Nur, and a television station, Al-Manar.

Q: Does Hizballah serve the interests of Iran and Syria?
A: Yes. Iran sees the Hizballah as its outstretched branch which provokes Israel, prevents any peace settlement in the Middle East, and as its partner in spreading the Islamic revolution around the world. The Syrians use the Hizballah to harass Israel, as the force which compelled Israel to leave southern Lebanon and the Golan Heights. Israel completed full withdrawal from Lebanon in the summer of 2000.

Q: How did Israel react to Hizballah provocation?
A: In 1993 and in 1996, Israel reacted militarily to continual Hizballah aggression. In 1993, hundreds of thousands of Lebanese fled southern Lebanon to the north, reaching as far as Beirut.

Q: Who helped Israel in southern Lebanon?
A: The Southern Lebanese Army militia, which included thousands of Christians, Druze, and even Moslems, helped Israel in southern Lebanon. They all wanted to see Syria and Iran out of Lebanese territory.

Q: What are the claims of Hizballah today?
A: Hizballah claims that Israel did not complete her withdrawal from southern Lebanon. The United Nations says just the opposite: that Israel did indeed complete a 100 percent withdrawal. Moreover, the Hizballah uses its support for the Palestinian *intifada* (uprising) as an excuse to continue to provoke Israel.

Q: How does Hizballah refer to Israel and the United States?
A: Israel is referred to as the "Small Satan" and the United States is called the "Big Satan."

Q: What are the religious aspects of the Hizballah opposition to Israel?
A: Israel, according to Hizballah, is considered an infidel state. The Jews, by the Koran, are the enemies of Islam. It is unacceptable to Hizballah that the Jews control Jerusalem, which to Islam is third in importance and holiness after Mecca and Medina.

The late Iranian leader Ayatollah Khomeini declared the last Friday of the month of Ramadan as Jerusalem Day. This has been observed since 1980. The Iranians have made this a day of demonstrations and parades for the sake of Jerusalem and its independence from the "infidel Jews."

Q: How do Hizballah and the Iranians view the September 2000 Palestinian uprising?
A: They see the present uprising as serving the goals of the Islamic revolution. The fight against Israel is not only for the Palestinians, but for all Moslems all over the world.

In January 2002, the general secretary of the Hizballah headed a religious convention in Beirut, Lebanon. Top representatives of Hamas and the Islamic Jihad attended, as well other Moslem clerics from Lebanon, the Palestinian Authority, Sudan, the Arab Emirates, Morocco, Algeria, and Jordan. At the end of the convention, the participants issued an official declaration supporting suicide bombings against Israel. They said that "the suicide attacks against Israel are legitimate according to the Koran." They consider the suicide attacks as "a strategic weapon which enable us to regain the strategic balance with the Zionist enemy."

In reaction to the declarations of the convention, U.S. National Security Adviser Condolezza Rice said the following: "The Lebanese government should do with Hizballah what the United States and other governments are doing with other terrorist organizations: freezing assets, not allowing them to operate freely, not allowing them to run arms freely, not allowing their territory to be used as sanctuary" (January 11, 2002, before the private Lebanese Broadcasting Corporation).

The U.S. State Department also accused the Iranian backed Hizballah of involvement in the arms smuggling ship that was intercepted by Israeli forces in the Red Sea. Hizballah never denied the charges, but has said that none of the crew were members of the organization.

The results of the Beirut convention of Islamic clerics may very well put Lebanon on the U.S. administration's anti-terror campaign list. The convention not only endorsed terrorism as the method by which "the Muslim world defends its honor and dignity," but it also voiced strong opposition to the inclusion of any of the Islamic groups on the U.S. State Department list of terrorist organizations.

The United States has unambiguously warned those regimes that sponsor terrorists that they will not escape punishment. The United States is determined, even if the process takes months or years to complete. The United States regards Hizballah as a terrorist organization, and the FBI has added the name of the former head of Hizballah's operational wing, Imad Mughniya, to the agency's "most wanted list."

All this is a clear signal to Hizballah sponsors — Lebanon, Syria, and Iran — that the United States will no longer accept attacks on civilians as a political tool. The world order changed dramatically on September 11, 2001.

Q: How does Hizballah see terrorist attacks?
A: To the Hizballah, the military and terrorist struggle against Israel is both compulsory and inevitable. Moslems must fight Zionism, and terrorism is the weapon of the weak against "Israeli aggression." Terror and only terror can exhaust Israel and lead to the final victory of the Moslems.

In its war against Israel, the Hizballah has known no limits. Its terrorists have kidnapped hostages, bombed embassies, hijacked planes, and attacked civilians as well as military personnel. In 1992, the Jewish Community Center in Buenos Aires, Argentina, was bombed. Hundreds died or were wounded. The building was razed to the ground. Although never publicly claiming responsibility for the attack, Hizballah was behind the crime.

The spiritual leader of Hizballah, Sheikh Fadlallah, encouraged suicide bombers and the murder of the innocent. He said, "When the goal of the war is just, the rule that prevails says that belief grants the fighter achievement and victory in every situation. The *shahada* (martyrdom) opens the gates of Paradise for him. Victory in the war promises him success in the next world. Death is not a tragedy. The martyr feels spiritual joy in his death."

The Islamic Jihad: Radical Militant Organization

The Islamic Jihad, like other Islamic organizations, bases its platform on radical and twisted Islam. This organization is infamous and known to be extremely dangerous and exceptionally cruel in its terrorist acts against whichever organization or people it deems to be the enemy. The joint goal of the Islamic Jihad factions and the Shiite Moslem terror organizations in Lebanon is the destruction of the state of Israel. This goal underlies the cooperation among these organizations and even leads to the transfer of activists from Palestinian terrorist organizations to factions of the Islamic Jihad.

Q: Where is the Islamic Jihad located?
A: The Islamic Jihad is known to have many cells in several Middle Eastern countries and apparently in Europe as well.

Q: What is the ideology of this organization?
A: All groups included in the Islamic Jihad share a fundamentalist Islamic ideology which espouses jihad against the infidels. The various cells in different countries generally act on their own initiative without coordination even within the same country. The Islamic Jihad is under the powerful ideological and religious influence of the Islamic revolution in Iran.

Q: Who supports the Islamic Jihad?
A: At times there is close collaboration between the Islamic Jihad groups and the Iranian regime. These groups receive aid and guidance from Iran in addition to generous financial support from other Arab and Islamic countries such as Libya, Syria, Sudan, Afghanistan, Pakistan, Saudi Arabia, and the wealthy Persian Gulf oil states. They also cooperate extensively with sundry Palestinian organizations.

Q: What are the aspirations of the Islamic Jihad?
A: The main aspiration of this group is to overthrow secular Arab regimes in order to establish an Islamic pan-Arab empire.

Q: How does the Islamic Jihad view the Jews and Israel?
A: Unique among other Islamic movements, the Jihad views war against the Jews and Israel as an initial essential step toward fulfilling

the goals of Islam. According to the Islamic Jihad, the only way to resolve the conflict with the Jews in Palestine is by direct and violent confrontation.

Q: Where does the Islamic Jihad expect the Jews to go?
A: One of the organization's leaders, Sheikh Tamimi, wrote in 1990. "The Jews have to return to the countries from which they came. We shall not accede to a Jewish state on our land, even if it is only one village" (*The Obliteration of Israel: A Koranic Imperative*, by Tamimi, 1992).

Q: How do they get their message across to the masses?
A: The messages of the Islamic Jihad ideology are disseminated among the activists through sermons in mosques in the territories, in books and articles in newspapers, and political indoctrination in Israeli prisons. It is important to note the spread of Islamic Jihad factions and their ideology amongst fundamentalist elements in the Israeli Arab population.

Q: What are the relations between the Islamic Jihad and the Fatah organization of Yassir Arafat?
A: According to the Islamic Jihad ideology, the "liberation of Palestine" is defined as the first and main objective on the road to an Islamic revolution throughout the Middle East. This has become the link between jihad groups in the territories and Jordan, and between them and Yassir Arafat's Fatah organization. The Fatah has sought to expand its circle of influence and supporters in the territories. It recruits a reserve of young, active personnel, prevents harmful competition within the religious factions and attempts to harness the jihad activists' religious fervor to escalate the "armed struggle."

Q: What caused a severe conflict between the Islamic Jihad and Fatah?
A: The unwritten covenant between these organizations ruptured severely in the wake of Arafat's proclamation of his willingness to recognize Security Council Resolutions 242 and 338. The Islamic Jihad construed this proclamation as recognition of the existence of the "Jewish entity." The harsh criticism that followed from the Islamic Jihad activists against the Fatah led to the termination of the Fatah's assistance and financial support of the jihad groups in the territories.

Q: What makes the Islamic Jihad so dangerous?
A: The fighters in this organization are indoctrinated to die for God's sake. This suicidal strategy is what makes the Islamic Jihad one of the most dangerous organizations of our times.

Q: What are the main differences between the Islamic Jihad and the Hamas?
A: The Hamas movement (military arm of the Palestinian Muslim Brotherhood) claimed that a solution to the Palestinian problem could come about only after an Islamic state would be established outside Palestine. The Islamic Jihad was convinced the order should be reversed: first a Palestinian state.

The Hamas and Islamic Jihad differed with respect to the importance of the Islamic revolution in Iran.

Both organizations differed with regards to the timing of launching jihad against the Jews. The Muslim Brotherhood and the Hamas believed they had to develop their military power in Gaza and the West Bank by first implementing Islamic indoctrination which would lead to the armed struggle. The Islamic Jihad countered that the armed struggle was a divine obligation and should be implemented immediately.

Q: According to the Islamic Jihad, what dangers does Israel pose to Moslems?
A: The Islamic Jihad considers Israel the spearhead of the imperialist West in the heart of the Muslim world. Accordingly, Israel must cease to exist as the first step toward the return of all Moslems to the faith and the establishment of an Islamic state on all Muslim territory. Therefore, the Palestinian problem is central to this Islamic revolution. The jihad groups invoke the attitude toward Palestine in the Koran and in Islamic religious law to support their claims.

No doubt, Iran is the patron and promoter of the Islamic Jihad. In the late 1970s, after having established their status firmly in Iran, the Iranian fundamentalist revolutionaries began to spread the Islamic revolution to areas heavily populated by Shiite Moslems and to other Arab countries. It was for this purpose that Iran set up the Islamic Revolutionary Council. It was instructed to coordinate the activities of pro-Iranian organizations in the various countries.

Just after the outbreak of Operation Peace for Galilee, the first active cells of the Islamic Jihad surfaced in Lebanon. Leaving their bases in West Beirut and the Beka'a Valley in Lebanon, the jihad groups attacked South Lebanese Army targets, the Israel Defense Forces, and Westerners in Lebanon.

To sum up, the Islamic Jihad has been one of the most active terror organizations in the territories and in Israel over the last few years. Its members have stabbed civilians, carried out murderous suicide attacks, such as forcing an Israeli bus off a cliff, have set fields and forests on fire in Israel, and killed Palestinian "collaborators."

AL-QAEDA: WORLD NETWORK OF TERROR

In our internal work in the Israeli intelligence, we spotted Al-Qaeda. Already in 1998, we thought Al-Qaeda to be a very dangerous organization and that it should be the first priority. It is difficult to enter into the core of the organization. It is the terror of zealots with very high motivation, with extreme ideological and sharp thinking, with unusual religious commitment coupled with the complete conviction that their cause is just. This is not the Palestinian terror that we are familiar with — that we can locate its headquarters, its foundation, its various branches and infrastructure. Bin-Laden (Al-Qaeda) is a coalition of many local organizations. This organization is on the move, dispersed and without a territorial base. It emerges, appears, disperses, and spreads. Today it is here and tomorrow it is there. It is very difficult to fight. — Ilan Mizrachi, Vice-Chairman, Israeli Mossad, *Ma'Ariv*, March 28, 2003

Al-Qaeda is one of the most dangerous and cruelest of all terror organizations in the world. The tragic events of September 11, 2001, in New York and Washington, D.C. proved just how dangerous and cruel this organization could be.

Al-Qaeda was established by Osama Bin-Laden in the late 1980s, with the aim of bringing together the Arabs who were fighting in Afghanistan against the Soviet invasion. This organization helped finance, recruit, transport, and train Sunni Moslem extremists for the Afghan resistance.

Q: What was the main goal of this organization?
A: The goal was to establish a pan-Islamic Caliphate throughout the world. This was to be achieved by working with allied Moslem extremist groups to overthrow regimes it considered "non-Islamic." Another goal was to expel Westerners and non-Moslems from Moslem countries.

Q: According to Al-Qaeda, what is the duty of a true Moslem?
A: In February 1998, Al-Qaeda issued a statement under the banner of "The World Islamic Front for Jihad Against the Jews and Crusaders." It was made clear in the statement that it was the duty of all Moslems to kill American citizens — military or civilian — and their allies all over the world.

Q: What are some of Al-Qaeda's known terrorist acts?
A: It is known that Al-Qaeda conducted the bombings of the United States embassies in Nairobi, Kenya, and Dar es Salaam, Tanzania, in August 1998. At least 301 persons were killed in those attacks and 5,000 others were injured. Al-Qaeda also claims to have shot down U.S. helicopters and to have killed American military personnel in Somalia in 1993. Three other bombings against American troops are attributed to Al-Qaeda as well in Aden, Yemen, in December 1992. This terrorist organization was part of the futile attempt to destroy the World Trade Center in 1993 which it unfortunately succeeded to destroy in the September 11, 2001, attacks.

Q: What other international plots was Al-Qaeda involved with?
A: Al-Qaeda was the mastermind behind these foiled plots across the globe:

- The assassination attempt of Pope John Paul II during the pontiff's visit to Manila in late 1994.

- The simultaneous bombings of the U.S. and Israeli Embassies in Manila and other Asian capitals in late 1994.

- The in-flight bombing of at least a dozen U.S. trans-Pacific flights in 1995.

- The assassination attempt of U.S. President Bill Clinton during his visit to the Philippines in early 1995.

It is known that Al-Qaeda continues to finance, train, and to provide logistic support to terrorist groups around the world that support these goals.

Q: How strong is the Al-Qaeda organization?
A: Al-Qaeda is known to have had between several hundred to several thousand members. It also serves as an umbrella organization for a worldwide network that includes many Sunni Moslem extremist groups such as Egyptian Islamic Jihad, the Islamic Movement of Uzbekistan, some members of Al-Gama'at Al-Islamiyya, and the Harakat Ul-Mujahidin.

Q: Where are its forces located?
A: Until the American incursion into Afghanistan, Bin-Laden and his key officers resided in Afghanistan, and the organization maintained terrorist training camps there. Moreover, Al-Qaeda is known to have a worldwide reach with cells in numerous countries which are reinforced by its ties to extremist terrorist networks.

Q: Who is Osama Bin-Laden?
A: Bin-Laden is the son of a billionaire Saudi family. It is believed that he inherited an estimated $300 million which he used to finance the Al-Qaeda organization.

Q: What are Al-Qaeda's other sources of money?
A: It is known that Al-Qaeda also maintains moneymaking front organizations. It solicits donations from like-minded supporters and illegally siphons funds from donations to Moslem charitable organizations.

IMAD MUGNIYAH: THE SATAN-MINDED TERRORIST

On October 10, 2001, Imad Mugniyah was included on the FBI's most wanted list of terrorists. Mugniyah is suspected in the bombings of the Israeli Embassy in March 1992 and a Jewish community center in Buenos Aires in July 1994. These bombings resulted in the death of 119 innocent people. Prior to the September 11, 2001, attacks in America, U.S. officials considered Mugniyah — a founder of the Hizbullah terrorist organization — responsible for the deaths of more Americans around the world than anyone else. The United States also blames Mugniyah for the 1983 suicide bombing in Lebanon which killed 241 U.S. Marines.

Q: What is known about Mugniyah?
A: Imad Mugniyah is the very opposite of Osama Bin-Laden. He has mastered many skills, is more professional than Bin-Laden and he operates as a faceless terrorist.

Q: Why has it been so difficult to apprehend Mugniyah?
A: Mugniyah has cleverly kept his face hidden and he is believed to have had plastic surgery twice over the years. Intelligence sources simply do not know what he looks like or where he is located. They believe he might be in Iran or perhaps in Lebanon's Beka'a Valley. For these reasons, he is referred to as the man of a "thousand faces," and he remains so illusive.

Mugniyah is known to be the commander of the Hizbullah terrorist organization and leads units abroad.

Q: What other crimes is he suspected of having committed?
A: Western Intelligence sources also suspect him in the bombing of the U.S. Embassy in Beirut, Lebanon, in April 1983. Sixty-three people died in the bombing. He is also suspect in the kidnapping of numerous Western hostages in Beirut in the mid-1980s. Two U.S. hostages — William Buckley, CIA station chief in Beirut, and Lt. Col. William Higgins, a Marine officer serving with United Nations forces in Lebanon — were both murdered.

Q: What else is known about Mugniyah?
A: Mugniyah is a Lebanese about 40 years of age. He is the grandson of a clergyman and was close to Yassir Arafat and his Fatah organization until the Lebanon War. He joined the ranks of Hizbullah in 1982 and quickly rose to power as chief of the organization's security apparatus. He is the Hizbullah's leading terrorist today.

Q: Does Mugniyah have any known connections with other terrorist groups and organizations?
A: Yes. Mugniyah has close ties with the PLO, Iran, and the Islamic Jihad in Lebanon, which is expressed in joint operations.

Q: What message has the West relayed to Syria, Iran, and Lebanon?
A: Mugniyah is the military arm of the Hizbullah, which is based in and carries out terrorist attacks in Lebanon and abroad. Hizbullah is assisted financially and militarily by Iran and Syria. Mugniyah also serves as the terrorist arm of Iran, acting against political

opponents to the fanatic Iranian regime. He is known to have been involved in the killing of exiled Iranian opponents to the regime in Europe.

Inclusion of Mugniyah's name on the FBI's most wanted list is a clear and overt warning to Iran, Syria, and, to a lesser extent, Lebanon. Bear in mind that U.S. President Bush has spoken quite bluntly not only about holding terrorists responsible, but any states that harbor or assist such terrorists and their organizations.

AYMAN ZAWAHIRI: THE KILLER PHYSICIAN

Dr. Ayman Zawahiri is a licensed physician, yet he is also a murderer. He initiated and caused the death of thousands of innocent people, mostly Americans. He is known today as one of the most dangerous terrorists in the world and his name tops the list of the FBI's most wanted.

In February 1998, Zawahiri, together with Osama Bin-Laden, established the terror organization named the "Islamic Front Against the Crusaders and the Jews." A few months later, 224 people were murdered — Americans and other nationals — when the American embassies in Kenya and Tanzania, Africa, were bombed. Two years later, the U.S. destroyer, the USS *Cole*, was attacked while docked in Yemen. Seventeen American sailors were killed. Then on September 11, 2001, the World Trade Center was destroyed in New York and the Pentagon was attacked leaving thousands dead and wounded.

It is common knowledge that Bin-Laden's Al-Qaeda terrorist organization was responsible for these killings. Few people know that the mastermind behind these attacks and the person reponsible for recruiting the fanatic Islamic terrorists who would carry out the attacks was Dr. Ayman Zawahiri.

Q: Who is Zawahiri?
A: Ayman Zawahiri is an Eygptian physician, fluent in English and French, and is a member of one of the most aristocratic families in Egypt. He is also Bin-Laden's personal physician.

Q: When did Zawahiri meet Bin-Laden?
A: They met in Afghanistan in 1987 and have been together ever since that time.

Q: What is known about Zawahiri?
A: Besides being an arch terrorist, he is fanatically religious and is known to be a good organizer. In one of his rare interviews, which was aired on Al-Jazira Television, he said that he would not mind to die for the sake of Allah. It is clear that the theory commonly accepted today — that fanatic Islamic fundamentalism takes root among the impoverished and miserable masses — is not the case with Zawahiri. This infamous physician was raised among the wealthy in a luxurious villa in Cairo.

On October 6, 1981, Egyptian President Anwar Sadat was murdered by a group of Islamic fanatics. Zawahiri was brought to trial and found guilty for supplying the weapons used by Sadat's assassins. He was sent to prison for a few years and was released in 1987. He traveled to Afghanistan where he met and teamed up with Bin-Laden.

In Afghanistan, Zawahiri started recruiting young Moslems to join Al-Qaeda. These young Moslems received terrorist training and were readied to act on call against American, Western, and Israeli interests.

Q: How did Zawahiri spread his beliefs?
A: He issued a monthly bulletin entitled *Alfath*, which means "the occupation." He used this paper to explain the motives behind his activities against the West, especially the United State, Israel, and Jews throughout the world.

In 1991, Zawahiri was elected leader of the Egyptian terrorist organization called "the Egyptian Jihad." He decided to act against the Egyptian regime led by Hosni Mubarak. In 1993, the Egyptian premier, Atef Sidki, narrowly escaped an assassination attempt on his life when a bomb exploded near him. A few months later, the minister of the interior, Hassan Alalfi was saved from a similar attack. In 1995, President Mubarak was saved from death as well.

Q: What happened after these failed assassination attacks?
A: Following the repeated failures at murdering Egyptian leaders, Zawahiri, together with Bin-Laden, changed direction. They concentrated their efforts on attacking U.S. interests in the Middle East, Africa, and later on in the United States.

In the aforementioned Al-Jazira Television interview Zawahiri said:

I came to the political conclusion that the biggest enemy which is behind all our troubles and disasters is the Jewish-Crusader [Christian] alliance. Yet today, more criminals can be found in the White House than in Israel.

Unfortunately, Zawahiri was able to fulfill his threats against the United States. The September 11, 2001, attacks on American soil were planned by Zawahiri and Khalid Shaick Muhammad. The latter was arrested in Pakistan by U.S. forces in March 2003.

NOTE: Some of the information in this chapter was taken from the International Institute, "I.C.T.," in Herzlia, Israel.

CHAPTER 3

HISTORY OF THE ISLAMIC ATTITUDE TOWARD CHRISTIANS AND JEWS AND NON-MOSLEM MINORITIES

When Islam was established in the seventh century C.E., there was a very active Jewish community in Medina in the Arab peninsula. The Jews of pre-Islamic Arabia were active advocates of their religion to the extent that several kings of Himyar, now Yemen, had converted to Judaism. Contemporary inscriptions described Abu Nuwas As'ar, the last Jewish king of Himyar, as a believer in one deity whom the king called Rahman, the Merciful One, as God was called in Judaism and later in Islam.

The prophet of Islam, Mohammed, was highly impressed by the Jewish religion and especially the idea of one God — monotheism. The influence of Judaism is felt almost everywhere in the Islamic holy book, the Koran. Moreover, Jewish law deeply influenced Mohammed as well. He sought closeness to the Jews and begged them to recognize him as a prophet.

Q: How did Judaism influence Mohammed?
A: In the early days of Islam, Moslems prayed in the direction of the Jews' holy city, Jerusalem, and observed the most solemn Jewish holiday, Yom Kippur (the Day of Atonement).

Q: When did they change these common customs?
A: Only later, when Mohammed reluctantly concluded that the Jews would not embrace him as their prophet and convert to Islam, did he substitute Mecca for Jerusalem, and the fast of Ramadan for Yom Kippur.

Q: What were other Judaic influences on Mohammed?
A: Mohammed based Moslem dietary laws upon Judaism's laws of Kashrut: "You are forbidden carrion, blood, and the flesh of swine; also any flesh of animals sacrificed to idols" (Koran 5:3). The five daily prayers of Islam are likewise modeled on the thrice daily service of the Jews.

Q: How does Mohammed relate to Abraham, the "father of monotheism"?
A: Second in importance only to his adoption of the Jews' God was Mohammed's adoption of the Jews' founding father, Abraham, as Islam's founder. In Sura 2, verse 125, Mohammed writes how Abraham and his son Ishmael converted the *Kaaba* (the holy rock of Arabian paganism) into the holy shrine of Islam.

Q: What did Mohammed want from the Jews of Arabia?
A: Believing himself to be the final and greatest prophet of basic monotheism, and having adopted so much of Jewish thought and practice, Mohammed appealed to the Jews of Arabia to recognize his role and to adopt Islam as the culmination of Judaism.

Q: Why did the Jews reject Mohammed?
A: The Jews rejected Mohammed's claims on the grounds that what was true in his messages was not new, and that what was new was not true. Islam may have served as a religious advance for Arabian pagans, but for the Jews it was merely another offshoot of Judaism.

Q: Did Mohammed ever read the Bible?
A: No. Mohammed was illiterate. Yet Moslems are proud that despite his illiteracy, their prophet could produce a unique book such as the Koran. Mohammed had heard stories from the Bible and tried to remember them, not all the time successfully.

Q: Is there an example?
A: Yes. Mohammed's references to the Bible were often erroneous. In Sura 28:38, for instance, he has Pharaoh (from the Book of Exodus) ask Haman (from the Book of Esther) to erect the Tower of Babel (which appears at the beginning of the Book of Genesis).

Q: What are other deterrents to Jewish acceptance of Mohammed?
A: In the Koran, 33:50, for example, Mohammed exempts himself from his own law limiting a man to four wives, and in 4:34 he instructs men to beat disobedient wives. Finally, Mohammed's suspension of many Torah laws invalidated him in the eyes of the Jews.

Q: What made Mohammed even more furious with the Jews?
A: The Jews not only rejected his prophecy, but they publicly noted the errors in Mohammed's biblical teachings and may have even ridiculed his claims to prophecy.

Mohammed the Prophet against the Jews

Ibn Khaldun (1332–1406), the great Arab historian, in *The Muqaddamah* (Introduction to History), defines the loss of collective consciousness of the children of Israel, their dispersion throughout the world, their alienation from the rest of humanity, and their living a life of disgrace and degradation. He even claims that the Jews were infected with such evil character traits as corruption and deceitful plotting.

As a result of their rejection of him, Mohammed turned against the Jews and their religion and he never forgave them. Mohammed's angry reactions to the Jews were recorded in the Koran, giving millions of Moslems throughout history "divinely based" antipathy to the Jews.

Q: What did Mohammed change?
A: First and most significantly, he changed Abraham from a Jew to a Moslem: "Abraham was neither Jew nor Christian. [He] surrendered himself to Allah. Surely the men who are nearest to Abraham are those who follow him, this Prophet. . . ." (Koran 3:67–68)

Q: What was his view about certain Jewish laws?
A: Mohammed said that the Torah laws had been given to the Jews as punishment for their sins: "Because of their iniquity we

forbade the Jews good things which were formerly allowed them."
(Koran 4:160).

Q: What was his accusation against the Jews?
A: Mohammed charged the Jews with falsifying their Bible by de-
liberately omitting prophecies of his (Mohammed's) coming. For
example, in the Koran (2:129) Mohammed has Abraham mouth a
prophecy of his coming. Mohammed charged that the Jews "extin-
guished the light of Allah" (Koran 9:32) by having removed such
prophecies from their Bible.

Q: How else does Mohammed accuse the Jews?
A: Mohammed asserted that Jews, like Christians, were not true
monotheists, a charge he substantiated by claiming that the Jews
believed the prophet Ezra to be the son of God. "And the Jews say:
Ezra is the son of God. . . . And Allah fights against them. How
perverse are they. . . ." (Koran 9:30)

Q: What can be concluded?
A: These anti-Jewish fabrications, articulated by Mohammed as reactions to the Jews' rejection of him, have ever since been regarded
by Moslems as God's word. As such, they have formed the basis
of Moslem anti-Semitism until the present day. Though originally
directed against specific Jews of a specific time, these statements
often have been understood by succeeding generations as referring
to all Jews at all times.

By the Jews remaining Jews they constituted a living refutation.
Thus, under Islam, Jew-hatred was ultimately Judaism-hatred. Any
Jew who converted to Islam was accepted as an equal. Important
to note is the fact that Christians under Moslem rule fared little
better. Moslems and their laws generally dealt harshly with both
Christians and Jews.

The Moslem legal code, which prescribed the treatment of
Jews and Christians, or Dhimmis — as they are both referred to in
Islam — follows in the next pages.

> *If anyone desires a religion other than Islam, never will
> it be accepted of him and in the hereafter he will be in the
> ranks of those who have lost* — Koran, Sura 3: 85

The Dhimmi: Jews and Christians, Second-Class Citizens

The famous claim of Arab propaganda is the following: Jews and Christians were treated fairly under the rule of Islam. They were protected and enjoyed civil and religious rights. The main reason for the Arab-Israeli conflict is Zionism. Zionism as a political and national movement is alien to the region. It destroyed the good Moslem-Jewish relations that have prevailed for generations and has caused the Arab-Israeli conflict.

The Jews are considered to be cursed and Christians are seen as hate-ridden: Allah himself is said to have stirred hostility and strife among various Christian communities as a punishment for their refusal to accept the Prophet Mohammed's message (Koran 5:15). With the exception of a few, Jews are inherently deceitful (Koran 5:14). Worse than that, the Koran states that the Jews of Eilat not only broke the laws of the Sabbath but scornfully persisted in their wrongdoings. As a result, they were severed from society and "changed into detested apes." (Koran 7:167)

The Dhimmis, as inferior scriptural communities, were required by law to pay a skull tax (the *jizya*) in return for which they were allowed to practice their religions and to maintain their local institutions. However, all this was in the context of certain infirmities, besides the *jizya* tax, imposed upon them by the Moslem majority. In Islam's view, these minorities were to be tolerated as a sign of their powerlessness under Islam. Islam would care for them in this way so long as they demonstrated their own inferiority by recognizing the legitimacy of Moslem rule over them. Any attempt on the part of the minorities to seek independence would be a violation of the contract.

Q: When did the Dhimmis come to the region?
A: Jews and Christians had been living throughout the Orient, Egypt, and North Africa for centuries before they were overrun in the seventh and subsequent centuries by successive waves of Bedouin invaders from Arabia who, under the banner of Islam, subjugated peoples and territories from India to Spain.

Q: *What was the status of Jews and Christians?*
A: Their status was that of *Ahl al-Dhimma* — protected peoples. In short, they were considered peoples tolerated in the Moslem lands: *"Dar al-Islam"* (House of Islam).

Q: *How did the Jews live in these regions?*
A: Up to the last decades of the 19th century, and even into the 20th, the Jews in most of North Africa (until European domination, i.e., Algeria, 1830; Tunisia, 1881; Egypt, 1882; Libya, 1911; Morocco, 1912), Yemen, and other Moslem lands of the Orient were still obliged to live in isolated groups amidst the general population.

Q: *How did life compare for the Christians?*
A: The indigenous Christian populations had fared no better. Throughout the Islamic lands they had, like the Jews, been reduced to the inferior status of Dhimmis and had been virtually eliminated from North Africa by the 12th century during the Almohad persecutions.

Q: *What was the attitude toward the Dhimmis?*
A: For twelve hundred years, the Dhimmis were tolerated in Moslem lands on the terms laid down in the covenant of Umar, the refusal or infringement of which could incur the death penalty.

Q: *What is the contemporary attitude of Islam toward the Jews?*
A: The Dhimmi status was referred to by an Egyptian, Abu Zahra, at an important conference of theologians (1968) held at the Islamic University of Al-Azhar in Cairo under the patronage of then President Nasser: "But we say to those who patronize the Jews that the latter are Dhimmis, people of obligation, who have betrayed the covenant in conformity with which they have been accorded protection. . . ." President Sadat's declaration on the feast of Mohammed's birth (April 25, 1972) also relates to this basic Islamic Dhimmi concept: "They (the Jews) shall return and be as the Koran said of them: 'condemned to humiliation and misery'. . . . We shall send them back to their former status."

Q: *What about the Arab attitude toward the Jews in the medieval era?*
A: In a bitter anti-Jewish ode against Joseph Ibn Nagrella, the Jewish minister of the Moslem ruler of Grenada, Spain, Abu Ishaq, a well-known 11th century Arab jurist and poet wrote, "Put them

back where they belong and reduce them to the lowest of the low
. . . turn your eyes to other [Moslem] countries and you will find
the Jews there are outcast dogs. . . . Do not consider it a breach of
faith to kill them. . . . They have violated our covenant with them
so how can you be held guilty against the violators?"

Q: *What was the result of such hatred?*
A: Nagrella and an estimated five thousand Jews of Grenada were
subsequently slaughtered on December 30, 1066.

Q: *Is this the only case?*
A: Throughout their history in Moslem lands, Jews and Christians
have suffered time and again from pogroms and humiliation.

Q: *Is there any testimony of modern historians to prove this?*
A: Yes. Antoine Fattal, in his authoritative study on the legal status
of non-Moslems in Moslem lands, has written: "The Dhimmi is a
second-class citizen. If he is tolerated, it is for reasons of a spiritual
nature, since there is always the hope that he might be converted."
Likewise, Louis Bardet, a Catholic theologian and a respected Ori-
entalist, one of the leaders of the contemporary "dialogue" between
Islam and Christianity, has stressed, "The Dhimmi should always
behave as an inferior; he should adopt a humble and contrite attitude. For example, on the payment of the *jizya*, or poll tax, the *qadi*,
on receiving the money, must make as if to give the Dhimmi a light
slap in the face so as to remind him of his place. The Dhimmi should
everywhere give way to the Muslim. . . . If Islam did not invent the
ghettos, it can be said that it was the first to institutionalize them."

Lebanese Maronite bishops issued a resolution in April 1975
protesting "vigorously against the abuse of sacredness of churches
and places of worship, desecration of Holy Places, firing at monasteries, hospitals, and ambulances . . . attacks on ecclesiastics . . . as
well as monks and nuns."

The world-renowned Jewish historian Albert Memmi described the life of the Jews in Moslem countries thusly:

> *Ever since the days of the Abbasids it has been part of
> the Charter of Omar that, to put it briefly, the Jew is at best
> protected like a dog that is part of the chattels. But let him
> raise his head or behave like a human being, and he must be
> beaten . . . to remind him of his condition.*

We always get what may have been the mistake of Deir Yassin thrown in our faces. Good heavens! We have suffered a hundred, a thousand Deir Yassins! And not only in Russia, in Germany, or in Poland, but actually in Arab lands with the world never caring.

THE YELLOW BADGE: CHRISTIAN OR MOSLEM

The historian Robert Brunschwig remarked: "Islam subjected the Dhimmis to special fiscal and vestimentary obligation." He noted that toward the end of the 12th century, in the Almohad empire (North Africa and Spain), the Jews were compelled to wear a distinctive mark, besides ridiculous clothing. He wrote, "Would it not be strange if it were the Almohad example which decided Christendom to adopt the same sort of measure? The Jews were first compelled to wear a distinctive badge in Christian lands at the beginning of the 13th century."

Q: What about Jewish rights in the Golden Age?
A: Bernard Lewis, the much-respected historian and co-editor of *The Encyclopedia of Islam*, emphasized in a 1968 article, "The golden age of equal rights was a myth, and belief in it was a result, more than a cause, of Jewish sympathy for Islam. The myth was invented in 19th century Europe as a reproach to Christians — and taken up by Muslims in our own time as a reproach to Jews."

A Romanian Jew, Benjamin II, who traveled extensively (1846–1851) during five years in the Orient and the Maghreb, drew a revealing comparison: "How happy I would be if [by my book of travels] I could interest them [the Jews of Europe] in the plight of their co-religionists who are the victims of oriental barbarism and fanaticism. Our strong and free brethren who have the good fortune to live under liberal regimes, where they are governed by wise laws and are treated humanely, will understand how deplorable and urgent is the abnormal situation of their brethren in the Orient. Religion demands it, humanity requires it."

THE LAND TAX AND THE SKULL TAX

Q: What is the kharadj?
A: The *kharadj* is a tax levied on the lands left to the indigenous dhimmis. This tax symbolized the Arabization of the land of the

dhimmis, meaning its addition to the patrimony of the Arab-Islamic community. In the early period of colonization, lands given in fief were exonerated from the *kharadj*.

Q: What is the jizya?
A: Each male dhimmi, with the theoretical exceptions of the aged, invalids, and slaves, had to pay a poll tax, the *jizya*, which symbolized the subjection and humiliation of the *dhimmis*.

Q: What is known of other taxation or ransoms paid by the dhimmis?
A: The *dhimmis* also were compelled to pay double the taxes of the Moslems. In addition, ransoms were frequently extorted from the local Jewish and Christian communities under threat of collective sanctions, including torture and death.

Generally speaking, the traditional approach of the Moslem Arabs to the Jews and Christians has been ambivalent: ethnic kinship and cultural affinity, on the one hand, together with a belief in Arab political superiority and religious supremacy, on the other. Thus, the image of the Jew as an enemy of the Moslems evolved in the classical Moslem literature and particularly in modern Arab literature into a demonological stereotype of a Jew who is also the enemy of mankind.

HUMILIATION AND DISCRIMINATION AS A WAY OF LIFE FOR CHRISTIANS AND JEWS IN ARAB COUNTRIES

In order to demonstrate his lower status and to show his poverty and misery, the dhimmi was forbidden to do certain things and at the same time was obliged to do others.

Q: What was forbidden the Jews and the Christians?
A: The dhimmi was forbidden the following on pain of death:
- to carry or possess weapons
- to raise a hand against a Moslem, even against an aggressor unjustly determined to kill him
- to ally himself with the enemies of the Arabs
- to criticize Islam, the prophet, or the angels
- to convert to any religion other than Islam, and having converted to Islam, to revert to one's original religion

- to be linked by marriage to a Moslem woman
- to hold a position giving him authority over a Moslem.

Q: What was the dhimmi obliged to do?
A: The dhimmi was obliged to:

- live separated from Moslems, in special quarters of a town, the gates of which were closed every evening, or as in Yemen, outside the limits of towns inhabited by Moslems
- to have lower houses than those of Moslems
- to practice their religion secretly and in silence
- to bury their dead hastily
- to refrain from showing in public religious objects, such as crosses, banners, or sacred texts
- to distinguish themselves from Moslems by their exterior aspect
- to make haste on the streets, always passing to the left (impure) side of a Moslem, who was advised to push them to the wall
- to walk humbly with lowered eyes
- to accept insults without replying
- to remain standing in a humble and respectful attitude in the presence of a Moslem

The dhimmis were forbidden to ride horses or camels since these animals were considered too noble for them. Donkeys were permitted, but they could only ride them outside town perimeters and they had to dismount on sight of a Moslem. In certain periods they were forced to wear distinctive badges in the public baths, and in certain regions were even forbidden to enter them at all.

Any litigation between a dhimmi and a Moslem was brought before an Islamic tribunal where the dhimmi's testimony was unacceptable.

CHAPTER 4

MODERN HISTORY — NATIONAL INDEPENDENCE FOR ARABS, MISERY FOR JEWS AND CHRISTIANS

Q: When did the Jews gain equal rights in Arab countries?
A: It was only after the establishment of European protectorates in all of North Africa, Egypt, and the Orient (with the exception of Yemen, where the Jews had to wait till 1949–1950, when they were airlifted to Israel in "Operation Magic Carpet").

Q: How long did the Jews enjoy equal rights?
A: Under European rule, Christians and Jews enjoyed physical security, and some even a certain affluence, which lasted for two or three generations.

Q: When did the Jews' situation worsen?
A: As each Arab country won its national independence, the situation of the minorities worsened, often becoming intolerable. More than one thousand Jews were killed in anti-Jewish rioting 1938–1949: in Baghdad (1941/46/48); Tripoli (1945–48); Aden (1947); Aleppo (1945/47/48); Damascus (1938/45/49); Oudja, Djerade, Cairo (1948); etc. Similar tragedies occurred during the same period to many indigenous Christian groups throughout the Arab world.

Q: What can be said about Arab opposition to Israel since her establishment in 1948?

A: The general Arab opposition to the existence of an independent sovereign State of Israel in its ancient homeland has its roots in traditional Islamic attitudes and dhimmi concepts. The contemporary hostile Arab attitudes toward Jews and other minorities is not something unusual in the Arab world. What was unusual, for the *dhimmis*, was the relative calm of the preceding two or three generations during the period of European domination.

Q: What about Moslem opposition to Christian Lebanese?

A: In 1860, the brutal massacre of several thousand Christians in Syria and Lebanon occurred soon after the passing of the Hatti-Humayun edict (1856), which granted equal rights with Moslems to Christians and Jews.

JEWS AND CHRISTIANS: BROTHERS IN TROUBLE IN THE MIDDLE EAST

> *We have in the Lebanese experience a significant example that is close to the multi-religious state we are trying to achieve.* — Yassir Arafat, The Economist, April 12, 1975

> *Land of tolerance, human synthesis, fraternal and peaceful. This Lebanon, thus made by the grace of God and the merit of its people, is it not a symbol of what the world could be, delivered from the reign of violence and undertakings inspired by religious or racial exclusivism?* — Suleiman Franjieh, former Lebanese president at the United Nations, 1974.

Both the former Lebanese president and the PLO chairman did not realize how quickly developments in Lebanon would prove that these beautiful declarations have no foundation.

The PLO terrorists in Lebanon, who fled Jordan in September 1970, came to Lebanon and made life miserable in their host country — Lebanon. In 1975, a civil war broke out between the Moslem minority and the Christian majority. The PLO terrorists joined the Moslems against the Christians. The Lebanese civil war lasted about one decade. Tens of thousands died and many others were injured. The damage to Lebanon's economy was enormous. In 1976, the

Syrian Army entered Lebanon in order to impose a cease-fire, yet the Syrian forces have remained in Lebanon till this very day.

Jews as well as Christians are dhimmis and, therefore, should be treated accordingly. The case of Lebanon, where the Arab Christians have had to fight for their existence against Moslem aggression, is another proof of the Moslem attitude toward non-Moslems. Lebanon exposes the true face of the Arab world, showing that its claims of tolerance for people of different religions is a lie. According to Islam, Jews and Christians are equal to each other, but are, by no means, equal to Moslems.

The Jews as well as the Christians understood that in order to survive and to face Arab aggression against them, they would have to cooperate and help one another.

Q: What was the reason behind Archbishop Moubarak's support for a Jewish state?
A: The words of Archbishop Moubarak expressed the fear and the concern of the Christians in Lebanon who knew how dire their fate would be if the Moslems achieved political control in the country.

Q: What encouraged the Christians?
A: The fact that Jews established their state in the region, despite Arab opposition, encouraged the Christians to feel that they were not alone in their fight against Moslem enmity. Some believed that Jews and Christians were like "brothers in trouble," capable of uniting their forces against Moslem opposition to their independence.

Q: How did the Jews view the Christian-Jewish cooperation?
A: In the early 1940s, Abraham Stern-Yair, the leader of the Lehi-Fighters for Israel's Freedom movement — wrote that the term "Hebrew nation" does not apply only to the tribe of Israel. It includes another important and large tribe — the Phoenicians (ancient Lebanese). These two groups are brethren in both language and culture.

Q: What is known about the massacre of 1860?
A: In 1860, the Lebanese Druze attacked the Christian Maronites. Thousands of men, women, and children were murdered. The Christians sent forth a desperate plea for help to the European powers in order to save them from complete annihilation.

Q: Who came to the aid of the Christians?
A: Sir Moses Montefiore, the well-known British Jewish leader, astonished by the disaster that befell the Lebanese Christians, did his utmost to assist them. After receiving the tragic report about the 20,000 Christians dead, he approached the *Times* (London) in the middle of the night insisting that it publish the story about the plight of the Christians in order to awaken world public opinion to their misery. He then set up a fund to help the survivors of the pogroms and included money of his own in the fund.

Q: Who else helped the Christians?
A: Adolph Cremieux, a Jewish minister in the French government, joined Montefiore's efforts and later persuaded and encouraged his government to send troops to Lebanon in order to rescue the remnant Christian population.

Q: How did the Christians express their thanks and appreciation for such help?
A: The Maronite Patriarch, Antoine Arida, who at that time was a child, was miraculously saved from death and later extolled Jewish assistance to the Christians during those dark days. He later appeared in synagogues throughout Beirut, praising the Jewish community not only for its help, but also for calling on the world to rescue the Christians. Arida also sent a telegram to the director of the Alliance Jewish School in Beirut, in which he wrote, "We will not forget the generous help of Alliance."

Q: Is there any other testimony concerning Arab hatred for Christians?
A: Yes. British Arabist Gertrude Bell recounted how the Moslems, upon hearing of the Japanese victories over Russia, 1904–1905, would shake their fists at the Christians, saying, "The Christians are suffering defeat. Now we too will shortly drive you out and seize your goods."

Q: What happened to the Christians in southern Lebanon?
A: Following the First World War, Syria was given to France by the League of Nations as a mandate territory. Arab nationalists subsequently called for a revolt against French rule, including its Christian supporters. As a result, Arab nomads brutally attacked the Christians of southern Lebanon as well as the Jewish community. Many fleeing Christians found shelter in Jewish settlements,

especially in Metula (a town in Israel situated near the Lebanese border).

Q: What was the result of the Arab pressure against the Christians?
A: As a direct result of the pogroms and vehement hostility, a large number of Syrian and Lebanese Christians emigrated to America, establishing an Arab Christian diaspora *(mahgiar)* at the end of the 19th century and beginning of the 20th century.

For centuries, Christian minorities in the Middle East have faced physical and spiritual threat from Islam, Copts, Assyrians, and the south Sudanese are the present-day targets.

The Christian Aramaic population in Lebanon has long been abandoned by the West. In 1990, Syria invaded and dominated the Christian enclave in central Lebanon and many Christian leaders were subsequently killed by Syrian-supported Moslems. Most of the Christian resistance elements in Lebanon have been virtually neutralized, either by force or by buying them out.

Commenting on this issue, the president of the expatriate World Lebanese Organization, Dr. Walid Phares, said the following:

> *The Lebanese Christians, and those of southern Lebanon in particular, should be guaranteed protection from Arab domination, particularly Syria's occupation. . . . The immediate threat from which the Christian people of Lebanon should be protected is the advance of Islamic fundamentalism. . . . Today, Lebanon is obliterated by a conglomerate of Syrian-fundamentalist forces. The duty of any Christian leader — secular or spiritual, in the Middle East and in the world — should be the support of this endangered community by any means. — Middle East Intelligence Digest, February 1994*

In April 1981, the Syrian army bombarded the Christian town of Zahle. It is a town located in Lebanon's Beka'a Valley and is populated by 200,000 Greek Catholics. Not one European country condemned the attacks nor did any intervene on behalf of the Christians. Neither did the United Nations, the United States, the Arab League, nor the Vatican.

The only country to intervene on behalf of the Christians was Israel. Across the country, Israeli rabbis prayed for the safety and wellbeing of the Lebanese Christians while Israeli forces attacked Syrian helicopters that were transporting troops into the area.

The Dhimmi State of Israel

The goal of our struggle is the end of Israel, and there can be no compromise. — Yassir Arafat, *Washington Post*, March 29, 1970

The state of Israel's establishment is totally unaccepted by the Moslems. Israel, they believe, inflicted injustice upon the Palestinian Arabs by taking their homes and their country. Moreover, the most serious problem is the fact that the Jews, who are dhimmis, not only established their state in the midst of the Moslem world, but also defeated and even humiliated the Arab Moslem armies, time and again, within one generation. This course of events is contradictory to the spirit and laws of the Koran. The conclusion, according to the Moslems, is that Israel must disappear.

The jihad "War of Ramadan," known to the world as the 1973 Yom Kippur War, was officially declared by the Moslem authorities in Egypt, Syria, and Saudi Arabia as jihad (holy war), which the Moslem is commanded to wage against the infidels, the enemies of Islam. In a pamphlet specifically published by the Egyptian Ministry of War at that time, entitled "Our Faith Our Way to Victory," Chief of Staff Shazli, referring to a verse from the Koran, addressed himself to the troops in these words: "The Jews have overstepped their bounds in (acts of) injustice and conceit. Kill them wherever you find them."

Q: Why do the Moslems refuse to accept the state of Israel in their midst?
A: The Moslem Arabs refuse to accept Israel as a reality in the region. The reason is simple: Israel has traumatized the Arab political consciousness. Why? Traditional Arab domination has produced feelings of superiority among the Arabs. These feelings were confirmed by the abasement of the dhimmi. If, however, the dhimmi can achieve equal rights, then the superior feels himself doubly inferior and unquestionably humiliated.

Q: What is the Arabs' reaction to this situation?
A: The less the Israeli image of a Jew fits into the dhimmi stereotype — as a servile, cowardly, debased being — the more violent

and bloodthirsty becomes the efforts of the ancient oppressor to force the victim back into his low status.

Q: What should be Israel's image?
A: Israel is regarded as the dhimmi state. If such a state rebels against Arab domination, it must be condemned to destruction. Jews must return to their dhimmi image and status.

Q: What is the background to Arab behavior toward the Jews?
A: In this sense, Arab treatment of Jewish minorities in its midst is rooted in the Islamic approach to Jews.

Q: What does Israel do to the Arab image?
A: The creation of the state of Israel is regarded in the Arab world as an unacceptable reversal of history. Furthermore, it is an intolerable insult to the might and "manhood" of the Arab world. This trauma produced the attempts to strangle the Jewish community under the mandate, to crush the infant state of Israel, to the many Arab-Israeli wars that followed Israel's independence, to the maintenance of a permanent state of war in the periods between the actual wars, to the famous "three no's" of the Khartoum Conference in 1967, and to the Palestinian Covenant — which calls for Israel's demise.

Q: What is Israel?
A: Israel is the only free, democratic state in the entire Middle East. The following is an excerpt from the Declaration of Independence of the State of Israel, May 14, 1948: "The State of Israel will insure complete equality of social and political rights to all its inhabitants irrespective of religion, race, or sex; it will guarantee freedom of religion, conscience, language, education, and culture; it will safeguard the holy places of all religions; and it will be faithful to the principles of the Charter of the United Nations."

> *It would have been better for the suiciders who destroyed the World Trade Center on September 11, 2001, had they destroyed the Israeli Knesset instead. This would have better served the struggle of the Palestinian people.* — Sheikh Dr. Muhammed Sayyid Tantawi, highest Islamic spiritual leader in Egypt, Al Bayan, Persian Gulf paper, May 11, 2002

PART II:

RADICAL AND ISLAMIC ARAB STATES

CHAPTER 5

STRATEGIC GOALS OF THE WEST'S ENEMIES

IRAN: POLICY OF FANATICISM AND TERROR

The U.S. has a major problem with Iran over its support for terrorist activities against the United States and in the Middle East. When we questioned those who carried out the explosion in the Khobar complex [U.S. military installation in Saudi Arabia], they clearly mentioned training and finance provided by Iran. [Nineteen U.S. servicemen were killed in the attack.] — Condolezza Rice, U.S. National Security Advisor, *Al-Hayat*, Lebanese daily, February 21, 2002

Iran's desire to acquire weapons of mass destruction is further proof of the deep-rooted hostility felt for Western civilization among fanatic Moslems. The radical ayatollahs ruling Iran today want Islam to prevail throughout neighboring countries. They seek duplication of the Iranian regime.

Iran is today both bigger and stronger than Iraq and, therefore, Iran poses the greatest danger to the stability of the Middle East.

Q: How does Iran view terror?
A: Since the Islamic Revolution in 1979, Iran views terrorism as a legal means by which to further its ideology and strategic aims that include:

- exporting the revolution

- assisting Islamic groups and organizations worldwide, especially in the Middle East

- attacking Israel and attempting to sabotage the political process

- destabilizing the regimes of more pragmatic Arab countries

- eliminating the opposition to Iran's regime from within

Q: Which Iranian organizations are involved in this policy?
A: The "Guardians of the Revolution," various government ministries, intelligence forces, the Office of Foreign Affairs, etc.

Q: When did the United States sever relations with Iran?
A: Diplomatic ties between Iran and the United States were severed after the Islamic Revolution in 1979 and the takeover of the U.S. Embassy in Teheran.

> *Teheran has again shown itself to be the world arsenal of terror. Iran's ayatollahs have been escalating their sponsorship of terrorist war — yesterday on the 'Great Satan' of America, today on Israeli Jews, tomorrow on the whole non-Islamic world.* — William Safire, *New York Times*, January 10, 2002

Q: What is Iran's position regarding the peace talks between Israel and the Palestinians?
A: Since the Madrid Conference in 1991, Iran has done its utmost to disrupt the peace process. It has supported all the Palestinian factions that oppose this process and has undermined Arafat's position in the Palestinian Authority after he signed the Oslo Agreement in September 1993.

> The government and people of Iran are of the opinion that the Israeli entity is false and artificial. In fact, there is no nation named Israel. . . . The Zionists scraped together some people from all over the world and, based only on racism, brought about the Zionist regime by virtue of the conquest of Palestine.
> — Ali Khameini, president of Iran, addressing Iranian Air Force personnel, Radio Teheran, February 8, 1996

Q: How does Iran refer to Israel?
A: Iran refuses to recognize Israel's existence and refers to Israel as "the occupation regime of Al-quds [Jerusalem]."

> When others talk about liberating Palestine they mean the "annexed territories of 1967." We mean all Palestinian land. . . . Iran is the only country which is opposed to the basic existence of Israel. — Iran's Foreign Minister Velliati interview in *Salaam*, February 6, 1996

Q: Which terrorist groups enjoy the material support of Iran?
A: Iran supports the following Palestinian factions: Hamas, Islamic Jihad, Ahmed Jibril, Palestinian Front for the Liberation of Palestine — General Command. These organizations have stated publicly their connections and cooperation with Iran. Moreover, most of these Palestinian organizations participated in the "Conference for the Support of the Uprising" organized by Teheran, December 4–6, 1990, and October 19–22, 1991.

Q: How does Iran support the "martyrs"?
A: In February 1996, leaders of ten Palestinian opposition organizations met in Damascus, Syria, with Iran's Vice-President Habibi. Habibi stressed Iran's support for a coordinated and continued struggle against Israel and praised the "martyrs."

Q: How does Iran specifically support the Palestinian Islamic Jihad and Hamas?
A: The Palestinian Islamic Jihad terrorist group enjoys the full support of the Iranian regime in training, finances, weaponry, etc. Some of these terrorists were known to have infiltrated Israel, after their training, and were apprehended by Israeli forces.

The Hamas leaders are known to have visited Iran since October 1995, where they met with high-ranking Iranian officials. They received military assistance, training, and finances. They were also trained in Hizballah camps in southern Lebanon by the Iranian "Guardians of the Revolution." This included training and preparations for suicide attacks in Israel.

Q: How does the Hizballah enjoy the support of Iran?
A: The Hizballah organization is the spearhead for Iran in its use of terrorism in general and in its fight against Israel in particular. These are just a few of Hizballah's large-scale attacks:

- In 1982, Hizballah bombed the United States Embassy in Beirut, Lebanon, killing 61 and wounding 120.

- On October 23, 1983, Hizballah was responsible for the suicide bombing of U.S. Marine headquarters in Beirut.

- On October 23, 1983, Hizballah bombed the French army barracks in Beirut, killing 74.

Iran gives millions of dollars annually to the Hizballah and ships weapons and ammunition to them as well as training the terrorists. It is publicly known that Hizballah terrorists are also trained in Iran at the Imam Ali training base in northern Iran. This includes courses for officers, company commanders, commandos, and courses in communications.

> *Iran's Hashemi Rafsanjani reminded us recently of the glorious day "when the Islamic world acquires atomic weapons." He acknowledged that in a nuclear exchange the nations of Islam would suffer damage, but only one great nuclear blast "would destroy Israel completely."* — William Safire, *New York Times*, January 10, 2002

Data on Iranian terror:

March 1996: A major shipment of arms and explosives destined for Iranian terrorists based in Germany was discovered at the Belgian port of Antwerp. Security sources indicated that the shipment was to be used in terrorist attacks against Israel and Jewish targets in Europe.

January 1996: Three Iranian trucks loaded with arms were intercepted by Turkish authorities on their way to Lebanon. They were intended for use against Israel via Turkey and Syria.

April 1996: Thirty Iranian planes landed in Damascus Airport, Syria. They were loaded with a cargo of ammunitions and weapons. The destination was Lebanon.

The following is an excerpt from the text entitled: "The Involvement of Arafat, PA Senior Officials, and Apparatuses in Terrorism against Israel, Corruption and Crime." The text was prepared by a team headed by Dani Naveh, Israeli Minister of Parliamentary Affairs, and was published in April 2002.

Chapter IV — Cooperation Between the PA [Palestinian Authority] and Terror-Sponsoring States

1. The PA holds contacts with the "axis of evil" states — Iran and Iraq, as well as with Saudi Arabia. The accumulating information, based, among other things, on captured documents, indicates that the PA receives money, arms, and moral support from these states.

2. The major role which the PA and its apparatuses played in the armed struggle against Israel brought about a change in Iran's attitude toward it. Until the Intifada, Iran viewed the PA as a "traitor" which seeks a political settlement with Israel; following the latest confrontation, the Palestinian apparatuses are considered by Teheran as the leaders of the violent struggle. On this background, the Iranian leader published (*Al Mastakabal*, September 2000) a religious decree permitting cooperation with the PA and Fatah. In our assessment, in the future the Iranian policy toward the PA will depend on its policies and activities toward Israel, and the PA's return to the political track will lead to the severing of the ties established with Iran during the past.

3. The improved relations were prominently reflected in the cooperation during the Karine-A affair, which

constituted only one expression of the continuing Iranian effort, which was significantly enhanced since the outbreak of the Intifada — to smuggle arms and force multipliers in the PA areas. This in order to create a "Lebanonization" of the conflict, escalate the confrontation between Israel and the Palestinians, and disrupt any attempt to calm the situation and stabilize a cease-fire. All this, in the framework of Iran's call to implement the "Lebanese model" in the PA as an essential stage on the path to Israel's destruction in the more distant future.

4. On this background, Iran expresses persistent and declared support for suicide attacks (in an interview in *Der Spiegel* on September 24, 2001), Foreign Minister Kharazi stated that the suicide attack in the Dolphinarium disco in Tel Aviv was not an act of terror since Israel is an "occupying power." Ayatollah Atma Fadal Lankarani, a senior cleric in the Shi'ite world who resides in Qom and is identified with the conservative camp, also published a religious decree on January 7, 2001, according to which, since the Palestinians have no other choice than to endanger their lives in suicide attacks in order to defend their state, such activities are permitted.

5. The bottom line — Iran draws much encouragement from the PA's turn to the route of terror (according to its method "legitimate resistance") and perceives the situation as an historical "window of opportunities" to achieve its ideological goals (the destruction of Israel, which the Iranian regime continues to espouse) and its strategic goals (Israel's weakening and containment in the framework of Iran's attempts for regional hegemony). Since September 11, 2001, the escalation in the conflict serves Iran in an additional aspect, as reflected in the words of Majlis member and presidential advisor, Mohtashemi Pur (April 23, 2002), who claimed that the United States will not attack Iran and Iraq as long as the Palestinian crisis continues, and therefore Iran must "increase the strength" of the Palestinians and "prevent Israel from any possibility of solving the crisis in the Middle East" (p. 59–60).

We shall fight together, as one Moslem nation, under one flag. — Yassir Arafat, in Teheran, "Voice of Fatah," Beirut, February 19, 1979

The foundation of the Islamic regime is opposition to Israel, and Iran's continuous issue is the obliteration of Israel from the region. — Supreme leader Ayatollah Ali Khamenei, January 2001

IRAN: TERROR AGAINST JEWS AND ISRAELIS

In March 2003, the government of Argentina issued an arrest warrant for four Iranian citizens, including two former ministers. Argentina accuses these Iranians of being actively involved in the planning of the bombing of the Jewish community center in Buenos Aires in 1994. In that terrorist attack, 85 people were murdered, mostly Jews, and well over one hundred others were wounded. The community center was destroyed.

The arrest warrants were issued for Ali Falnan, who was in charge of Iranian intelligence; Ali Akbar Farwaresh, who was Iran's minister of education; Mohsen Rabbani, Iran's cultural attache in Buenos Aires; and Ali Balash Abdai, a member of the Iranian intelligence. Three of the four were in Buenos Aires a short time prior to the terrorist attack.

The Argentinian judge who issued the warrants said that the radical Iranians were behind the crime in 1994 and that the time had come for those responsible for the crime to be brought to justice.

The Argentinians continued by accusing people in the highest echelon in Iran for being involved as well. They mentioned Ali Haminai, the Iranian spiritual leader, as well as Hashemi Rafsangiani, the former president of Iran. Both men knew about the plans to destroy the Jewish center, yet did nothing to stop it. The crime was committed by the Hizballah terrorist organization. This organization enjoys the financial support of Iran, and its terrorists are trained by the Iranians.

Israeli intelligence has more information about this terrorist attack. According to the Israeli intelligence, the decision to destroy the Jewish community center was made in July 1994 by the Iranian Supreme Council. The man who committed the crime,

Ibrahim Hasin Bero, was a member of the Hizballah terrorist organization. He agreed to serve as the "martyr." He arrived in Argentina a few days before the attack and spoke with his family in Lebanon by telephone just a few hours before exploding himself and killing the 85 victims.

According to Argentinian intelligence, the bombing which destroyed the Israeli Embassy in Buenos Aires in March 1992 was also committed by the Hizballah with the cooperation of Iran.

Q: How long was the Israeli investigation?
A: Eight and one-half years.

Q: Who participated in the meeting in which the destruction of the Jewish community center was discussed?
A: The meeting was held in August 1993 with the participation of Ali Haminai, the Iranian spiritual leader; the former Iranian president, Rafsangiani; the minister of intelligence, Ali Falahian; and the former foreign minister, Akbar Ali Wilayati.

Q: What was decided at that meeting?
A: It was decided to destroy the Jewish community center and to begin all necessary preparations to carry it out. Ali Haminai issued a fatwa justifying the terrorist attack. It was decided as well that Ali Falahian, the minister of intelligence, would be in charge of the attack.

Q: Who was appointed to carry out the attack?
A: Falahian asked Imad Mugniyah, the Hizballah member, to plan and carry out such attacks abroad. On October 10, 2001, Mugniyah was included on the FBI's most wanted list of terrorists (see the chapter on Mugniyah). Mugniyah received the help and cooperation of the Iranian authorities. He was experienced, and the leader of the terrorists who destroyed the Israeli embassy in Buenos Aires in March 1992. The suicide bomber, Ibrahim Hasin Bero, member of the Hizballah, was chosen by Mugniyah to carry out the attack on the Jewish community center.

Q: What did Israeli intelligence discover about the events prior to the attack?
A: Hasin Bero called his family in Lebanon a few hours before blowing himself up. He told his family members that he was going to

join his brother in heaven. His brother was killed in August 1989 in Lebanon in an exploding car near an Israeli military position in southern Lebanon.

On September 9, 1994, the Hizballah terrorist organization declared in Lebanon that Hasan Bero was killed in southern Lebanon. By doing so, the Hizballah was attempting to conceal Hasan Bero's involvement in the crime in Buenos Aires.

Ten days before the attack, the Iranian ambassadors in Argentina, Uraguay, and Chile were ordered back to Iran for consultations. They were not at their posts in the embassies when the attack occurred.

Q: Who purchased the explosives?
A: The Iranian intelligence purchased the huge quantity of explosives that was needed to destroy the building. Moreover, they made certain that the crime would be committed immediately after Hasin Bero's arrival in Argentina. The suicide bomber arrived and found a car loaded with explosives waiting for him. The car was located in a parking lot in the vicinity of the community center.

Iran, one of the most fanatic states in the world, is also included in U.S. President Bush's list termed "Axis of Evil." As long as this blindly fanatic and highly dangerous regime exists, the world cannot expect to sleep quietly.

> *Iran must stop its pursuit of weapons of mass destruction and the ability to produce them.* — Colin Powell, U.S. Secretary of State, *Jerusalem Post*, March 29, 2003

IRAN'S NUCLEAR THREAT

In 2002–2003 more facts and details were discovered about the Iranians' intentions to accumulate a variety of weapons of mass destruction. One can only imagine the danger to the world in general and to Israel in particular if the fanatic and radical Iranian leaders succeed in putting their hands on such weapons. In the aftermath of September 11, 2001, the threats of fanatic terrorists must be taken seriously. Bear in mind that Iran does not recognize Israel's right to exist and has declared publicly time and again that its goal is Israel's destruction.

Iran now openly says it is pursuing a complete nuclear fuel cycle. We completely reject Iran's claim that it is doing so for peaceful purposes. . . . After all, Iran is in possession of a great amount of energy of a non-nuclear nature as a result of their gas and oil supplies. — Ari Fleischer, White House spokesman, March 2003

According to various reports, Iran has a nuclear program that is far more advanced than has been previously reported. U.S. administration officials have long accused Iran of trying to develop nuclear weapons.

Q: What did Time magazine reveal in March 2003?
A: *Time* magazine wrote that the United Nations inspectors had discovered that Iran's uranium-enriched facility is "extremely advanced," to the point that it violates the Treaty on the Non-Proliferation of Nuclear Weapons. Enriched uranium is known for its use in producing nuclear weapons.

Q: What was found by United Nations representatives?
A: In February 2003, Mohamed ElBaradei, director general of the International Atomic Energy Agency, visited the Iranian facility in Natanz. The facility was designed to enrich uranium. *Time* magazine quoted diplomatic sources who reported that ElBaradei found the plant much further along than previously believed. Work on the plant involves hundreds of gas centrifuges ready to produce enriched uranium, and "the parts for a thousand others [are] ready to be assembled" as well. Elbaradei found the plant "extremely advanced," according to these same diplomatic sources.

Q: Has Iran denied its intentions?
A: No. Iran has confirmed two nuclear plants — one in Natanz and the other near Arak. However, Iran claims that its nuclear program is aimed at building power plants. In February 2003, Iranian President Mohammed Khatami said the following: "Iranian experts have acquired the knowledge for civilian application of the nuclear technology." He added that nations have a right to do so.

Q: Is Iran in violation of the Non-Proliferation Treaty?
A: Yes. The United Nations Atomic Energy Agency has defined Iran's adding of uranium to some centrifuges as a test to be a

"blatant violation" of the non-proliferation treaty. Iran is a signatory on that treaty.

Time magazine quoted Jon Wolfstahl of the Carnegie Endowment for International Peace as having said the following: "If Iran were found to have an operating centrifuge, it would be a direct violation (of the treaty) and is something that would need immediately to be referred to the United Nations Security Council for action."

Bear in mind that Iran, along with Iraq and North Korea, was among the countries labeled part of the "axis of evil" by U.S. President Bush in his State of the Union address in January 2002.

Q: What has the United States revealed about Iran's nuclear capabilities?
A: The U.S. State Department said in December 2002 that it had recent satellite photos which reinforce the belief that Iran was "actively working" on a nuclear weapons program. U.S. Secretary of State Colin Powell said the following in an interview on CNN on March 9, 2003: "Here, we suddenly discover that Iran is much further along — with a far more robust nuclear weapons development program — than anyone said it had."

Q: What has the United States concluded from its findings?
A: Colin Powell said, ". . . it shows you how a determined nation that has the intent to develop a nuclear weapon can keep that development process secret from inspectors and outsiders." (CNN interview, March 9, 2003)

Condoleeza Rice, U.S. national security adviser, said that the findings "do not surprise us at all. . . . We've said all along that there are real problems with Iran and its so-called peaceful nuclear programs. It's been couched as a peaceful program, but we've been one of the lone voices that said the Iranians are a problem" (excerpt from an interview on ABC's "This Week").

Q: Which country supplied the reactor to Iran?
A: The Russians. U.S. President Bush asked the Russians to end its work with Iran on nuclear reactors. He insisted that Tehran was trying to develop nuclear weapons. Moscow refused.

Q: What is Israel's reaction?
A: Israel has said that it is deeply alarmed by these developments. In a 1981 air attack, Israel destroyed an Iraqi nuclear plant. A

senior Israeli official has said that the news is "a huge concern" because Iran denies Israel's right to exist and is a principle sponsor of the Hizballah terrorist organization. Hizballah has carried out attacks against Israel and is on the United States's list of terrorist organizations.

The assumption now is that Iran may achieve nuclear weapons by the year 2006. It is clear that the only super power that may stop Iran is the United States.

IRAQ: CRUELTY AND VICIOUSNESS AS A WAY OF LIFE

And the angel of the Lord said to her, Behold thou art with child and shalt bear a son and shalt call his name Yismael [the biblical Arabs]. And he will be a wild man, his hand will be against every man, and every man's hand against him. — Genesis 16:11–12

"Oh people of Iraq, oh people of rebellion and defiance. I see many heads that the time has come to cut them off." These were the words of the legendary Islamic general Alhaggiag Ibn Yousouf. He was commander of the Islamic forces at the beginning of the Islamic era in the seventh century C.E.

General Ibn Yousouf was sent to Iraq by the prophet Mohammed's followers since the Iraqi people were known to be rebellious, defiant, stubborn, and very cruel. Ibn Yousouf was known as a brilliant fighter and as a cruel man himself. After a long and bitter battle against the rebellious Iraqi leader, he succeeded in crushing the uprising.

Immediately after his brief speech, Ibn Yousouf took his sword and, one by one, cut off the heads of the Iraqi leaders. Iraq was tranquil and silent for many years after.

By Arab standards, the Iraqi people are considered the cruelest of all. In July 1958, the 23-year-old Iraqi king Faisal was murdered in a coup d'etat. The leader of the coup was General Abd AlQarim Kasem. He ordered that the young king be killed, his feet then to be tied to the back fender of a car, and that his body be dragged through the streets of Baghdad. He ordered the Iraqi masses to come out into the streets in order to witness this act of brutality.

In 1963, General Abd AlQarim Kasem was himself over-thrown by his deputy, General Abd AlSalam Aref. Knowing quite well that his fate was execution, General Kasem requested one thing from General Aref. He pleaded: "Kill me, but don't do to me what I did to King Faisal." His dying request was respected. In the 1958 coup d'etat, the Iraqi prime minister, Nouri AlSaeed, a very well-known figure, was assassinated as well. A few years later, General Aref died in a plane crash.

Saddam Hussein is infamous in Iraqi history as one of the cruelest and most vicious leaders to ever have ruled in Iraq. When King Faisal's body was dragged through the streets of Baghdad in July 1958, Saddam Hussein was about 20 years old. He was among the masses who cheered the brutal behavior.

During the years 1981–1988, Saddam Hussein fought a war he initiated against his neighbor state, Iran. The war ended with the death of hundreds of thousands of Iraqis and Iranians and count-less more maimed or wounded. Hussein did not hesitate to use poisonous gas to kill the Iranians. Moreover, the Iraqi president killed thousands of Iraqi citizens of Kurdish descent in the town of Halabtscha in northern Iraq. In that horrendous attack, men, women, and children were indiscriminately slaughtered. By using these poisonous gases, the Iraqi dictator became the first head of state to use outlawed gas to murder the masses since the Second World War.

After the first Gulf War, Saddam Hussein's two sons-in-law fled to Jordan, fearing for their lives. Saddam Hussein then con-vinced them to return to Baghdad, assuring them that they would be safe. Believing their father-in-law, the men returned to Iraq. Two days after their return, they were murdered by Saddam's agents.

The Iraqi president never hesitated to kill all those who oppose his rule. During the Iraqi-Iranian war, one of Saddam's ministers suggested that in order to end the war and any further casualties to Iraq, perhaps Saddam should step down temporarily. The idea was for Saddam Hussein to return to power immediately following a cease-fire agreement with Iran. Saddam Hussein's reaction to this suggestion was quick in coming. He ordered his agents to kill the minister. The following day, the minister's wife came to beg for his life. Saddam Hussein had the man murdered and had his body sent in a coffin to his family.

During his reign, Saddam Hussein had his political rivals in Iraq either killed, tortured, or imprisoned. His two sons, Udai and Kosai, served as his watch dogs.

Ameen Paris Rihani, an Arab historian, characterized the Arabs neighboring Iraq in the lower Arab peninsula thusly:

> The people of Yemen and Asir are still savage; not one of them would trust his brother. They live in perpetual fear and anxiety. . . . They are like wild beasts which fear everything and everybody that may come near them. As to the Yemen . . . all our people are armed, all fight, and all kill for the least thing. We are very jealous of our rights. . . . If in this village two houses would suddenly engage in a fight, the entire population would split into two parties and join in the fight. War could break out in the village. When it subsides, and only then, would the people ask what the cause of the fighting was. They fight first, and then inquire as to the cause of the fight. This is our way of life in Yemen. We fight our own relatives. The brother would fight his own brother, the son his own father. . . . — From *Muluk Al-Arab*, (Kings of the Arabs, 3rd edition, Beirut, 1953

The Egyptian historian, Ahmad Utman, expressed his opinion about democracy in the Arab world. Speaking on Al-Jazira television in March 2003, he said the following:

> Had we changed the present Arab dictators by other Arab leaders, the new leaders would do the same as their predecessors. The reason for this would be the fact that the Arab nations are under cultural and moral collapse.

Whoever thinks that the people of Iraq are the unwilling victims of a terrible dictator, Saddam Hussein, does not know the reality of the Arab world. There are 21 Arab states. None of them is democratic. The various Arab nations: Egypt, Syria, Libya, Algeria, etc., all accept the dictatorships and lack of freedom of speech as something natural and as their way of life.

This is a copy of a flier that was distributed in Ramallah on the West Bank during the coalition war against Saddam Hussein's regime in Iraq (March 2003). It reads: "Kill the Americans and British who are the enemies of Islam."

The uprisings that have occurred in the Arab world since Israel's establishment in 1948 have had nothing to do with the desire for democratic rule. The uprisings and coups d'etat occurred because of thirst for power — mainly groups of military officers being forcibly removed by a group of opposing military officers.

The Arab nations are still awaiting the emergence of their own Thomas Jefferson or Mikhail Gorbachov.

THE U.S. AND BRITISH-LED COALITION WAR FOR DEMOCRACY IN IRAQ, SPRING 2003: THE AFTERMATH

O daughter of Babylon [Iraq], you devastator; Happy shall he be who requites you with what you have done to us. Happy shall he be who takes your little ones and dashes them against the rock. — Psalm 137:8–9

Flee from the midst of Babylon, let every man save his life. Be not cut off in her punishment, for this is the time of the Lord's vengeance. . . . Suddenly Babylon has fallen and been broken; wail for her. Take balm for her pain; perhaps she may be healed. — Jeremiah 51:6–9

The coalition war waged in the spring of 2003 for "Iraqi Freedom" proved, once again, that the United States is the sole superpower in the world. The removal of the evil regimes of the Taliban and Bin-Laden in Afghanistan and of Saddam Hussein in Iraq has made the world far safer. Radical Islam, which threatened and continues to threaten today the Western world, suffered a severe blow. The removal of the brutal Iraqi regime sends a clear message and warning to other regimes and Islamic organizations around the world such as Iran, Syria, Hizballah, and Hamas.

The combined efforts of France, Germany, and Russia to prevent the military action proved unsuccessful. Besides demonstrating their shortsightedness, these countries proved their preference for their own selfish economic interests over the safety of the nations of the world and the welfare of the Iraqi people, their well-being, and their future.

Any individual with an appreciation for a life of freedom would like to see Iraq democratic. The success of a thriving free and democratic Iraq can have an enormous effect on the other dictatorial Arab and Islamic regimes in the area.

"La liamrica la lisaddam, naa'm naa'm lilislam" (translation: "No to America no to Saddam, yes to Islam"). These and similar slogans were chanted by hundreds of thousands of Iraqis in one of the demonstrations after the war of 2003.

Wishful thinking is one thing, reality is quite another. It is indeed difficult to speak about democracy in the Western sense of the word when referring to the Arab nations for a number of reasons.

1. In all of the Arab world, there is not even one single democracy. The history of the Arab world since 1948 is a story marked by murder, subversion, coup d'etats, persecutions, civil war, hatred, and bloodshed. Hundreds of thousands of Arabs were murdered by fellow Arabs. Many hundreds of leaders, presidents, kings, ministers, religious leaders, and other dignitaries were assassinated. At different times, the Arab armies fought one another and caused tens of thousands of casualties.

It can now be seen that Arabs themselves, citizens of the same country, not only cannot coexist but collide day and night. — The late King Hussein of Jordan interview with *Newsweek* editor Arnaud de Borchegravé

2. Iraq, besides being an Arab state, is also composed of various groups of population, such as the Kurds in the north, the Shi'ite Moslems in the south, and the minority of the population which is Sunnite Moslems. The fanatic Shi'ites may very well want to see an Islamic state rather than a democracy.

The United States cannot afford to give this majority the option to control the country and to replace Saddam Hussein's dictatorship with a fanatic Shi'ite Islamic regime, styled after Iran, and which would be even worse. The fateful mistake was made in 1921 when the British administration established Iraq by combining three different Islamic communities headed by the Sunni minority.

3. Democracy, as a way of life and as a value, developed over hundreds of years in Europe before becoming the common way of life. The masses were educated about their rights and duties and then learned to appreciate a life of freedom. The Arab states, on the other hand, were established in the 20th century. The educational system in the Arab states never considered democracy as a solution or as a preferred system to that under which they lived for hundreds of years. The attempt to impose democracy in these countries by outsiders, may not be accepted and it may not work.

4. Between the years 1921 and 1958, Iraq enjoyed a kind of democracy: elections were held, political parties were established, a parliament was formed, there was a modified free press, etc. However, all these signs of democratic rule were associated with the British colonial power. Moreover, it is associated with the corrupted Iraqi higher echelon which led to a deteriorating economy. The Iraqi try at democracy did not work.

In July 1958, Iraq's first coup d'etat occurred. The military junta, headed by General Adi AlQarim Qassem, murdered Iraqi King Faisal and took control of the country. Between 1958 and 2003, the Iraqi people have lived under the rule of dictators.

5. Iraq is very different from other Arab states. In Jordan, the kingdom has been ruled by the Hashemite dynasty from King Abdullah to his grandson, the late King Hussein, and through his

son Abdullah today. The kingdom is called the Hashemite Kingdom of Jordan.

The same can be said of Saudi Arabia which is named after the founder of the kingdom, Ibn Saud.

In cases of a homogeneous society, it is easy to find a common symbol with which the masses can identify. In Iraq, the situation is very different. The Kurds have nothing to do with the Shi'ites and the Sunnis have nothing to do with either. The Kurds have never hidden their national aspirations to attain statehood independent of Iraqi or any other rule. The Shi'ites, although different from neighboring Iranian Shi'ites, believe that as the majority in Iraq, they should have control of the country. The Sunnis, located in central Iraq, feel that they are the most developed and are, thereby, the best suited to rule Iraq. These deep-rooted rifts among the Iraqi population may make it more difficult to establish a democracy in the Western sense of the term.

6. Throughout the history of Iraq, as well as the history of most Arab countries, the military has always played an important role. The position of the various Arab armies was not only to defend the country from foreign aggression, but to defend it from internal opposition. Whenever there was a lack of stability or any sign of a threat — either external or internal — the army was always there. For the Iraqi masses, democracy would entail a revolution in their way of thinking.

Islam is a dominant factor in most of the Arab states. To teach religious Moslems — not to mention fanatic Moslems — to forego the Islamic way of thought and instead to adopt a democratic way of life, is a very difficult mission at the very best. The only way in which to establish a lasting democracy is through education, mainly among the younger generation. The name of the game is education and time.

> *The argument we would be starting a democratic wave in Iraq is pure blowing smoke. You have 22 Arab governments and not one has made any progress toward democracy, not one. . . . You don't go from an 'authoritarian' dictatorship to a democracy overnight, not even quickly.* — Jessica T. Mathews, president, Carnegie Endowment for International Peace, quoted in *Outpost*, March 2003

Saudi Arabia: Not a Friend of the United States

> *To listen to Saudi officials, or read the Arab press, you would never know that most of the hijackers [of the September 11, 2001, attacks on America] were young Saudis, or that the main funding for Osama Bin-Laden — a Saudi — has been coming from wealthy Saudis, or that Saudi Arabia's government was the main funder of the Taliban.* — Thomas Friedman, *New York Times*, October 16, 2001

The United States considers Saudi Arabia a friend and an ally to America. The United States sells weapons to the Saudis as well as hi-tech products, etc. America buys oil from the Saudis.

The Saudi regime is known to be highly corrupted and ineffectual. Opposition to the Saudi regime from within and without is very strong.

When Iraq, Saudi Arabia's eastern neighbor, invaded Kuwait in August 1990, the Saudis knew that the only power that could force Iraq out of Kuwait is the United States. The Saudis reasoned that in the event of a military threat from Iraq, they would always ask America for protection.

Yet despite continual support from the United States, the Saudis are, by no means, friends of the United States. Or in the words of a prominent government Saudi cleric, Sheikh Saad Al-Buraik:

> *I am against America until this life ends, until the Day of Judgment. . . . My hatred of America, if part of it was contained in the universe, it would collapse. . . . She is the root of all evils and wickedness on earth. . . . Oh Muslim, don't take the Jews and Christians as allies. . . . Muslim brothers in Palestine, do not have any mercy, neither compassion on the Jews, their blood, their money, their flesh. Their women are yours to take, legitimately. God made them yours. Why don't you wage jihad? Why don't you pillage them?* — Excerpt of his speech in a Riyadh government mosque and quoted by Cal Thomas, *Star Ledger*, April 30, 2002

Q: Who are the majority of Al-Qaeda terrorists?
A: It became public knowledge in January 2002 that from 158 incarcerated Al-Qaeda terrorists in Guantanamo, Cuba, 100 are

Saudis. An additional 240 from 250 detainees in Pakistan, suspected as members of Al-Qaeda, are Saudi citizens as well.

> *If the United States wants to prevent big terrorist attacks, there is one government over any others that must have reforms or to be changed. This is not the government of Saddam Hussein, but the House of Saud.* — Tom Gross, *National Review*

Q: Does Saudi Arabia support terror?
A: Yes. The Saudis never denied their financial support for the Palestinian terrorists. Their so-called *shahids* (martyrs) and their families enjoy financial support from Saudi Arabia. Moreover, it is known that Saudia Arabia supports the fanatic terror organization Hamas.

Q: How much financial support are we talking about?
A: According to Ahmad Muhammed Ali, chairman of the Saudi Bank, over the years the bank has paid $429.7 million to Palestinian Authority employees and $22.8 million was paid to the martyrs of the uprising.

Q: Who else is involved?
A: Prince Naif, the minister of interior, declared in January 2002 that Saudi Arabia will pay $5,333 to each member of a martyr's family.

On January 22, 2002, in an interview on the Arab cable network Al Jazira, Abdallah Bin-Matruk Al-Hadel, a spiritual leader of great influence in Saudi Arabia, lavishly praised Osama Bin-Laden and called the Jews "monkeys" and "pigs." He said that the Islamic nation that brought forth Bin-Laden is a strong and big nation. Matruk advised the United States to expel the Jews from U.S. soil.

It is a known fact that, directly or indirectly, Saudi Arabia supports international terrorism against the United States and Israel. In 1999, Jack Kelley, a reporter for USA Today, revealed that prominent Saudi businessmen had transferred billions of dollars to New York and London bank accounts. These accounts were linked to Osama Bin-Laden, who was relatively unknown at the time.

Q: How is Saudi money connected to Bin-Laden?
A: Jack Kelley explains: "The money was deposited into the accounts of Islamic charities, including Islamic Relief and Blessed Relief, that serve as trusts for Bin-Laden."

After the September 11, 2001, tragedies, the American authorities have closed down some of these organizations and many others are under investigation.

Here is one example in which the Saudis raised money for the Palestinian terrorists. Sheikh Saad Al-Buraik, the aforementioned Saudi government cleric, hosted a two-day telethon that raised $109 million for the families of "martyred" Palestinian fighters.

Q: Does Saudi Arabia cooperate with the United States in its investigations into terrorist acts and their financial funding against the United States?
A: The Saudis have offered only minimal cooperation to U.S. authorities, particularly with regard to the June 1996 terrorist bombing of the Khobar Towers in Dhahran, Saudi Arabia. In that attack, 19 American air force personnel were killed and hundreds more were wounded. The American administration tries to put a good face on Saudi behavior. However, reality shows that the Saudis are blocking the investigation of their nationals. Moreover, they refuse to clamp down on funding of Bin-Laden's network, and they opposed American use of their air facilities in Saudi Arabia in the coalition's war against the Taliban.

Q: How is Saudi doctrine spread in the United States?
A: The Saudis are a major source of funding for mosques in the United States which preach a radical Wahhabite ideology. In the November 2001 issue of *Commentary*, Daniel Pipes quoted Muhammad Hisham Kabbani, who is considered to be one of the rare moderate Muslim leaders. Kabbani says that extremists have taken over 80 percent of the mosques in America, as well as schools, youth groups, community centers, political organizations, professional associations, etc. All these groups advocate replacing the present order in the United States with that of an Islamic one.

Q: Did the Saudi ambassador to the United States, Prince Bandar, cooperate with American authorities in their investigation into the September 11, 2001, attacks?

A: No. Instead of helping the American authorities, Prince Bandar managed to get dozens of Saudi nationals out of the United States before they could be held for questioning.

> *Who hath gathered wealth [of this world] and arranged it. He thinketh that his wealth will render him immortal. Nay, but verily he will be flung to the Consuming One. . . . It is the fire of Allah kindled.* — 1 Koran, Sura CIV: 2–4, 6

> *The incredible lies in Saudi newspapers accusing Jews of draining the blood of young Muslims for festival pastries, and inventing an anti-Semitic Benjamin Franklin to justify the murder of Jews throughout the world. Anyone who believes that Saudi Arabia is a "moderate" country after all this should be forced to read Mein Kampf daily for a year, to perform a comparative analysis of Saudi publications, and to memorize Hitler's peace plans for Czechoslovakia and the Sudetenland.* — Michael Ledeen, Zionist Information News Service, July/August 2002

The Saudis fulfill, literally and word for word, what the Koran prescribes as just punishment. "Stealing is punished by the amputation of the hands" (Koran, Sura 5, verse 41). "Adultery is punished by public flogging" (Koran, Sura 22, verse 2).

- Do you know that Saudi Arabia is the only country in the world which has a verse from a holy book — the Koran — decorating its flag?

- Do you know that in Saudi Arabia people who have committed a crime can be punished by having their hands or heads cut off?

- Do you know that people in Saudi Arabia who are found guilty are sentenced to hundreds of lashes in a humiliating manner?

- Do you know that Saudi Arabia annually contributes hundreds of millions of dollars to Syria and tens of millions of dollars to the PLO?

- Do you know that Saudi funding to Syria and the PLO has enabled them over the years to purchase millions of dollars worth of Soviet arms? It has also enabled Syria to pay for the presence of 5,000 Soviet military and technical advisors on Syrian soil.

- Do you know that during the years 1967–1985 the income from oil of Saudi Arabia and Kuwait was $830 billion? Yet their contribution to their brethren — the Palestinian refugees — was only $84 million.

- Do you know that the contribution of the United States to UNRWA (United Nations Relief and Welfare Agency) for Palestinian refugees since 1950 is over $1,500 million?

- Do you know that Saudi Arabia refuses to utter the word "Israel" in a normal way? No credence can be given to Israel's recognition because Saudi Arabia has insisted time and again that no such recognition is implied.

- Do you know that Saudi Arabia has for years prevented Egypt's full return to the Arab world as long as Egypt adheres to the peace treaty with Israel?

For the Saudis, the Koran is the constitution. Here are some of the Saudi beliefs:

- "Men are superior to women" (Sura 2:228).

- Women have half the rights of men:
    1. as a witness in court (Sura 2:282),
    2. in inheritance (Sura 4:11).

- "A man may beat his wife" (Sura 4:34).

- "A man may marry up to four wives at the same time" (Sura 4:3).

In an article in the *National Interest* (winter 2002/2003), Daniel Pipes, the world renowned Mideast expert, described how the

Americans cooperated with Saudi demands or limitations with regard to Christian holidays. He wrote the following:

> Mail to U.S. military and official government personnel enters the kingdom on U.S. military craft, and American officials in Saudi Arabia follow Saudi wishes by seizing and disposing of Christmas trees and decorations and other symbols of the holiday. They seize and destroy Christmas cards sent to Americans who receive their mail through a Saudi postal box, and even tear from the envelope U.S. stamps portraying religious scenes.

In that same article, Daniel Pipes succinctly expressed the Saudis' cooperation with U.S. efforts to track the financing of Al-Qaeda thusly:

> The Saudis cooperation with our efforts to track down the financing of Al-Qaeda appears to be somewhere between minimal and zero.

> . . . members of the governing board of the Riyadh Christian Fellowship were suddenly picked up and taken to the Ministry of Interior for lengthy interrogation. . . . the government's major complaint was that the Christians had a governing board and a bank account for the congregation. . . . New rules were issued — no governing board, no bank account, and no large meetings. . . . sources confirmed that the Christians promptly met all the conditions. . . . all members of the board were again rounded up and interrogated. They were ordered out of the country within 24 hours. — Michael Collins, The Christian Science Monitor, August 8, 1983

Syria: A State of Terror

> Over the decades, Syria acquired non-conventional weaponry, engaged in narcotics trade, networked with communist and anti-Western countries from Cuba to North Korea, and became a key actor in the proliferation of terrorism in the Middle East and beyond. — Mordechai Nisan, Hebrew University, October 2, 2001

Despite the emergence of Iraq as the most radical Arab state, Syria is still the leader of the Arab "rejection front." She was behind all the most radical Arab resolutions against Israel. She is continually making all the necessary preparations to achieve a military strategic balance with Israel. Syria's rejectionism has found different expressions on numerous occasions.

Q: How does Syria regard Israel's right to exist?
A: According to Syrian Information Minister Ahmad Iskandar, in *Ar-Rav Al-Am*, on December 18, 1982: "Syria is still the only Arab state that adheres to the resolutions of the Khartoum Conference of 1967, which decreed: No peace, no recognition, and no negotiations with Israel. Syria will always adhere to these 'resolutions.' "

Q: What are its views about UN Resolution 242?
A: According to Syrian Foreign Minister Abd al-Halim Khaddam, on Radio Damascus, July 7, 1980: "The Zionist entity is only temporary. . . . UN Security Council Resolution 242 has to be rejected."

> *The people of Syria are Allah's lash in His land. He wreaks His vengeance through them against whomsoever He wishes among His slaves. It is unthinkable that those who are double faced among them should prosper over the faithful. They will certainly die out of grief and desperation.* — The Islamic holy Hadith

Q: What about the Camp David Accords?
A: According to Syrian Information Minister Iskandar in *Al Akhbar* (Jordan), November 5, 1978: "We want a firm stand against the Camp David agreements. . . . We want joint Arab action against the agreements. . . . We reject the Camp David agreements."

Q: What was Syria's attitude toward the Israeli-Lebanese agreement of 1983?
A: At the beginning of 1983, Lebanon and Israel reached an agreement which terminated the state of war and established good neighborly relations between the two countries. The Syrians rejected and opposed this agreement. Radio Damascus on June 3, 1983, expressed President Assad's position:

> *Assad stated that Syria will spare no efforts to frustrate the agreement. . . . The agreement, therefore, will fail. . . .*

Almost every significant terrorist group operating in the Middle East or western Europe has connections with Syria, as do some groups from other regions as well. These connections are made either through the provision of training facilities or through cooperation with Libya and Iran. The Syrian government, which controls most of Lebanon, exploits its freedom in that country to sponsor a variety of terrorist organizations using training facilities in the Beka'a Valley. These include a large number of Palestinian groups.

Furthermore, Syria has set up a solid organizational infrastructure for its terror activities in the major capitals of Europe. This network is under the authority of the Syrian embassies, enabling terrorists to pass as diplomats and to use the diplomatic corps for the transfer of arms.

Q: What kind of cooperation exists between Syria, Libya, and Iran?
A: In three successive conferences in 1982, in Tripoli on February 4, in Teheran on April 13, and in Damascus on August 23, Libya, Syria, and Iran agreed to a division of labor. Syria would sponsor Jibril, Habash, Hawatmeh, and the Musa factions of the PLO; Libya would assume joint responsibility for Abu Nidal with Syria; and Iran would oversee the fundamentalist groups such as the Hizballah, the Islamic Jihad and the radical wing of Amal.

Q: What were the results of such cooperation?
A: The results were soon to follow: the bombing of a club in West Berlin, the aborted attempt to bomb the El Al Airline offices in London, a similar attempt in Madrid, the bombing of City Hall in downtown Paris, etc.

Q: Which terrorist groups operate from Lebanon with the assistance of Syria?
A: The Syrian government, which controls parts of Lebanon, exploits its freedom in that country to sponsor a variety of terrorist organizations using training facilities in the Beka'a Valley. These include a large number of Palestinian groups, the Armenian Secret Army for the Liberation of Armenia (ASALA), the Popular Front for the Liberation of Oman, the Democratic Front for the Liberation of Somalia, and the Eritrean Liberation Front.

Q: When did Islamic terrorist organizations gain their foothold in Syria?
A: Fanatic Islamic terrorist groups, such as Hamas, the Islamic Jihad, etc., set up headquarters in Damascus in the 1990s.

Q: Where were these terrorist groups located?
A: At least five terrorist training bases were located in the vicinity of the Syrian capital — Damascus — and in Lattakia. Other bases were set up in the Beka'a Valley in southern Lebanon.

Q: Is there concrete evidence that Syria is indeed training terrorists?
A: Yes. At his trial in Rome, the Pope's assailant, Mehmet Al Agca, testified that he and other members of the Grey Wolves, an extremist Turkish gang, were trained in Lattakia, Syria, and taught by Bulgarian and Czech experts.

Q: Why did Syria establish terrorist training bases in Lebanon?
A: Terrorist training bases were set up in southern Lebanon to deflect charges of Syria directly supporting terrorism. The close proximity to the Syrian border ensured complete Syrian control over these bases and their activities.

Q: What is the Syrian reality today?
A: There has been no change. Syria supports the Hizballah, the Islamic Jihad, the Hamas, and other radical Islamic organizations. U.S. President Bush categorized these groups as terrorist organizations in 2002 and he called upon Syria to end its support for them.

> *In January 2001, Bashar (Assad) made a state visit to Teheran, accompanied by several high-ranking ministers. The hosts and guests issued a joint communique praising the heroic Intifada and all groups fighting for the liberation of Arab lands controlled by "barbaric" Israel. — Outpost, July–August 2002*

Syria: The Massacre of 28 Israeli POWs

> *Evil shall come from the north on all the inhabitants of earth.* — Jeremiah 1:14

During the Yom Kippur War of 1973, 28 Israeli troopers were captured by the Syrian forces. They were prisoners of war, yet despite that, they were murdered in cold blood by the Syrian troops, thus violating one of the main paragraphs of the Geneva Convention.

Q: Did the Syrian authorities attempt to cover up this sad story?
A: No, on the contrary. They boasted about it.

Q: How?
A: The Syrian minister of defense awarded the state's highest medal — for the cold-blooded murder of Israel POWs and for eating human flesh.

Q: Was the event publicized in Syria?
A: The following is a translation from the minutes of the session as published in the Syrian *Official Gazette*, of July 11, 1974:

> *There is the outstanding case of a recruit from Aleppo who killed 28 Jewish soldiers all by himself, slaughtering them like sheep. All of his comrades-in-arms witnessed this. He butchered three of them with an axe and decapitated them. In other words, instead of using a gun to kill them, he took a hatchet to chop their heads off. He struggled face to face with one of them and, throwing down his axe, managed to break his neck and devour his flesh in front of his comrades.*
>
> *This is a special case. Need I single it out to award him the Medal of the Republic? I will grant this medal to any soldier who succeeds in killing 28 Jews, and I will cover him with appreciation and honor for his bravery.* — General Mustafa Tlas, Syrian Minister of Defense, 12th Session of Parliament, December 1, 1973

Q: Where is Mustafa Tlas?
A: Until the end of 2003, Mustafa Tlas served as Syria's minister of defense.

Q: Was this sad story adequately covered by the world media?
A: No. The story is hardly known.

Q: Did the United Nations discuss or condemn this murder?
A: Not at all.

Syrian Terror against Its Own People: Confessions of Akram Ali Bishani

Whoever says "no" to President Assad is likely to find himself a head shorter. — Mustafa Tlas, Syrian Defense Minister, *New York Times*, September 12, 1984

Since coming to power in 1970, the late former Syrian president, Hafez al-Assad, had accumulated a long record of gross violations of human rights. During recent years, more severe measures were taken as a result of an increase in opposition activities. A report by the International Commission of Jurists in Geneva spoke of detentions without trial, and torture to extract information. Families of those held are generally not informed of arrests and they find real difficulty in tracing the whereabouts of their relatives. At times, if the suspected person could not be found, members of his family were imprisoned instead.

> *Amnesty International report cites six cases of alleged mass political killings said to have been carried out by the security forces between March 1980 and February 1982. They include the reported killing on 27 of June 1980 of between 600 and 1,000 inmates of Palmyra Prison (Syria).* — Amnesty International briefing, London, November 1983

Here is one example of mass murder — one day in which 550 people were massacred:

Akram Al Bishani and Issa Ibrahim Fayyad were two members of the terrorist gang of five which was sent to Jordan from Syria to assassinate the prime minister of Jordan. The terrorists were arrested and the following are excerpts from Bishani's confession regarding mass killing committed in the Palmyra Prison.

Q: What are the operations which you were entrusted with during your service at the Defense Battalions (Saraya Al-Difa's, a special brigade of the Syrian army)?
A: I was entrusted with two operations.

Q: What was the first operation?
A: "The operation of Palmyra Prison on June 26, 1980. . . . We were awakened at 3 A.M. and told that there was a meeting in full

battledress with weapons. . . . We were met by Brigadier Mouieen Nassif, chief of the brigade. He addressed us: 'Today you will be attacking [the Moslem Brothers'] largest center which is the Palmyra Prison.' . . . We mounted the planes led by the commander of the 138th brigade. Brigadier Suliman Mustafa, an Alawite . . . we reached there at about 6:30 A.M. of the same day . . . in the prison we were divided into six smaller groups or more. My group was of about eleven persons. . . .

"My group was led by Captain Munir Darwish. They opened a dormitory door, wherein there were about 60 to 70 persons. . . . Then he said, 'There is one who has not died yet and we want to machine-gun him.' The total of those whom I machine-gunned was about 15 persons; the total of those killed in the prison of the Moslem Brothers was about 550 persons. . . ."

In its report from 1983, Amnesty International stated: "Syrian security forces have practiced systematic violations of human rights including torture and political killing and have been operating with impunity under the country's emergency laws. There is overwhelming evidence that thousands of Syrians not involved in violence have been harassed and wrongfully detained without chance of appeal and in some cases have been tortured, others are reported to have 'disappeared' or to have been the victims of extra judicial killings carried out by security forces."

Radio Damascus reported: "Before dawn on September 26, 1976, three PLO terrorists, captured after they attacked the Semiramis Hotel in Damascus, were hanged in a public square of that city where their bodies remained suspended for hours. The terrorists admitted under interrogation that they belonged to the Al-Fatah wing of the PLO."

Q: What was Assad's reaction to this brutality?
A: Commenting on the attack, President Assad declared: "We condemn this act of terror, committed by a gang of traitors and criminals. We refuse to bargain with them."

Q: What does Syria think of the PLO?
A: Referring to those who sent the terrorists to Damascus, the Syrian president added, "The only thing these PLO leaders wanted was to attack Syria, despite its sacrifices on behalf of the Palestinians."

Syria: The Killing of 20,000 Moslems in Hama

Assad: a lion in Lebanon yet a rabbit in the Golan Heights. — A Palestinian saying (*Assad* in Arabic means "lion")

I went to Hama ten weeks afterward, when the city was reopened to foreigners. I have seen many scenes of destruction in the Middle East, but never anything like Hama. Whole neighborhoods had been plowed up like cornfields and bulldozed as flat as parking lots. Seeing a stoop-shouldered old man with a checkered headdress shuffling along a stretch of rubble the size of four football fields, I asked him where all the houses were. "You are standing on them," he said. And where, I asked, were all the people who used to live there? "You are probably standing on them, too," he answered, shuffling away. Thomas Friedman, *New York Times Magazine*, October 7, 1984

The Hama massacre occurred in February 1982, and was the bloodiest massacre committed by Hafez al-Assad, the late former president of Syria. The victims were members of the Moslem Brotherhood which opposed the Alawite regime of President Assad.

Q: How serious was the massacre?
A: According to the study carried out by Amnesty International: "When law and order was restored, estimates of the dead on all sides ranged from 10,000 to 20,000."

Q: What did the Syrian regime do to cover up its crime?
A: At the time of the massacre, the Syrian regime of President Hafez al-Assad had hermetically sealed off the entire city to the outside world, as heavy artillery and aerial bombing pounded away at positions held by his bitter opponents — the Moslem Brotherhood.

Q: How many Syrian troops were involved in the massacre?
A: According to the Amnesty International study, some 6,000 to 8,000 soldiers including units from the 21st mechanized brigade of the 3rd armored division, were reportedly dispatched to the city.

Q: What did the Syrian troops do to the city?
A: The study says that ". . . old parts of the city were bombarded from the air and shelled in order to facilitate the entry of troops and tanks along the narrow roads. . . ."

Q: What did the State Department's human rights report of 1983 say about the massacre?
A: "Evidence on the number of people killed is scanty because the government restricted access to the city for some time, and has attempted to stifle information on events there. Nevertheless, there have been press accounts that several thousand persons were killed."

Q: What did the Washington Post *write about the massacre?*
A: The *Post* reported a few weeks after the massacre that as many as 20,000 orphans may have been created during the ordeal.

Q: What did the Moslem Brotherhood sources say?
A: Moslem Brotherhood sources say that as many as 30,000 people may have been killed.

Q: What do the Syrians say about the massacre?
A: The Syrian governor of the area insisted that only 1,200 were killed on both sides.

Q: What happened on February 19, 1982?
A: Amnesty International has heard that there was, among other things, a collective execution of 70 people outside the municipal hospital in February 1982; the Hadra quarter residents were executed by Syrian troops that same day.

Q: What were some of the means used to crush the resistance?
A: Cyanide gas containers were alleged to have been brought into the city, connected by rubber pipes to the entrances of buildings believed to house insurgents, and turned on, killing all the buildings' inhabitants. Amnesty International reported that people were assembled at the military airfield, at the sports stadium, and at the military barracks, and left out in the open for days without food or shelter.

Q: What are the conclusions of the National Security Agency (NSA), which took before-and-after photographs of the massacre and devastation in Hama?

A: The "before" picture showed an ancient Arab town complete with small streets and alleys, a large marketplace, and a large number of mosques. The "after" picture clearly showed that virtually all had been leveled during the massacre, including the numerous mosques. The reason was clear — the Moslem Brotherhood had based themselves in the mosques. By destroying them, the Syrian government believed it could deal a complete blow to the Moslem Brotherhood.

Q: Why was there no coverage of these atrocities in the American media?
A: American television networks neglected to cover the massacre for one simple reason. The Syrian government did not permit any camera crews into the area. It is very hard indeed to make the nightly news programs in the United States without some good, vivid footage to back up a story.

Q: Did the Arab League condemn the murder of thousands of Arabs and the demolishing of numerous mosques?
A: Not at all.

Q: Was there even a meeting of the United Nations Security Council to discuss the tragedy?
A: Not at all.

Q: What are the consequences of the Hama massacre?
A: If Syrian President Assad could slaughter so many of his own people, Moslems and Arabs, one can only imagine what his son, Bashir Assad, president of Syria today, would do to the Jews, should they ever fall into his hands.

> *Political liberty can exist only when there is peace. Social reform can take place only when there is peace.* — U.S. President Woodrow Wilson

In October 1983, Syrian television showed 16-year-old girls, trainees in the Syrian Ba'ath Party militia, fondling live snakes as President Assad and other Syrian leaders looked on approvingly. The girls suddenly bit the snakes with their teeth, repeatedly tore off flesh and spat it out as blood ran down their chins. After this, militiamen strangled puppies and drank their blood.

Syrian Terror against Political Opponents

> *It is not only in internal affairs that the Syrian government has elevated extremist violence to an instrument of state. During 1980 and 1981, Syrian agents went on the offensive in Beirut (Lebanon), shooting and killing several Lebanese and western journalists in order to discourage reporters from writing negatively about Syria. As a member of the press corps at the time, I can testify that the campaign had its intended effect. Although unflattering stories about Syria still go out, there wasn't a journalist in Beirut who didn't think twice, or even three times, about writing ill of the Syrian regime.*
> — Thomas Friedman, *New York Times Magazine*, October 7, 1984

The Syrian regime has made it a policy to murder political opponents and to destroy their homes and offices. Opposition to the Syrian regime is considered treason and deserves death. This policy has been conducted inside as well as outside Syria.

Q: What happened to the pro-Iraqi weekly Alwatan Al-Arabi in Paris?
A: On April 22, 1982, Syrian agents planted a bomb in the building housing the editorial offices shortly after it had published an interview with a Moslem Brotherhood leader.

Q: Why was France chosen as the venue of Syrian terror?
A: Paris was chosen partly because some leaders of the Syrian opposition were residing there and partly because of differences between Syria and France regarding the Middle East in general and Lebanon in particular.

Q: What was the reaction of France?
A: The French government recalled its ambassador to Syria for consultations.

Q: What are the aims of Syria's terror operation?
A: Syria has three main aims: 1. Israeli targets, 2. elements of Syrian opposition, and 3. various Arab elements connected with the Syrian opposition.

Q: What are the Syrian targets in Lebanon?
A: Syria considers Lebanon to be an integral part of Syria. Therefore, Syria operates against various elements which it believes are interfering with Syrian interests in Lebanon.

Q: Is the Lebanese media free to criticize Syria?
A: One particular group that is targeted — Arab and western journalists who report on Lebanon and Syria in ways which do not suit Syria — has been subjected to a campaign of intimidation and terror.

Q; What happened to Salim Al-Luzi?
A: Mr. Al-Luzi, the editor of *Al-Hawadeth*, was murdered in March 1980. His hands had been burned by acid to symbolize the fate awaiting anyone who dares to write critically about Syria.

Q: Who else was murdered?
A: On March 16, 1977, the Lebanese leftist leader Kamal Jumblat was murdered. Perhaps this is the main reason why Walidi Kamal's son, is pro-Syrian. He does not want to suffer the same fate as his father.

Q: What happened to the Lebanese president-elect, Bashir Gemayel?
A: Mr. Gemayel was murdered in September 1982 because his views concerning Lebanon differed from those of Syria.

Q: What is the reason behind the Syrian hatred toward Premier Michel Aoun?
A: Mr. Aoun's "mistake" was to ask the Syrian troops to leave Lebanon and to let the Lebanese run their own affairs. Michel Aoun was forced to flee to France.

Q: Were other top Lebanese political leaders murdered?
A: In addition to the aforementioned murders, other top political leaders were killed as well: Tony Franjieh, son of the former president of Lebanon, was murdered in his home in June 1978; Imam Musah Sadr, religious leader, disappeared in Libya in September 1978; Rashid Karame, prime minister of Lebanon, was murdered in June 1987; and Rene Awwad, president elect of Lebanon, was murdered in November 1989.

The following is a partial list of terrorist activities over the last few years which Syria is known to have perpetrated or in which she has played an operational role:

- October 4, 1976: A Syrian intelligence agent seized on the Iraqi border admitted that he had been sent to carry out attacks against Iraqi government institutions and to murder Syrian exiles in Iraq.

- March 26, 1979: An explosive device was thrown at the Israeli Embassy in Ankara, Turkey. The "Eagles of the Revolution" claimed responsibility.

- March 27, 1979: Two attacks in Paris, one against a Jewish restaurant, the other against a store owned by Jews.

- April 2, 1979: RPG missiles — Soviet anti-tank weapons — were fired at the American Embassy in Beirut. The "Eagles of the Revolution" claimed responsibility.

- April 7, 1979: A time bomb was discovered at a French cinema where a Jewish culture week was being held. *As-Saiqa* — a Syrian-controlled terrorist group — claimed responsibility.

- July 21, 1980: Salah A-Din Al-Bitar, a founder of the Ba'ath Party who had been exiled from Syria, was murdered in Paris. It appears that this was the start of activity against Syrian opposition figures abroad.

- January 31, 1981: The Syrians dispatched a terrorist cell to assassinate the prime minister of Jordan, Mudar Badran.

- March 17, 1981: At Aachen, West Germany, the wife of Issam Al-Atar, a Moslem Brotherhood leader, was killed. The action was apparently aimed at Atar himself, but he was not at home.

- May 1, 1981: Heinz Nittel, chairman of the Austria-Israel Friendship Association and a member of the

Vienna City Council was murdered in Vienna by the Abu Nidal group, operating under Syrian aegis.

- **August 29, 1981:** Two terrorists attacked a synagogue in Vienna with machine guns and grenades, killing two people and wounding 19 others. The Abu Nidal group claimed responsibility.

- **January 4, 1982:** The Turkish security authorities announced that the terrorists, who in 1979 and 1980 blew up the Iraqi oil pipeline which passes through Turkey, had been sent by Syria.

- **January 11, 1982:** An attack on a supermarket in Amman, Jordan, was carried out by personnel from the Syrian Embassy. As a result, the Syrian third secretary was expelled.

- **March 26, 1982:** Three Syrians were expelled from West Germany after being arrested there in late February with arms in their possession.

- **April 24, 1982:** An explosive device was detonated next to the offices of a French news agency in Beirut.

From 1982, Syria became the patron and supporter of the Hizballah terrorist organization which took over southern Lebanon. For more details, refer to the chapter on the Hizballah.

Turkey, a member of NATO and close ally of the United States, has fought long battles with Kurdish rebels that have operated under the shield of Syrian sanctuary provided in the Lebanese Beka'a Valley in Lebanon.

PKK (Kurdistan Workers Party) fighters were trained in Syrian-directed camps. Its leader, Abdullah Ocalan, resided in Damascus. In 1993, an agreement was reached putting an end to Syrian involvement following a wave of attacks against Turkish targets in Western Europe. The agreement later collapsed due to Syria's violation of the agreement and, in 1998, Turkey mobilized its forces for war against Syria. As a result, Syria gave in and ended its support for Kurdish rebels.

U.S. Secretary of Defense Donald H. Rumsfeld warned Syria on Friday to stop sending military equipment to Iraqi forces. "We have information that shipments of military supplies have been crossing the border from Syria to Iraq, including night vision goggles. These deliveries pose a direct threat to the lives of coalition forces. We consider such trafficking as hostile acts and will hold the Syrian government accountable for such shipments. There is no question but that to the extent military supplies, equipment, or people move borders between Iraq and Syria that it vastly complicates our situation." — *Jerusalem Post*, March 30, 2003*

From the mid-1960s through the Al-Aqsa intifada of October 2000, Israel — as America's strategic ally — has continually suffered from Syrian-sponsored Palestinian and Islamic terrorism. Damascus has provided ideological, logistical, and military support for terrorist organizations warring against Israel.

Syria is patron for the Popular Front for the Liberation of Palestine (PFLP) and the Hizballah. Ramadan Abdullah Shallah, leader of the Palestinian Islamic Jihad group, has headquarters in Damascus. It is from these offices that he leads continual urban and rural attacks against Israeli civilians. The goal is to take over Palestine.

In April 1986, Nizar Hindawi attempted to blow up an El Al plane in London. Hindawi was caught hiding in the home of the Syrian embassy's attache, directly linking Syria to international terrorism.

In 1992, the Syrian-supported Lebanese Hizballah terrorist organization bombed the Israeli embassy in Buenos Aires, Argentina. In 1994, the Hizballah group attacked a Jewish Community Center in Buenos Aires. The terrorists were aided by Iranian intelligence and logistic support.

In September 2001, Israeli security services uncovered a Hamas terrorist cell in Samaria. The Palestinian members of the cell were former students in Damascus who were recruited by Syria for terrorist attacks against Israel.

The new Syrian president, Bashar Assad, was described in the New York monthly, *Outpost* (July–August 2002) thusly: "In

Syria, Bashar Assad came to power after his father lowered the age requirement for president." Assad senior is a hard act to follow for brutality, but the son was swift in implementing control through a policy of intimidation, fear, and anti-Western rhetoric. He greeted the pope in Damascus with a barrage of anti-Semitic slurs:

> *There are always those who seek to recreate [Jesus'] journey of suffering and pain among people. . . . We see our brothers in Palestine being killed and tortured. We see them [Israel] attacking sacred Christian and Muslim places in Palestine. . . . They try to kill the principle of religions in the same mentality in which they betrayed Jesus Christ. . . . We expect you to stand by them [the Palestinians] against the oppressors so that they can regain what was unjustly taken from them.*

When the war against Iraq broke out in the spring of 2003, Syria supported the regime of Saddam Hussein. The Syrian regime, under President Bashar Assad, was the only Arab country to support the wicked regime of Saddam Hussein. The Syrians helped the Iraqi leader by:

1. sending weapons to Saddam Hussein to use in the Iraqis' fight against U.S., British, and coalition forces,
2. encouraging the Syrian people to demonstrate against the United States, and
3. giving shelter to the Iraqi leaders.

> *I also believe there are some things that we need to do that are more urgent. . . . One of those is to deal with these training camps . . . particularly in Syria and Lebanon, where the next generation of terrorists are being prepared.*
>
> *I think we should first give the Syrians and the Lebanese an opportunity to clean up their own house. But then I think that is a much more immediate threat to the security of the United States of America, in my judgment, than Saddam Hussein.* — Senator Bob Graham, chairman, Senate's Select Committee on Intelligence

Syria refused to accept the advice of the United States not to intervene. The Syrians were convinced that America would fail in Iraq.

> *Syria is dangerous because it has chemical weapons, because she is making severe efforts to manufacture biological weapons, and because the terror organization Hizballah obeys her orders and is under her control.* — Ariel Sharon, prime minister of Israel, *Yediot Aharonot*, April 16, 2003

The Iranians use Syrian territory to help Hizballah provoke and attack Israel.

> *A lot of people are happy when [the U.S.] is touched by catastrophe from God. That's because of your stupid policies.* — Ahmed Jibril PLO leader speaking with *U.S. News*, Jibril's headquarters, Damascus, May 22, 1989

Syria considers the Americans to be the devil of the Middle East and the Israelis their agents in the area. Since Israel is an enemy, whoever supports Israel is an enemy as well. Syria, therefore, should do everything possible in order to damage American interests in the area, including killing American citizens and cooperating with the United States' greatest rivals — the Communist countries.

> *At every major diplomatic turn, Syria stood in the way of America's efforts on behalf of security, peace, and prosperity in the Middle East. In 1978, Damascus was a key actor in the Arab regional alignment against the Camp David Peace Accord between Israel and Egypt that President Carter mediated.* — Mordechai Nisan, Hebrew University, Jerusalem

The following is a list of Syrian terrorist attacks against American targets:

- 1970: The Popular Front for the Liberation of Palestine (PFLP) — a Syrian-supported terrorist group — hijacked three passenger planes. One Pan-Am and one TWA were blown up in Jordan.

- 1973: Fatah's Black September group killed 29 passengers on a Pan-Am plane at Rome Airport.

- June 1985: An Islamic group hijacked a TWA flight over Europe and forced it to land in Beirut. U.S. Navy diver Robert Stetham was murdered on board the plane.

- 1985: In Rome Airport, 14 people were killed by the Abu Nidal group; 5 were Americans.

- December 1988: Pan-Am flight 103 exploded over Lockerbie Scotland. 270 passengers died, 175 were Americans. The United States blamed Libya for the attack, but evidence existed that Syria was also involved.

- 1988: An American passenger was killed on board a Kuwaiti airplane which was hijacked by Hizballah.

- 1973: PLO murdered U.S. Ambassador Cleo Noel in Khartoum, Sudan.

- June 16, 1976: U.S. Ambassador Francis E. Meloy Jr. was murdered with his economics assistant, Robert O. Warring, in Lebanon.

- March 1984: U.S. diplomatic official William Buckley, the political attaché at the U.S. embassy was abducted and murdered in Lebanon.

- February 1988: U.S. officer William Higgins was murdered by Hizballah. He commanded UNIFIL (United Nations Interim Forces in Lebanon).

- 1984: Malcolm Kerr, president of the American University in Beirut was murdered.

- 1986: Peter Kilburn, librarian at the American University in Beirut was murdered.

Kidnappings

In the 1980s, the following staff at the American University of Beirut were kidnapped: University President David Dodge; Dean of Agriculture Thomas Sutherland; member of the engineering department Frank Reiger; and university comptroller Joseph James Cicippio. David Jacobsen, director of the University Hospital in Beirut, was abducted in 1985.

Also abducted was member of the Associated Press staff Terry Anderson; American Cable News personnel Jeremy Levin; and Presbyterian minister Benjamin Weir.

As a result of the wave of abductions and assassinations in Lebanon, many U.S. journalists fled Lebanon.

> *It is astounding that Damascus could deceive America by its cosmetic gesture of helping to have hostages released after the Syrians themselves had masterminded these kidnapping operations in Beirut.* — Mordechai Nisan, Hebrew University

Attacks

- April 18, 1983: A truck-bomb attacked the United States Embassy in Beirut. Sixty-three people died; 17 were Americans.

- October 23, 1983: A truckload of explosives bombed the U.S. Marine compound in Beirut; 241 American Marines died. Hizballah claimed responsibility.

- September 1984: The U.S. Embassy Annex in East Beirut was attacked, leaving 20 people dead.

- 1991: U.S. troops training in Germany were bombed by the PFLP-GC of Ahmed Jibril.

- 1996: A truck-bomb exploded at the Khobar Towers — a U.S. military housing complex in Dhahran, Saudi Arabia; 19 people died.

> *Be not envious of evil men, nor desire to be with them. For their hearts study destruction and their lips talk of mischief.* Proverbs 24:2

> *The way of the wicked is like darkness, they know not at what they stumble.* — Proverbs 4:19

A report on state-sponsored terrorism prepared for the Senate Sub-committee on Security and Terrorism states: "According to intelligence analysts, the two trucks used in the October 23, 1983, bombing of the U.S. Marine headquarters in Beirut were rigged by Syrian professionals stationed in the Beka'a Valley (Lebanon) and even driven into Beirut along a route guarded by Syrian militias." White House sources report that American intelligence intercepted the names and ranks of the Syrian officers directly involved in preparing the blow — 241 U.S. Marines died in the incident.

Q: *What is the meaning of American-Israeli relations?*
A: A Syrian daily concludes "that the Zionist entity implements aggressive and expansionist action in the region only after total agreement with the U.S. administration." In Syrian parlance, Zionism is but a symptom of imperialism, and they are "two sides of one coin"; if the American influence in the Middle East could be eliminated, the Israeli challenge would be greatly reduced, if not ended.

Q: *In light of all this, who, according to Syria, is the source of evil?*
A: After the 1982 conflict in Lebanon, the Syrian prime minister stressed that "the war was not merely between Syria and Israel, but between Syria and those behind Israel." The United States, not Israel, is the "essence of evil." Assad has been quoted as saying that "the United States is the primary enemy."

Q: *Did Syria hit American targets in Lebanon.*
A: Yes. Top American officials have reached complete agreement that Syria had a major role in the October 1983 bombing of the U.S. Marine barracks in Beirut. Former Secretary of Defense Caspar Weinberger accused the Syrian government of "sponsorship and knowledge and authority" for this crime and former Secretary of State George Shultz said that "Syria must bear a share of responsibility." President Reagan stated that Syria "facilitates and supplies instruments for terrorist attacks on the people of Lebanon."

Q: *Who are the other enemies of Syria?*
A: In Syrian opinion, Israel is by no means the only American lackey in the Middle East. The revolt by the Moslem Brotherhood in 1980 was blamed on American agents as well: "The weapons are Israeli, the ammunition from Sadat, the training is Jordanian,

and the moral support is from other parties well known for their loyalty to imperialism."

Q: What was Syria's reaction to the murder of Egypt's President Sadat?
A: When Anwar Al-Sadat was killed, Syrian radio broadcast a speech celebrating the event and calling for the death of other Arab "traitors" including King Hussein of Jordan and Saddam Hussein of Iraq.

Q: In light of this, what is the best choice for the Arabs?
A: According to Syria, the Arabs face the following choice: either "submit to hostile United States or choose a strategic alliance with the friendly Soviet Union."

Q: Has Syria actually threatened the United States?
A: Syrian rulers from time to time explicitly threaten the United States, as when the prime minister asserted in 1980: "If I were able to strike at Washington, I would do so." A 1982 newspaper editorial called on the Arabs to "strike at every type of U.S. interest, to behead the snake." These threats are not idle. There have been repeated attacks against American soldiers and diplomats, perhaps the most spectacular being the Katyusha artillery rocket barrage in May 1983 on Secretary Shultz as he spent the night in the U.S. ambassador's residence in Beirut.

> *The one who digs a pit shall fall into it.* — Proverbs 26:27

In 1983, Syrian President Assad forced the Lebanese government to cancel its peace treaty with Israel. In 1984, Lebanon nullified the agreement which was signed during the Reagan administration in Washington.

In 1991, during George Bush's administration, the Hizballah — supported by Syria — organized mass demonstrations in Lebanon in opposition to the Madrid Peace Conference. Many banners read: "Death to America."

There has been a strategic link between Lebanon and Teheran via Syria, which became a formidable axis of Middle Eastern and worldwide terrorism since the 1980s. Syria succeeded in transforming the "Switzerland of the Middle East" (Lebanon) into a terrorist puppet-state which has continually attacked the Western world across the globe.

> *In 1989, production of hashish in Beka'a Valley, Lebanon — under Syrian control — was an estimated $100 million yearly. Heroin refining laboratories to process opium from Afghanistan and Iran were additional sources of enormous income for Syria.* — Mordechai Nisan, Hebrew University

PART III:

PEACE ACCORDS AND ATTEMPTS TO ACHIEVE PEACE

CHAPTER 6

ISRAEL AND HER NEIGHBORS AT THE NEGOTIATING TABLE

I may forgive the Arabs for killing our dear sons, but I will never forgive them for teaching our sons to kill. — Golda Meir, Israeli Prime Minister

Since its establishment, Israel has sought peace with her neighbors. Time and again, all her requests for direct negotiations with neighboring Arab countries were rejected. The Arab countries claimed instead that the only possible solution to the conflict is the military option, the option that would eventually put an end to Israel's existence.

My soul has long dwelt with haters of peace. Whenever I speak about peace they start a new war. — Psalm 120:6–7

After the Arab defeat in the Six Day War of June 1967, the Arab leaders met in Khartoum, Sudan. After three days of debate, the Arab leaders decided on September 1, 1967: "Kings and presidents have agreed to unified efforts at international and diplomatic levels to eliminate the consequences of aggression and to assure the withdrawal of the aggressor forces of Israel from Arab lands, but within the limits to which Arab states are committed: no peace with Israel, no negotiations with Israel, no recognition of Israel, and the maintenance of the rights of Palestinian people in their nation."

At that time, the Soviet bloc played a crucial role in inciting the Arab leaders against Israel. The Russians supplied the Arab states with huge quantities of sophisticated weapons in addition to their guaranteed political support in the world arena and especially in the United Nations.

In 1977, the late Egyptian President Anwar Sadat was the first Arab leader to break the Arab unity against Israel. On November 19, 1977, he made his historic visit to Israel. As a result of this visit, the two countries embarked upon historical negotiations which led to the 1978 Camp David Accords and the 1979 Israel-Egypt Peace Treaty. Since then, peace has been maintained along the countries' mutual border, and cooperation between the two states is slow but steady.

In October 1991, the United States, together with Russia, succeeded to convince the Arab states to attend the Madrid (Spain) Peace Conference. The purpose of the conference was to begin discussion on the issues that divided Israel and her neighbors. Syria, Jordan, Lebanon, and a Palestinian delegation all attended the conference. The Palestinian delegation participated as an integral part of the Jordanian delegation since Israel refused to allow the PLO terrorist organization to attend independently.

> *Witness what Arafat said to the former president of Indonesia, Aburrahman Wahid, who had asked why the Palestinian leader rejected Israel's offer at Camp David, "Look, we've got 150 years, and we'll throw them into the sea."* — Mortimer Zuckerman, editor, *U.S. News & World Report,* July 15, 2002

THE MADRID PEACE CONFERENCE

The Madrid Conference of October 1991 was the base for the peace negotiations that were subsequently conducted. The conference was held as a direct result of very intensive diplomatic efforts carried out mainly by America immediately following the defeat of Iraq's Saddam Hussein in the Gulf War of January 1991.

Q: What did the invitation to the conference intend?
A: The invitation called for the convening of an opening conference in order to set up two separate yet parallel negotiating tracks: the bilateral track and the multilateral track.

Q: What was the mandate of the conference?
A: The conference was intended to serve as an opening forum for all parties involved. The conference had no power to impose solutions or to veto any agreements.

Q: How long did the conference last?
A: The Madrid Conference convened on October 30, 1991, and lasted for three days. It was agreed that the conference would only be reconvened with the agreement of all participants.

Q: What was unique about this conference?
A: The Madrid Conference marked the first ever direct talks between Israel and Syria, Lebanon, Jordan, and the Palestinians.

Q: What was the purpose of the bilateral talks?
A: There were four separate sets of bilateral talks. The negotiations with the three Arab states were aimed at achieving peace treaties. The talks with the Palestinian delegation were based on a two-stage formula: first, a five-year interim with self-government arrangements and, second, negotiations on the permanent status issues.

Q: What was the purpose of the multilateral talks?
A: The purpose of the multilateral talks was to build confidence among the regional parties with setting a common goal of co-operation in the building of the Middle East of the future. The talks convened in Moscow in January 1992. They included five separate forums attended by delegations of the area as well as representatives of the international community. The talks focused on the issues facing the Middle East: arms control, environment, refugees, economic cooperation, and water. The talks then continued periodically in locations around the globe, including the Middle East.

The following diagram is taken from the booklet *The Middle East Peace Process — An Overview*, published by the Ministry of Foreign Affairs in Jerusalem, November 1999.

- The purpose of the bilateral negotiations is to resolve the conflicts of the past.

- The goal of the talks with the Arab states is to conclude bilateral peace treaties.

- The talks with the Palestinians are aimed at achieving a settlement in two stages, over five years.

- The purpose of the multilateral talks is to build the Middle East of the future.

- Issues of regional concern are discussed in a forum which fosters cooperation and builds confidence between the parties.

PEACE WITH JORDAN

Over the years, the late King Hussein of Jordan met covertly with various Israeli leaders at different times prior to the Madrid Peace Conference. Traditionally, Jordan's policy was never to be the first Arab state to sign a peace treaty with Israel. As a result of this policy, Jordan was the second following Egypt's precedent.

Q: When did talks with Jordan begin?
A: The bilateral talks between Israel and Jordan were initiated at the Madrid Conference and continued for approximately two years in Washington, DC. The talks culminated in the signing of the Israeli-Jordanian Common Agenda on September 14, 1993.

Q: When was the first public meeting held between King Hussein and the late Israeli premier, Itzak Rabin?
A: On July 25, 1994, King Hussein met with Prime Minister Rabin for the first public meeting between the Jordanian monarch and an Israeli prime minister. The meeting was held in Washington and resulted in the Washington Declaration, co-signed by Hussein, Rabin, and President Clinton, who signed as a witness.

Q: What were the main points of the Washington Declaration?
A: 1. The termination of the state of belligerency between Jordan and Israel.
    2. Both countries agreed to seek a just, lasting, and comprehensive peace based on United Nations Resolutions 242 and 338.

3. Israel would respect the special role of the Hashemite Kingdom of Jordan over sites holy to Islam in Jerusalem.

Q: What other issues were decided upon?
A: The two countries decided on mutual cooperation on other vital issues: tourism, water sources, commercial trade, finance, and joint projects between the two states. The outcome of these talks has been incorporated in the peace treaty between Jordan and Israel, signed on October 26, 1994.

Q: What is the importance of this treaty?
A: The signing of this peace treaty is of great importance to both Jordan and Israel equally for these reasons:

1. It is a peace treaty with an Arab country which fought against Israel in the past.

2. Jordan has the longest and most complicated border with Israel.

3. The peace treaty may prevent the establishment sometime in the future of a very dangerous and threatening Arab eastern front against Israel. Such a front would include Jordan, Syria, Iraq, Lebanon, and other Arab states that might join their ranks.

4. After signing a peace treaty with Israel, Egypt was excommunicated from the Arab world. It was of great importance for another Arab state to join ranks with Egypt and to sign a peace treaty with Israel. Together they could withstand the Arab world's united stand of animosity against Israel.

5. With secured peace on her southern border (with Egypt) and her eastern border (with Jordan), Israel could allow herself feelings of security and confidence. Bear in mind that these two countries attacked Israel in the 1967 Six Day War.

Q: Israel proved itself a true partner for peace with Jordan. Who were the real enemies of Jordan?
A: Since its establishment, Jordan has been under Syrian threat to its north and under Palestinian threat from within. Although

Israel was publicly considered "the enemy," Jordan always knew Israel would help Jordan to defend herself in the event she would be threatened by the Syrians, the Iraqis, the Palestinians, or any other country.

Q: Can an example be cited to confirm this argument?
A: Yes. In 1970, Syrian forces entered Jordan in order to topple King Hussein's regime. It was Israel's threat to intervene in favor of King Hussein that finally deterred the Syrians.

Q: What are other aspects of the Israeli-Jordanian Peace Treaty?
A: Another aspect of the treaty deals with the normalization of relations between the two countries. There is cooperation in transportation and roads, postal services, telecommunications, environmental issues, energy, health, agriculture, etc. Economic cooperation is considered one of the strongest pillars of peace. It is vital to the promotion of secure and harmonious relations between the two countries.

Q: What marks the main step of the peace treaty?
A: Full diplomatic relations between Israel and Jordan were established on November 27, 1994. This was marked by the appointment of respective ambassadors and by the opening of embassies in both countries.

In addition, in August 1995, the Jordanian parliament rescinded its participation in the Arab boycott against Israel.

CHAPTER 7

AMERICA AS MIDEAST BROKER

ISRAEL-PLO ACCORDS

Since the establishment of the PLO, Israel's policy was consistent — no recognition of this organization. Israel considered the PLO a terror organization whose members are terrorists, not guerilla fighters fighting for national purposes.

THE OSLO AGREEMENT AND INTERIM AGREEMENT

In 1992, the Likud government, under Yitzhak Shamir, lost the elections and the Labor Party took power under the leadership of the late Yitzhak Rabin. When the Labor Party came into power, leftist elements in the Labor Party, such as Yossi Beilin, Ron Pundak, and others, had been having contacts with the PLO leadership. The secret meetings were held in Oslo, the capital of Norway.

Q: What were the results of the Oslo talks?
A: As a result of these talks, Israel recognized the PLO as a partner for peace.

Q: What did the PLO give in return for Israel's recognition?
A: On September 9, 1993, Chairman Arafat sent a letter to Prime Minister Rabin stating that the PLO:

1. recognized the right of Israel to exist in peace and security
2. accepted UN Security Council Resolutions 242 and 338
3. commited itself to a peaceful solution to the conflict
4. renounced the use of terrorism and other acts of violence
5. assumed responsibility over all PLO elements to ensure their compliance, to prevent violations and to discipline violators
6. affirmed that those articles of the PLO Covenant which denied Israel's right to exist were now inoperative and no longer valid
7. undertook to submit to the Palestinian National Council for formal approval of the necessary changes to the covenant

Q: What was the most symbolic step taken to affirm the new relations between the PLO and Israel?
A: The most dramatic and symbolic gesture that marked the new relations between Israel and the PLO was the historic handshake between Prime Minister Rabin and Chairman Arafat at the signing of the Declaration of Principles on the White House lawn on September 13, 1993.

The Declaration of Principles included arrangements for Palestinian self-rule in Gaza and Jericho, the elections of a Palestinian Council, and extensive economic cooperation between the two parties. In addition, the declaration included a set of general principles and guidelines regarding a five-year interim period of Palestinian self-rule.

It was agreed that talks would start no later than the third year of the five-year interim period to discuss the permanent status. The agreements reached in these negotiations were to take effect after the five-year interim period.

Q: What are the toughest issues in the declaration?
A: The toughest issues concerned Jerusalem, refugees, settlements, security arrangements, and borders which were to be excluded from the interim agreements. It was agreed that the outcome of the permanent status talks should not be prejudged or pre-empted by the interim arrangements. During this period, the Israeli government retained sole responsibility for foreign affairs, defense, and borders. Israel's position on Jerusalem remains unchanged. Prime Minister Rabin stated, "Jerusalem is the ancient and eternal capital of the Jewish people." The fundamental Israeli position calls for an undivided Jerusalem under Israeli sovereignty, with religious freedom for all.

Q: Why didn't the Israeli government make its position clear on these issues?
A: The Israeli delegation to the talks was very enthusiastic to reach a historic agreement and believed that some compromise on these tough issues could be reached in the end. Others are convinced that the Israeli delegation was inexperienced and not strong enough to reach a better or more defined agreement.

The Gaza-Jericho Agreement was signed on May 4, 1994. The Transfer of Power was signed on August 29, 1994. The Interim Agreement was signed on September 28, 1995.

The Interim Agreement enabled the Palestinians to run their own affairs in different fields, to elect their leadership, and to open an era of cooperation with Israel. In return, the Palestinians were to educate their people to an atmosphere of peace and mutual cooperation. In addition, they were to revoke the Palestinian National Covenant which calls for the destruction of Israel.

> *Both sides have undertaken in the agreement to act to strengthen understanding and tolerance, prevent incitement and hostile propaganda, and will use the legal means at their disposal to prevent incitement on the part of groups or individuals. Both sides have pledged that their educational systems will act to advance peace between Israel and the Palestinians.*
> — From the Israeli-Palestinian agreement on the West Bank and Gaza Strip, September 28, 1995

Q: *Does the agreement mention the care of and access to Jewish holy sites in areas that are to be handed over to the Palestinians?*

A: Yes. The Palestinians agreed to protect the Jewish holy shrines. The agreement reads: "Responsibility over sites of religious significance in the West Bank and Gaza will be transferred to the Palestinian side. In area C this will be transferred gradually during the 'further redeployment phase,' except for the issues which will be negotiated during the permanent status negotiations. Both sides shall respect and protect religious rights of Jews, Christians, Moslems, and Samaritans; to wit:

- Protecting the holy sites
- Allowing free access to the holy sites
- Allowing freedom of worship and practice

The agreement guarantees freedom of access to and freedom of worship at the holy sites, and defines access arrangements for the holy places located in areas A and B. With regard to Rachel's Tomb in Bethlehem and Joseph's Tomb in Nablus, special arrangements are set out in the agreement which will also guarantee freedom of access and freedom of worship.

Q: *What is meant by Area A, Area B, and Area C?*

A: According to the agreement, the areas of Judea, Samaria, and Gaza fell into three categories:

Area A is comprised of six cities: Jenin, Nablus, Tul Karem, Kalkilia, Ramallah, and Bethlehem, and the city of Hebron, minus the Old City of Hebron, the Jewish Quarter, and everything that is linked from there to Kiryat Arba and the Tomb of the Patriarchs. In these areas, the Palestinian Council will have full responsibility for internal security and public order, as well as full responsibility for civil affairs.

Area B comprises the Palestinian towns and villages in the West Bank. Sixty-eight percent of the Palestinian population resides in these areas. The Palestinian Council will be granted full civil authority here as in area A. The council was charged with maintaining public order and Israel would have overriding security authority to safeguard its citizens and to combat terrorism.

Area C comprises the unpopulated areas of the West Bank. These areas are of strategic importance to Israel and the Jewish settlements. As a result, Israel retained full responsibility for security and public order. The council was to assume all civil responsibilities not related to territory, such as economics, health, education, etc.

The following is an excerpt from the Israeli Foreign Office pamphlet entitled *The Middle East Peace Process — An Overview*, Jerusalem, November 1999.

Milestones in the Implementation of the Interim Agreement

On January 20, 1996, following completion of the first stage of IDF re-deployment (with the exception of Hebron), elections were held for the Palestinian Council and for the head of the Palestinian Authority. Yasser Arafat was elected Ra'ees (head) of the Authority.

On April 24, 1996, the Palestinian National Council, convening in Gaza, voted 504 to 54, with 14 abstentions, as follows:

1. The Palestinian National Charter is hereby amended by canceling the articles that are contrary to the letters exchanged between the PLO and the government of Israel 9–10 September 1993.

2. Assigns its legal committee with the task of redrafting the Palestinian National Charter in order to present it to the first session of the Palestinian central council (24 April 1996).

[On December 14, 1998, the Palestinian National Council, in accordance with the Wye Memorandum, convened in Gaza in the presence of U.S. President Clinton and voted to reaffirm this decision.]

An agreement on a temporary international presence in Hebron was signed on May 9, 1996.

The Protocol Concerning the Redeployment in Hebron was signed on January 17, 1997. The Protocol was accompanied by a Note for the Record prepared by the U.S. Special Middle East Coordinator, confirming a series of agreements between the sides on non-Hebron issues and reaffirming their commitment to implement the Interim Agreement on the basis of reciprocity.

Q: What were other commitments made by the PLO in the agreement?
A: The PLO promised to fulfill specific obligations in six areas:

1. to strengthen security cooperation

2. to prevent incitement and hostile propaganda

3. to combat terrorist organizations and their infrastructure

4. to apprehend, prosecute, and punish convicted terrorists

5. to comply with requests for the transfer of suspects and defendants to Israel in areas under Israeli jurisdiction

6. to confiscate illegal firearms among the Palestinian population

Q: The PLO readily signed the agreement but has it lived up to its obligations?
A: Time and again the Palestinian Authority has violated many of the agreements reached. It did not end or prevent hostile propaganda against Israel, it does not combat terrorism or infrastructures of terrorist factions, nor does it confiscate illegal firearms and weapons. On the contrary, time and again Israel has caught the PLO smuggling weapons into Gaza and Judea and Samaria by land and by sea.

In March 1996, terrorist actions were carried out by Palestinian terrorists in Tel Aviv, Jerusalem, and Ashkelon. Scores of Israelis were killed and hundreds were injured. Shimon Peres, then leader of the Labor Party, lost the elections to Benjamin Netanyahu, leader of the Likud Party.

Q: Why did Shimon Peres lose the election?
A: Shimon Peres lost the 1996 election for two main reasons: first, the Israeli people did not think that Peres was strong enough to force Arafat's hand and demand that Arafat honor all his signed commitments, and second, the Israeli people began living with feelings of insecurity. Others felt that Peres's vision of a "New Middle East" was nothing more than a fantasy.

Q: What happened to the traditional support of Israeli Arabs for the Labor Party candidate?
A: A few weeks prior to the March 1996 elections, Israeli soldiers in southern Lebanon mistakenly shelled civilian targets. As a result, innocent Lebanese Arab civilians were killed. This mistake caused much agitation and anger amongst Israeli Arabs. Some decided not to vote for Shimon Peres, and others decided to boycott the elections altogether. Peres lost by a small margin.

Note: It is a fact that Shimon Peres has never won an election. He lost elections in 1981, 1984, 1988, and 1996. He is referred to as "the constant loser."

THE WYE RIVER MEMORANDUM

In October 1998, U.S. President Bill Clinton hosted a summit at Wye River, Maryland. Israeli Prime Minister Benjamin Netanyahu headed the Israeli delegation and Chairman Arafat represented the Palestinian people. Both Netanyahu and Arafat signed the Wye River Memorandum on October 23, 1998, at a ceremony that was attended by the late King Hussein of Jordan. The memorandum consists of steps to facilitate the implementation of the Interim Agreement signed on September 28, 1995.

As part of the memorandum, the Israeli government emphasized the principle of reciprocity. At a later date, Prime Minister Netanyahu would phrase it thusly: "If they (the Palestinians) give, they will receive. If they do not give, they will not receive."

Q: What are the main points of the Wye River Memorandum?
A: Israel agreed to the first and second redeployment and the transfer of lands to the Palestinian Authority: 13 percent from Area C (1 percent to Area A and 12 percent to Area B) and 14.2 percent from Area B to Area A.

With regard to security, the following measures were agreed upon:

1. The Palestinian side would make known its policy of zero tolerance for terror.

2. A work plan would be developed by the Palestinians and shared with the United States which would be implemented immediately.

3. A U.S.-Palestinian committee would meet weekly to review the steps being taken to end terrorism in addition to bilateral Israeli-Palestinian security cooperation.

4. The Palestinians agreed to apprehend individuals suspected of perpetrating acts of violence and terrorism.

5. The Palestinians would implement a program for the collection of illegal weapons and firearms.

6. Security between Israel and the Palestinians would include bilateral cooperation and exchange of forensic expertise, training, and other assistance, and the establishment of a high ranking U.S.-Palestinian-Israeli committee to meet at least biweekly to assess current threats and to deal with any impediments to security cooperation.

7. The Palestinian Authority would issue a decree banning all forms of incitement to violence and terror.

8. A U.S.-Palestinian-Israeli committee would meet on a regular basis to monitor cases of possible incitement to violence or terror. The committee would make recommendations and reports on how to prevent such incitement.

9. The Palestinian Authority agreed to provide Israel with a list of its policemen in conformity with prior agreements.

10. The executive committee of the PLO and the Palestinian Central Council would reaffirm Chairman Arafat's letter to President Clinton from January 22, 1998. The letter promised the nullification of the Palestinian National Charter provisions that were inconsistent with the letters exchanged between the PLO and the government of Israel on September 9 and 10, 1993.

Moreover, the Wye River Memorandum included the resumption of the permanent status negotiations. It was agreed that neither side would initiate any step that would change the status of the West Bank and the Gaza Strip in accordance with the Interim Agreements.

And they have healed the brokenness of my people superficially saying, Peace, Peace, but there is no peace. — Jeremiah 6:14

THE SHARM EL-SHEIKH CONFERENCE

The government of Benjamin Netanyahu lost the elections in the spring of 1999. The new government, led by Ehud Barak of the Labor Party, was determined to reach an agreement with the Palestinian Authority. The talks were conducted in Sharm el-Sheikh, Egypt, in September 1999 and continued at Camp David, Maryland, in the year 2000.

Q: When was the memorandum signed?
A: It was signed on September 4, 1999.

Q: What was the contents of the memorandum?
A: The Sharm el-Sheikh Memorandum restated the commitment of both sides to fully implement all agreements reached since September 13, 1993. The memorandum set out to resolve outstanding issues facing the present interim status, particularly those laid forth in the Wye River Memorandum. Its intention was to form a kind of bridge between the completion of the interim period and the beginning of the permanent status.

Q: What was mentioned in the memorandum about the permanent status?
A: It was agreed upon in the memorandum that negotiations on the permanent status would begin no later than September 13, 1999. The goal of these negotiations would be to reach a framework agreement on the permanent status within the next five months, which would lead to a comprehensive agreement on permanent status within one year.

Q: What other issues were included in the memorandum?
A: The Sharm el-Sheikh Memorandum also included the following issues:
1. further redeployment of Israeli forces
2. the release of Palestinian prisoners retained by Israel
3. the reactivation of all interim committees
4. the Palestinian Authority's pledge to continue fighting terrorism against Israel

Q: What was Israel's position with regards to the permanent status?
A: Speaking at the opening of the talks on September 13, 1999, Israel's foreign minister, David Levy, reiterated Israel's position on the negotiations on a permanent status agreement. He said, "We will not return to the 1967 lines — united Jerusalem will remain the capital of Israel — settlement blocs in the territories will remain under Israeli sovereignty — there will be no foreign army west of the Jordan River."

Q: What was the Palestinian position?
A: The Palestinians demanded Israeli withdrawal to the June 4, 1967, cease-fire lines; East Jerusalem would become the capital of the future Palestinian state; Palestinian refugees would have the right of return in Israel proper as well as to Palestinian lands; all settlements in Judea, Samaria, and Gaza would be evacuated.

The United Nations has stated: "All member states shall settle their international disputes by peaceful means." And, further: "All members shall refrain from the use of force against the territorial integrity or political independence of any state."

The PLO also has a charter which states: "The establishment of the State of Israel is null and void, regardless of the passage of time (Article 19). And, further: "Armed struggle is the only way to liberate Palestine" (Article 9).

THE CAMP DAVID CONFERENCE FAILURE:
SUMMER 2000

In the summer of 2000, the United States hosted peace talks in Camp David, Maryland. The conference was attended by President Bill Clinton, Prime Minister Ehud Barak, and Chairman Arafat. Each was accompanied by a delegation of advisors.

Q: What happened at that conference?
A: Israel's Prime Minister Barak came to this conference prepared to make far-reaching concessions, as suggested by President Clinton. The issues on the agenda were the partition of Jerusalem, the return of 97 percent of Judea and Samaria to the Palestinian Authority, and the agreement to discuss the Arab refugee issue.

Q: What was Arafat's reaction?
A: With regard to the Arab refugee issue, Chairman Arafat insisted that the Palestinian refugees be granted the right of return to homes and lands in Israel proper.

Q: Are there any Palestinian homes in Israel?
A: Arafat knows quite well that there are no Palestinian homes in Israel. Therefore, he knew from the outset that his demand would be rejected.

Arafat, time and again, has proven himself the master of double-talk. He says one thing to the leaders of the world, while doing just the opposite.

The following is an excerpt from a letter Arafat wrote to the then Foreign Minister of Norway, Johan Jorgen Holst, on September 9, 1993:

> *In light of the new era marked by the signing of the Declaration of Principles, the PLO encourages and calls upon the Palestinian people in the West Bank and Gaza Strip to take part in the steps leading to the normalization of life, rejecting violence and terrorism, contributing to peace and stability, and participating actively in shaping reconstruction, economic development, and cooperation.*

Even Arafat's own colleague, Mazen Izz al-Din, exposed that for the howler it was. On the Palestinian Authority's own TV broadcast, Din said, "One day history will expose the fact that the whole intifada and its instructions came from Brother Commander Yasser Arafat" (Mortimer Zuckerman, editor, *U.S. News & World Report*, July 15, 2002).

In September 2000, the PLO leader, Yassir Arafat, decided to pursue terror against Israel as a political weapon. Israel, on the one hand, believes that the differences between Israel and the Palestinians should be resolved around the negotiating table. Arafat, on the other hand, chose the option of terror to solve the differences.

It is clear that Arafat is responsible for all the bloodshed of Jews and Palestinians alike in what he calls the Al-Aksa Intifada ("the uprising of the Temple Mount"). In his cynical and blatant disregard for all agreements signed and the promises he has made over the years, Arafat has caused the death and injury of thousands on both sides with his continual use of terror. Arafat claimed that Premier Ariel Sharon's visit to the Temple Mount caused the uprising.

Q: Is there clear proof to Arafat's lie?
A: Yes. The truth was confirmed by the Palestinian media on December 6, 2000. The following was written in the semi-official Palestinian Authority daily, *Al-Ayyam:*

> *Speaking at a symposium in Gaza, Palestinian Minister of Communications, Imad Al-Falouji, confirmed that the Palestinian Authority had begun preparations for the outbreak of the current intifada from the moment the Camp David talks concluded, this in accordance with instructions given by Chairman Arafat himself. Mr. Falouji went on to state that Arafat launched this intifada as a culminating stage to the immutable Palestinian stance in the negotiations, and was not meant merely as a protest of Israeli opposition leader Ariel Sharon's visit to the Temple Mount.*

Q: What were the actual steps taken by the Palestinian Authority to start the uprising?
A: Yassir Arafat:

1. used official Palestinian media to incite his people to violence against Israel and Israelis;

2. authorized the Fatah militia — the *Tanzim* — to fire on Israeli civilians and soldiers, with weapons supplied by the Palestinian Authority; and

3. released dozens of Hamas and Islamic Jihad terrorists from Palestinian prisons, signaling to these organizations that they have a green light to launch attacks against innocent Israeli citizens.

Q: What were the results of these steps?
A: Arafat's policies resulted in a series of terrorist attacks in Israel, which caused the death and injury of hundreds of innocent men, women, and children.

Q: Why does Arafat use terror?
A: Since the establishment of the PLO in 1964, Arafat has never ceased using terror to gain political achievements.

It is not coincidental that the Al-Aksa intifada began at a time when Israel expressed her readiness to make far-reaching and unprecedented compromises in order to reach an enduring agreement with the Palestinian Authority. Arafat preferred to continue casting himself as a relentless revolutionary, sparing no acts of terrorism, in order to prevent being labeled as "weak" by Palestinian extremists. He chose to use terror as a negotiating tool.

Q: After the failed negotiations at Camp David in July 2000, what was then U.S. President Clinton's opinion of the situation?
A: Arafat dismissed all the proposals put forth by the United States government at Camp David, while Israel agreed to consider them. As a result, President Clinton placed the blame for the failure of the talks squarely at Arafat's feet. At the same time, he praised Prime Minister Barak.

Q: From Israel's perspective, what is the main issue now?
A: The main issue for Israel now is the Palestinian violation of the basic principle of the peace process. Tranquility is a basic requisite for conducting peace negotiations. This is why the Israeli government has decided that the first order of business in any contacts with the Palestinians will be ending the violence.

Q: The PLO claims that Israel is an occupying power that oppressively rules over the Palestinian people? What are the facts?
A: Since the outset of Israel-PLO talks and the September 13, 1993, Oslo Accords, Israel has been very generous in its approach toward Palestinian national aspirations. At that time, Arafat pledged to abandon terrorism and to commit to a negotiated solution. In exchange, Israel has agreed to the expansion of the Palestinian Authority's jurisdiction and authority over 97 percent of the Palestinian population in the West Bank and Gaza. That is the situation to date.

> *The man's [Arafat's] duplicity is the stuff of legend. Dennis Ross, the former U.S. envoy to the Middle East, wrote, "I've never met an Arab leader who trusts Arafat. . . . Almost all Arab leaders have stories about how he misled or betrayed them.* — Mortimer Zuckerman, editor, *U.S. News & World Report,* July 8, 2002

Sixteen Mistakes and Miscalculations
of the Oslo Agreement

In September 1993, the late prime minister of Israel, Yitzhak Rabin, and PLO leader Yassir Arafat signed the Oslo Agreement. The Israeli left, supported by the leftist-oriented media in Israel and the Arab Knesset Members, hailed the agreement. Whoever questioned the wisdom behind such a dangerous agreement marked by an abundance of non-calculated risks for Israel, was considered to be a right-winged fanatic who refused to opt for peace over war.

These same people, with their blindness or naiveté developed an entire theory about the peace process and how wonderful the situation would be at the end of the process. Unfortunately, reality proved that wishful thinking and euphoric dreams are one thing — reality is quite another.

The following is a list of 16 mistakes and miscalculations of the Oslo Agreement.

1. Legitimizing Arafat as a partner for peace

Bringing Arafat from Tunis to Judea and Samaria was the most crucial mistake. Yassir Arafat was a staunch supporter of Saddam Hussein of Iraq in the Gulf War of 1991. He was excommunicated by the Saudis, and the Kuwaitis expelled Palestinians from their territory. Arafat was a *persona non grata* throughout Europe, in the United States, and in almost all the Arab states. Shimon Peres and Yossi Beilin, two leftist politicians in Israel, along with other supporters of the left, brought Arafat from Tunis to Judea and Samaria. They claimed that Arafat is the only Palestinian leader with whom Israel can achieve peace since he is a pragmatic leader. They reasoned that if Israel does not negotiate with Arafat, the only other option would be the radical Islamic fundamentalists such as Hamas and the Islamic Jihad.

The sad reality is that not only did Arafat not fight the Hamas and Islamic Jihad, but his forces — the *Fatah* and the *Tanzim* — joined ranks with the Hamas and Islamic Jihad in their murderous terrorist attacks against the Israeli population. In just over four years since the outset of the September 2000 uprising, over 1,000 Israelis have been brutally murdered by Arafat and his gangs.

Q: Are you saying unequivocally that the Palestinian struggle is not aimed at liberating the territories that were conquered in 1967?

A: "Of course not. Of course not. The Palestinians have three stories. Their narrative in Arabic is one of mobilization for a war of jihad and non-recognition of Israel's right to exist. That narrative rejects any attachment between the Jewish people and the land of Israel, and it mobilizes the Palestinian people for a war with the goal of bringing about Israel's collapse" (Moshe Ya'alon, Israel chief of staff, interviewed by Steven Plaut, *Outpost*, September 2002).

2. Not keeeping a closer eye on what Arafat was saying

From the beginning, Yassir Arafat never hid his intentions or thoughts. He spoke to his people in Arabic about jihad and sacrifice, while speaking to the world in English about peace. Israeli leftist leaders were well aware of Arafat's deception, yet chose to keep quiet. Time and time again, these same leftist leaders went to Arafat to appease him and would plead for an audience with him.

Arafat's double-talk deception began the day after the signing of the Oslo Agreement. While addressing an audience in Amman, Jordan, Arafat explained that the Oslo process was only the first step in implementing the "stages plan." This is the PLO's infamous plan for the gradual destruction of Israel. Arafat hid nothing. Only the Israeli leftists hid the truth from themselves.

Q: So that means that in the present situation, leaving settlements (in Judea, Samaria, and Gaza) would be a mistake with potentially catastrophic implications?

A: "Today, any such departure under terrorism and violence will strengthen the path of terrorism and violence. It will endanger us" (Moshe Ya'alon, Israel chief of staff in an interview by Steven Plaut, *Outpost*, September 2002).

3. Imposing Arafat's rule over the Palestinians in the territories

The Palestinian people reside in Judea, Samaria, and the Gaza Strip. The PLO leadership that lived in Tunis were outsiders who self-appointed themselves to rule over the Palestinian populace.

Israeli policy prior to the Oslo Agreement had been to consider the PLO as an enemy and outsider. As a result, the PLO was not considered a partner in any future negotiations. The Oslo Agreement changed this policy. In effect, the agreement imposed the PLO terrorists' authority and rule over the Palestinian people in the territories. While Israel considered its argument with the Palestinians in the territories to be about final borders and future co-existence, the PLO questioned Israel's right to exist. The Palestinian National Covenant reads openly that Israel has no right to exist.

According to Arafat, the issue is not that Israel is being provocative, but Israel's being is provocative.

4. Creating a rift in Israel

The Israeli Knesset is made up of 120 parliamentary seats. At the signing of the Oslo Agreement, the Labor Party along with other leftist elements numbered 56 seats in the Knesset. The Oslo Agreement, so crucial to Israel's very existence, was first signed and then was brought to vote in the Knesset. It passed 61 to 59. Among the 61 supporters of the agreement were five Arab anti-Zionist members of the Knesset. The agreement passed on the basis of a single vote. One right-winged member of the Knesset was swayed to vote in favor of the agreement by a political bribe. Outraged by this parliamentary trick that approved the Oslo Agreement, Israel society was ripped into shreds. The planners of Oslo were to blame for such a rift.

5. Inexperienced Israeli negotiators

Among the Israeli negotiators in Oslo were leftist politicians Yossi Beilin, Ron Pundak, Uri Savir, and others. All were inexperienced in negotiating such an agreement involving the complexities of the conflict. Moreover, they lacked the know-how of negotiating with Arab leaders, not to mention PLO terrorists. They were inexperienced and naive, and whole-heartedly believed what the other side was telling them.

6. The Israeli Army was not consulted

The Israeli negotiators in Oslo wanted to keep the negotiations secret at all cost. When military issues arose during the talks with the Palestinians, high-ranking and experienced Israeli military personnel were not consulted at all. The result of this negligence was that the Oslo Agreement, according to Israel's former Prime Minister General Ehud Barak, was "full of holes like Swiss cheese."

7. Assuming both sides want peace

The Israeli side was eager to achieve peace. Israel was willing to compromise for the sake of peace. Israel, who captured the territories in June 1967 in a war of defense, was willing to make far-reaching and painful concessions for the sake of peace. Wishful thinking on the part of Israeli leftists reasoned the following: a Palestinian mother and a Jewish mother both want the same things for their children. Reality proved just the opposite. While Israeli children sang songs of peace and waved flags with the Star of David entwined with doves of peace, Palestinian children were being trained to become suicide bombers. Today, Palestinian mothers send their grown children to become *shahidim* — martyrs.

8. Fantasy vis-à-vis reality

Israel's then Foreign Minister Shimon Peres masterminded the slogan the "New Middle East." He envisioned the New Middle East becoming a true paradise once agreement was reached with the Palestinians. As this illusion was being shattered over and over again, Mr. Peres never let reality damage his fantasy. He refused to listen to reason, and stood steadfast with his visions of peace. Even after the Palestinians started the intifada with over 1,000 Israelis brutally murdered, Mr. Peres continued to claim that the Oslo Agreement was good. He continued to insist that Arafat is the partner for peace. This is the same Shimon Peres who once said that Israel should join the Arab League.

9. Arafat would crush internal Palestinian opposition

The late Israeli Prime Minister Yitzhak Rabin is known for his Hebrew saying regarding how Arafat would deal with his adversaries. Rabin said, *"Bli bagatz ubli betselem."* ("Without the Supreme Court and without the human rights watch dog.")

In this respect, he was right. Arafat has proved to be a leader with no respect for law, human rights, nor Western and democratic values. He is a dictator who cares only for his own interests and those of his supporters. He has crushed Palestinian opposition when he felt it endangered his rule.

Arafat saw Oslo as a Trojan horse and September 2000
as the moment of emerging from the belly of the horse. —
Moshe Ya'alon, Israel Chief of Staff, interviewed by Steven Plaut, *Outpost*, September 2002

10. The division of Palestine again

The Balfour Declaration of November 2, 1917, spoke about the Jewish national home on both sides of the Jordan River. Israeli policy after June 1967 was that Jordan is indeed a Palestinian state. At Camp David in 1978, the late Israeli Prime Minister Menachem Begin agreed to Palestinian autonomy, not to a Palestinian state. The Oslo Agreement strengthened the Palestinian claim to statehood in Judea and Samaria. Such a state would pose mortal danger to Israel's very existence.

At first a small state; and with the help of Allah, it will
be made large and expand to the east, west, north, and south.
. . . I am interested in the liberation of Palestine, step by step.
— Abu Iyad, second in command to PLO Chairman Yassir Arafat, *Al-Anba*, Kuwait, December 18, 1988

11. To leave main issues to the end of the process

The outstanding issues facing negotiators are: borders, Jerusalem, the refugees, and the settlements. These issues should have been discussed and decided upon at the very beginning. Leaving them for agreement in the end complicates even more the controversies facing Israelis and Palestinians. The impression is that the naiveté of the Israeli negotiators in Oslo together with their inexperience led to the uprising of September 2000.

12. Words for territory

Since the Oslo Agreement, it has been demanded of Israel to give up territory — territory she needs for her security. The Palestinians, in turn, were asked to promise they would live in peace. In the end, the Palestinians proved that they cannot be trusted. They used the territories they were given as a base of aggression against Israeli civilians.

13. Giving weapons to the Palestinians

Under the leadership of the late Yitzhak Rabin, the government of Israel gave thousands of weapons to the Palestinians.

Right-winged Israelis warned Rabin and Peres not to give arms to the Palestinians. They warned that such weapons might one day be used against Israel. Unfortunately, the right's warnings proved correct. The Palestinians use Israeli weapons in order to kill Israelis, not to maintain order in their authority.

14. The right is right; the left is wrong

The Oslo Agreement caused a serious rift in Israeli society. The right attempted to delegitimize Rabin. At the same time, the left did the same to critics of Oslo. Rabin himself mocked the settlers and even compared the Likud to the Hamas as partner to the anti-peace bloc. Israel might have suffered less from the period of self-deception following the Oslo Agreement had the left in Israel paid more attention to criticism from the right.

15. Going against the spirit of democracy

The anti-democratic way in which the Oslo Agreement was passed in the Israeli Knesset was discussed above (see number 4). The anti-democratic spirit of Oslo culminated in January 2001 at Taba. Prime Minister Ehud Barak was facing a landslide defeat in the upcoming election and he was left with a minority government. In spite of this, he offered the Palestinians greater concessions than those he offered at Camp David, six months earlier than the talks at Taba.

> The war of attrition against the Zionist enemy will never cease. . . . It is in my interest to have a war in the region, because I believe that the only remedy for the ills of the Arab nation is a true war against the Zionist enemy. — Yassir Arafat, *Al-Destour*, Lebanon, December 26, 1983

16. Breaking Israeli law

When the Israeli negotiators met with the PLO leaders in Oslo, they were doing so in direct violation of Israeli law. At that time, the PLO was considered, by law, to be an enemy. As such, all contact with the PLO was illegal. The Israeli negotiators, in their enthusiasm to achieve, blatantly broke the law.

To sum up, the results of these mistakes and misconceptions has cost Israel thousands of dead or wounded citizens and billions of dollars in economic damage.

Arafat's True Intentions: the Writing Was on the Wall

The situation in which he finds himself [Arafat] is largely of his own making. He's missed his opportunities, and thereby betrayed the hopes of the people he's supposed to lead. Given his failure, the Israeli government feels it must strike at terrorist networks that are killing its citizens. — George W. Bush, U.S. president, remarks from the White House rose garden, April 4, 2002

On June 8, 1974, the Palestinian National Council met in Cairo, Egypt. The major organizations belonging to the PLO were divided in their views as follows:

The "moderates" were those who held that the PLO will gain tactical advantage by participating in the Geneva Conference, and establishing a Palestinian state without renouncing the final objective, which is the destruction of Israel and Jordan. These organizations include the fatah (occupation) of Yassir Arafat.

The "radicals," led by George Habash, were against any settlement and participation in Geneva. They believe that the only way to solve the problem is by constant war.

The ultimate aims, therefore, of both groups are identical. They differ only in the timing of their tactics and strategies. While the moderates want to achieve their goal in stages, the radicals want the same goal all at once.

The main points of the Palestinian National Council of June 1974 were that the PLO:

1. should declare an independent Palestinian state on any territory evacuated by Israel (Article 2)
2. should use the Palestinian state as a base for war against Israel (Article 4)
3. should act in order to cause a war between Israel and the Arab states in order to put an end to Israel (Article 8)

Since the establishment of the PLO, Yassir Arafat and his colleagues have never hidden their true intentions. After the signing of the September 13, 1993, Oslo Agreement, the Israeli people expected to see a dramatic change from the Palestinian Authority. They expected the Palestinian Authority to prove its good intentions for peaceful coexistence with Israel. They awaited Arafat's concrete steps to end hostile Palestinian propaganda against Israel, to stop the spread of hatred and incitement in the Palestinian media, and to stop anti-Semitism. All that never happened. Arafat did not change and he never ceased terror against Israel. Israeli leaders and politicians, mainly those with a leftist orientation, believed that Arafat was merely paying lip service to his Arab rivals by continuing to use radical terminology and terror against Israel.

These Israeli politicians were left with their "wishful thinking." Arafat did not change.

> *The chairman of the Palestinian Authority has not consistently opposed or confronted terrorists. At Oslo and elsewhere, Chairman Arafat renounced terror as an instrument of his cause, and he agreed to control it. He's not done so.* — U.S. President George W. Bush, April 4, 2002

The following story reflects the PLO: A farmer was once requested by his neighbor to lend him his goat for a day. The following day, when the neighbor failed to return the goat, the farmer came to claim it. However, the neighbor described how the goat had died soon after he had borrowed it. Just then, the goat began to bleat. When the owner said he could hear his goat's voice, the neighbor demanded angrily, "Do you believe your goat and not me?"

When will the world believe the goat? The PLO, through its propaganda, wants the world to believe the neighbor.

> *I call on the Palestinian people, the Palestinian Authority, and our friends in the Arab world to join us in delivering a clear message to terrorists: blowing yourself up does not help the Palestinian cause. To the contrary, suicide bombing missions could well blow up the best and only hope for a Palestinian state.* — U.S. President George W. Bush, April 4, 2002

The following are just 15 out of hundreds of declarations made by the PLO over the years which prove the true intentions of Arafat and his colleagues. All these declarations were made before the Oslo Agreement.

At first a small state; and with the help of Allah, it will be made large and expand to the east, west, north, and south. . . . I am interested in the liberation of Palestine, step by step. — Abu Iyad, second in command to PLO Chairman Arafat, *Al-Anba*, Kuwait, December 18, 1988

The Palestinian state would be a skipboard from which we would be able to release Jaffa, Acre, and all Palestine. — Abu Iyad, *Al-Sakra*, PLO organ, Kuwait, January 6, 1988

We in the PLO distinguish between the PLO National Covenant and the political plans. The first includes the final political aim, the second includes the step-by-step road. — Abu Iyad, *Ukaz*, Saudi Arabia, November 22, 1988

The partitioning of Palestine in 1947 and the establishment of Israel is fundamentally null and void. — Article 10, PLO National Covenent

Three months ago I supported the idea to liberate Palestine at once. I was stupid. Now I am interested to liberate Palestine by stages. This is the art of liberation. — Abu Iyad, *Al Anba*, Kuwait, December 18, 1988

I want to tell Carter and Begin that when the Arabs set off their volcano, there will only be Arabs in this part of the world. . . . Our people will continue to fuel the torch of the revolution with rivers of blood until the whole of the occupied homeland is liberated, not just part of it. — Yassir Arafat, Beirut, March 12, 1979, after the signing of the Camp David agreement

The establishment of a Palestinian state in any part of Palestine has as its goal the establishment of a Palestinian state in all of Palestine. — Saleh Kalef, Arafat deputy, *Al-Siyassa*, Kuwait, December 12, 1988

[The PLO is] . . . opposed to a Zionist state. . . . Zionism is a racist movement (and) we don't want a racist state in this area. — Arafat speaking one week before the November PNC meeting in Algiers, *Los Angeles Times*, December 19, 1988

I want to release a part of this Arab territory and this cannot be released by war. . . . Afterwards we would liberate all the rest. — Nabil Sha'ath, Arafat's chief advisor, *Al-Anba*, Kuwait, March 28, 1989

The proclamation of the Palestinian state is the first step toward obliterating the new Zionist-facist state. — Abadallah Al-Khouran, PLO Executive Committee member, *Washington Post*, December 22, 1988

If we will gain independence on part of our land, we will not relinquish our dream of establishing a single democratic state over all of the Palestinian land. — Nabil Sha'ath, *Al-Siyassa*, Kuwait, January 29, 1988

The struggle with the Zionism enemy is not a struggle about Israel's borders, but about Israel's existence. We will never agree to anything less than the return of all our land and the establishment of the independent state. — Bassam Abu Sharif, PLO leader, Kuwait News Agency, May 31, 1986

The stage plan still exists. Its purpose is to serve the present interests, yet it does not contradict the Palestinian National Covenant. — Farouk Kaddoumi, *Al-Sakra*, Kuwait, October 18, 1988

Our first objective is to return to Nablus, and then move on to Tel Aviv. The day that we achieve independence will signify the defeat of Israel as a state. — Leila Khaled, Secretary General, PLO General Union of Palestinian Women, *Middle East Monthly*, London, January 1989

I shall make it very perfectly clear to you. We shall never recognize Israel, never accept the usurper, the colonialist, the imperialist. We shall never allow Israel to live in peace. — Farouk Khadoumi, head of the PLO Political Department, *Stern*, West Germany, July 30, 1981

Jordan is ours, Palestine is ours, and we shall build our national entity on the whole of this land after having freed it of both the Zionist presence and the reactionary traitor's [i.e., King Hussein's] presence. — Yassir Arafat, "A Letter to Jordanian Student Congress in Baghdad," as reported in the *Washington Post*, November 12, 1974

Not a weapon forged against you will succeed. Every tongue that accuses you in judgment will be refuted. Such will be the lot of the lord, the vindication I award them. It is the Lord who speaks. — Isaiah 54:17

Some of these declarations and additional findings were submitted to the U.S. Congress by the nation's State Department on March 19, 1990. The report stated:

1. PLO statements and actions continue to pursue a course of terrorism and the rejection of Israel's legitimate existence (p. 2–13).

2. The PLO Covenant stands as the ideological credo of the PLO, and the statements of PLO leaders point out that no attempt has been made by the PNC to repeal the Covenant or change any of its provisions advocating the elimination of Israel (p. 16–19).

3. The PLO's "Phased Plan" remains the key PLO strategy for implementing its Covenant, and PLO leaders reaffirm that the establishment of a Palestinian state in the territories would be just a prelude to expanding such a state in "all of Palestine" (p. 20–23).

4. All of the PLO factions which participated in the November 1988 PNC have engaged in infiltration attempts since December 1988, and Arafat, instead of trying to halt the terror operations, has endorsed them (p. 27–32).

5. The PLO has opposed the extradition and prosecution of PLO terrorists wanted for attacks abroad (p. 38).

6. The PLO has refused to acknowledge its responsibility for PLO terrorism, and has not compensated American victims (p. 38–39).

Again I will build you, and you shall be built. O maiden of Israel. . . . And you shall replant vineyards on the Samarian hills. . . . For thus says the Lord: Sing out joyously and exalt among the great nations . . . and give praise and say:

God has rescued His people, the remnant of Israel. — Jeremiah 31:4–7

The *Jerusalem Post* of July 3, 1990, put it thusly in its editorial:

As an organization, the PLO has never recognized Israel's right to exist. It has not changed its charter, which calls for Israel's destruction, nor has it disavowed the ten resolutions of the 'policy of phases' adopted by the PNC in Cairo in June 1974. Resolution Eight states that, after the establishment of a national independent fighting authority on any part of the Palestinian territory that will be liberated, 'the Palestinian authority will struggle to unite the confrontation countries to pave the way for the completion of the liberations of all the Palestinian territory.' All letterheads, maps, and emblems of the PLO, including those on official documents submitted to the UN, show the state of Palestine as covering the whole area from the Jordan to the Mediterranean. Israel, whose right to exist Arafat is presumed to recognize, does not exist on these maps.

The Oslo Accords were a Trojan horse, the strategic goal is the liberation of Palestine from the Jordan River to the Mediterranean Sea. — Faisal Al-Husseini, in his last interview, *Memri*, July 2, 2001

And to those who would try to use the current crisis as an opportunity to widen the conflict, stay out. Iran's arms shipments and support for terror fuel the fire of conflict in the Middle East. And it must stop. Syria has spoken out against Al-Qaeda. We expect it to act against Hamas and Hizballah, as well. It's time for Iran to focus on meeting its own people's aspirations for freedom and for Syria to decide which side of the war against terror it is on. — U.S. President George W. Bush, April 4, 2002

It doesn't matter if Arafat lives or dies, doesn't matter if he has electricity or not, doesn't matter if his cell phone works or not, doesn't matter if his toilet flushes or not. The issue is not Arafat. The issue is the terror war. — Michael Ledeen, Zionist Information News Service, July/August 2002

One Western observer expressed his opinion about terror thusly: "In the Middle East, terror is an endemic feature of local politics. Most of the terror is not anti-Israel or even anti-West, but intra-Arab and intra-Muslim. It is a way for Syria to check Jordan, for Syria to subvert Iraq (and vice versa), for Lebanese factions to deal with one another, and for Libya to tame its enemies everywhere."

This cartoon appeared in the Israeli daily *Ma'Ariv* on September 5, 2001. It depicts Arafat wishing his suicide bomber "success." The bomb was made in Durban, South Africa. The first week in September 2001, an international conference on racism was held in Durban. Arafat's Palestinian delegation incited the masses against Israel at that conference.

PART IV:

ARAFAT AND THE PALESTINIAN AUTHORITY: POLICY OF LIES, HATRED, AND FANATICISM

CHAPTER 8

INCITEMENT

TEACHING CHILDREN TO HATE

In light of the new era marked by the signing of the Declarations of Principles, the PLO encourages and calls upon the Palestinian people in the West Bank and Gaza Strip to take part in the steps leading to the normalization of life, rejecting violence and terrorism, contributing to peace and stability, and participating actively in shaping reconstruction, economic development, and cooperation. — Excerpt from Arafat's letter to then Foreign Minister of Norway, Johan Jorgen Holst, September 9, 1993

The Palestinian Authority, in gross violation of agreements signed, continually commits a severe crime by indoctrinating their young with deep feelings of hatred and the will to kill others.

These same children were sent by Arafat and the Palestinian Authority to run to the front lines to challenge and taunt the Israeli soldiers by throwing stones at them, by cursing them, and by spitting at them.

Arafat's misconception is that the more hatred and lies you spread, the more you benefit the Palestinian cause.

The Palestinian Authority employs thousands of teachers and spends tens of millions of dollars on textbooks, equipment, etc., each year. The purpose is one: to teach hatred and to incite the new generation of Palestinians to kill and to become suicide bombers. Examination of their textbooks reveals a wealth of rhetoric, anti-Semitism, and intolerance towards others, especially Christians and Jews.

Here are a few examples, all cited from official Palestinian textbooks in use to this day:

> The Jews have killed Muslim and Christian inhabitants of Palestine whose inhabitants are still suffering oppression and persecution under racist Jewish administration. — *Islamic Education for Ninth Grade*, no. 589, p. 182

> Learn from this lesson: I believe that the Jews are the enemies of the Prophets and the believers. — *Islamic Education for Fourth Grade*, part 2, p. 67

> In the textbook *Palestinian National Education for Second Grade*, no.519, p. 2, there is a map entitled "Our Country, Palestine" which depicts "Palestine" replacing all of Israel.

> Complete the following blank spaces with the appropriate word: "The Zionist enemy _____ civilians with its aircraft." — *Our Arabic Language* for third grade, part 2, p. 9

> The following is an excerpt from a poem entitled "Palestine": "My brothers: the oppressors [Israel] have crossed the borders, therefore we must wage jihad and redeem our land. Are we to let them steal its Arab nature? Draw your sword, let us gather for war with red blood and blazing fire. Death shall call and the sword shall be crazed from much slaughter. O Palestine, the youth will redeem your land." — *Reader and Literary Texts for Eighth Grade*, p. 120–122

> *For every evil, silence is the best remedy.* — The Talmud

All Palestinian Authority textbooks continue to teach non-recognition of Israel, whose name does not appear on any map. Israel's place on maps is marked "Palestine." Every reference to Israeli cities, regions, and geographic areas identifies them as part of "Palestine."

> *The new Palestinian schoolbooks [September 2000] make no attempt to educate for peace and coexistence with Israel. Indeed, the opposite is true. The peace process is not even referred to in the schoolbooks. The Oslo Accords are mentioned once, but are not defined as a peace process, rather as a point in time connected to the PLO's "liberation army forces entering Palestine."* — Palestinian Media Watch, by Itamar Marcus

> *The promotion of hatred and violence is pervasive in the Palestinian Authority's media, schools, summer camps, and religious sermons. The Palestinian Authority deliberately disseminates messages filled with anti-Semitic and anti-Israeli hatred with the clear aim of promoting violence against Israel and the Jewish people. These teachings foster an environment of hostility and violence, not peace and conciliation.* — U.S. Senator Arlen Specter, ZOA (Zionist Organization of America) pamphlet

"Shahada": Death for Allah

> *Arafat promised us the peace of the brave. Instead he gave us the peace of the grave.* — Ra'anan Gissin, spokesman, prime minister's office, Israel interview on CNN

Children in the Palestinian Authority are brought up to see death for Allah — *shahada* —as something expected of them. This message is obvious in the Palestinian Authority official media, in the written and electronic media, as well as in school textbooks.

The Palestinian Authority daily *Al-Ayyam* published a poem written by a 12 year old on November 13, 2002, expressing this longing. The children's section also included a political cartoon which equated an Israeli hand grenade and death with an American hamburger. Both sentiments — the yearning for shahada and the hatred of America — are integral parts of Palestinian Authority ideology and the children's opinions are an indication of the ways in which this ideology is being passed on to the next generation.

This is the poem in translation:

My Land
by Omar Ali Amda (6th grade)
I have responded to my country's call,
My honor shall not fall,
My shahada is in my hands.
I shall redeem my country with my soul
And protect my religion with my heart.
I am not troubled by the breaking of my bones,
I am not bothered by the demolition of my house.
Oh, occupier, hear me.

The Palestinian Authority has been teaching and encouraging their children to see shahada as something that is expected of them. In one televised gathering, Yassir Arafat himself was shown encouraging young children to seek death while he simultaneously glorified a famous child martyr. He is seen addressing the cheering and chanting children who filled an auditorium and called them all "colleagues, friends, brothers, and sisters of Paris Ouda" (a 14-year-old child who died in the conflict, who has since been turned into a heroic symbol by the Palestinian Authority). He continued by declaring that one of the children present would "raise the Palestinian flag over Jerusalem." The children's response was to combine the Jerusalem and shahada messages into one by chanting, "Millions of shahids marching to Jerusalem." The following is a translated excerpt from Arafat's speech to the Palestinian children which was aired on Palestinian Authority television on August 18, 2002:

Oh, children of Palestine. The colleagues, friends, brothers, and sisters of Paris Ouda. The colleagues of this hero represent this immense and fundamental power that is within, and it shall be victorious, with Allah's will. One of you, a boy or a girl, shall raise the [Palestinian] flag over the walls of Jerusalem, its mosques and its churches. . . . Onward together to Jerusalem.

This is not the first time that Arafat publicly supported the idea of child shahids. Time and again he has made it clear the importance he attaches to having dead Palestinian children to show the world. Arafat said the following on Palestinian Authority television in January 2002:

> Question: Mr. President, what message would you like to send to the Palestinian people in general and, particularly, to the Palestinian children?
> Arafat: . . . The child who is grasping the stone, facing the tank; is it not the greatest message to the world when that hero becomes a shadid? We are proud of them.

> *Suicide bombers kill and maim dozens at a time, with but one regret: that their victims are so few. What they truly strive to bring about is a Holocaust. They come as close to that end as their means will allow. My nomination for an appropriate descriptive term, then, is this: "genocide bombing."*
> — Steve Zak, *Washington Times*, December 4, 2002

Peace is not only a piece of paper signed by two leaders declaring that peace has been achieved between their two countries. A true and lasting peace is based on positive education amongst the people, especially among the younger generation. It should be an ongoing education teaching mutual respect and understanding. It should promote friendship and hope for a better future for both sides.

The Palestinian Authority is, in fact, doing just the opposite. Through its education and media it continues to spread hatred, fanaticism, and death. The damage is far more profound when such hatred is encouraged among the young. The new generation is encouraged to die for the cause besides murdering their Jewish neighbors.

Q: Can some examples be cited?
A: When asked by his Palestinian mother what he wants to be when he grows up, her two-year-old son answered, "A martyr" (*New York Times* article, October 29, 2000).

The Palestinian Authority Television aired a program in which a teacher appeared before her students and said, "Our blood is a sign of our fighting for our precious Palestine" (November 2, 2000).

Al-Hayat Al-Jadidah, the official Palestinian Authority daily, carried an interview with the father of an Arab youth killed while attacking Israeli civilians. He said that he has "great pride that his progeny has become a martyr" (November 2, 2000).

On November 8, 2000, this same newspaper, *Al-Hayat Al-Jadidah,* interviewed Ramadan Saal Abd Rabbo, a 13-year-old boy who was wounded. The boy said, "My goal is not to be injured, but rather something higher: martyrdom."

> *I will take my soul in my hand and toss it into the abyss of death and then either life that will gladden friends or death that will anger the enemy. The honorable soul has two objectives: achieving death and honor.* — A song sung by Palestinian schoolgirls, Palestinian Authority Television, October 27, 2000

For a few weeks in March and April 2002, Israel conducted a military operation in Judea and Samaria against the terrorist infrastructure of the Palestinian Authority. Tons of weapons, bombs, explosive devices, etc., were destroyed. Hundreds of terrorists were caught or killed in battle. The most astonishing find was the large number of boys who were ready to commit suicide, killing themselves along with innumerable innocent Israelis, for the sake of Yassir Arafat. They were all systematically brainwashed by Arafat's representatives. All were programmed to believe that their deaths would serve the interests of the Palestinian people and that they would remain for all eternity in paradise surrounded by 70 virgins.

The Palestinian Authority encouraged the sacrifice of their own children.

> *I will push my child to participate in the resistance, and I pray to Allah that my son ends his life as a shaheed.* — Chairperson, Hizbullah Women's Movement, Al-Jazira Television, December 13, 2000

> *I began to take action within the framework of the American University in Beirut, and to explain the priorities of the shaheed children — in the same way that we are educated to become doctors, they are educated to die like their fathers.* — Member of Hizbullah Women's Movement, Al-Jazira Television, December 13, 2000

"The Jews Are Monkeys and Pigs"

A continual and significant theme broadcast by the Palestinian Authority Television has been the promotion of anti-Jewish and anti-Israel sentiment. During one televised sermon, Jews were referred to as "cursed . . . the brothers of monkeys and pigs, with a stream of curses that will continue until the Resurrection." Attacking and afflicting Jews is presented as part of the destiny to be fulfilled by Muslims and Arabs. It is viewed as a religious obligation from Allah: "Allah loves those who fight on his behalf. . . . Allah said against the Jews . . . 'your Lord has declared that He will surely send against them [the Jews] until Resurrection, those who will afflict them with terrible torment. . . ." Interpreted by traditional Islam, this means that Muslims are the ones who will torment the Jews, until Resurrection.

The following are excerpts from a sermon by Dr. Mustafah Najem which was televised on Palestinian Authority Television on December 2002:

> *Praise be to Allah, who has cursed [the Jews], the brothers of monkeys and pigs, with a stream of curses that will continue until the resurrection of the dead. He has warned us against their evil and their arrogance, and has said; 'You will find that the most brazen among mankind, with hatred towards the believers, are the Jews and the idolaters' (Koran 81:5). It is not foreign to them to shed our blood. They murder and slaughter us, demolish our homes, and destroy everything that is important to us. . . . The Jews are Jews, and we are forbidden to forget their character traits even for a moment, even for a blink of an eye. Oh servants of Allah [Muslims], the Jews are those who tried to murder your prophet in order to expunge the call [to Islam]. It is no wonder that it has been legitimized [for them] to kill and slaughter us. . . . Our enemies are waging a war against us, against Islam and the Muslims in particular, against those who demand their rights, and against any Muslim who seeks to hold his head up. They are trying to subdue us with hard oppression. Such are the Jews, who are fighting us during our peaceful festival, and also during the holy months, because they are idolaters,*

heretics, whose faith is false. While we are the believers in the truth and in the true faith. . . .

Anti-Semitism and racism are basic tenets of the Palestinian Authority in which both the Jews and the Jewish religion are defined as evil by nature. The following statement by Abd El-Aziz Shahin, Palestinian Authority minister of supplies, was televised on the official Palestinian television network on December 12, 2002:

> *Since the 19th century the Zionist mind has been built upon the killing of the Arab people. They do not want a single Arab on Palestinian soil. This is a matter that exists with every Zionist, whether he is right-wing, center, or left-wing . . . because the Zionist education . . . in their religious schools, where they learn that they are the chosen people of God and we are the others, we are considered the stage between the Jew and the monkey. This is a basis of the Jewish religion, and from this comes the killing of the Arab people in Palestine.*

> *At a ceremony in Gaza, under the heading "Palestine and Iraq in the same trench," 25 Palestinian families of shahids received grants from Saddam Hussein totaling $280,000. Sketches of Arafat and Saddam Hussein appeared together on a poster beside the Iraqi and Palestinian flags. During the ceremony support was expressed for Iraq in its battle with the United States and one of the speakers, the poet Omar Halil Omar, "praised the role of Iraq and the Commander Saddam Hussein, and stressed that Iraq's land will be a graveyard for the American soldiers. . . ."* — Al-Hayat Al Jadida, December 19, 2002, from Palestinian Media Watch, Dr. Itamar Marcus, December 19, 2002

ANTI-SEMITISM IN ARAFAT'S SERVICE

> *If you do a content analysis of the Palestinian Authority's media, it is worse than the Nazis' propaganda.* — Ra'anan Gissin, spokesman for the Prime Minister of Israel, *Philadelphia Inquirer*, March 26, 2001

A question seldom asked is: How can the Arabs, who are a Semitic people themselves, be anti-Semitic? According to both

Judaism and Islam, Abraham was their forefather. He had two sons: Isaac from his wife Sarah, and Yishmael from Hagar. Yishmael is the father of the Arab nation.

Arab hatred for Israel and Zionism soon expanded into hatred toward expressions and descriptions of Israel to "prove" their claim that Israel is evil, wicked, corrupted, depressive, racist, etc. The Jews who support Israel are just the same in their eyes. This is how anti-Israel feelings among Arabs emerged into anti-Semitism slogans.

> *There is, of course, no difference whatsoever between anti-Semitism and the denial of Israel's statehood. Classical anti-Semitism denies the equal rights of Jews as citizens within society. Anti-Zionism denies the equal rights of the Jewish people to its lawful sovereignty within the community of nations. The common principle in the two cases is discrimination.* — Abba Eban, former foreign minister of Israel, *New York Times*

It is clear that Palestinians cannot, on the one hand, spread hatred among their people while, on the other hand, strive for peace. Peace and hatred are diverging concepts.

> *Israel will not negotiate under terror. If the Palestinians are interested in negotiations, I suggest to Arafat that he make a 100 percent effort to stop terror. . . . The Palestinians are the aggressors.* — U.S. President George W. Bush, *Yediot Acharonot*, August 26, 2001

> *There is no alternative to the destruction of Israel. . . . This book is dedicated to the fighters of the expulsion of the enemy [Israel] from our land.* — Excerpt from official Palestinian textbook, sixth grade, *Palestine Our Homeland*

One of the most notorious libel texts used by anti-Semites against the Jewish people is the *Protocols of the Elders of Zion*. In this book, the Jews are described as traitors, liars, thieves, and conspirators who seek to control the world. The Palestinian Authority never hesitated to use portions of this infamous text to justify its own positions. Here are a few examples:

Protocols of the Elders of Zion *proves Jews seek to conquer the world with the secret plan of Israel and world Jewry to "hold the reins of most of the newspapers" in order to "have the means to propel and to influence."* — *Al-Hayat Al-Jadidah*, Palestinian Authority daily, January 25, 2001

We must expose the Zionist-Colonialist plot and its goals, which destroy not only our people but the entire world" — Abdel Jawad Saleh, PA minister of agriculture, *Al-Hayat Al-Jadidah,* November 6, 1997

Q: How does the Palestinian Authority view Jewish influence in the United States?
A: Hafez al-Barghouti, editor of the Palestinian Authority's daily, *Al-Hayat Al-Jadidah,* referred to the United States Congress as "the Judaized Congress."

Q: How does Al-Hayat Al-Jadidah characterize the Jews?
A: In an October 31, 1997, article, the Palestinian Authority daily characterized the Jews as "those who spread death and murder and spill blood and who are said to be our cousins and, like us, 'the children of Abraham,' despite the fact that Abraham did not immigrate to Poland, did not visit New York and New Jersey, and did not live in Russia."

Q: What rights do the Jews have to nationhood?
A: According to *Al-Hayat Al-Jadidah* from September 2, 1997, "These Zionists are not fit to establish a nation or to have their own language or even their own religion. They are nothing more than a hodgepodge."

Q: What other stereotypes are applied to the Jews?
A: On September 1, 1997, *Al-Hayat Al-Jadidah* said the following: "The conflict between the Jews and the Muslims resembles the conflict between man and Satan." On August 5, 1997, this same Palestinian Authority daily declared, "Generosity is an Arab custom and stinginess is a Jewish custom."

In the *New York Times* of August 1996, Arafat called Israel "a demon" that "swallows up everything." At a press conference with Hillary Clinton, then the first lady of the United States, Arafat's wife, Suha, accused Israel of "daily and intensive use of poisonous gas," causing "cancer and other horrible diseases" among Palestinian Arab women and children. She also claimed that Israel has contaminated 80 percent of Palestinian Arab water sources with "chemical materials." (Reuters, November 11, 1999)

The Germans know how to get rid of the Jews. — *Haj Amin El Husshni*, November 1943

Beware of the treasonous Jews. — Palestinian Authority school textbook, ninth grade, *Islamic Education*

The following are a few examples of how Arafat spreads hatred and incitement through his official media.

On July 21, 2000, the official Palestinian Authority Television repeatedly broadcasted video clips of violence against Israeli soldiers and military parades while the announcer described Israeli soldiery as "Satan's agents" and "enemies of mankind."

On July 28, 2000, the official Palestinian Authority Television broadcasted a speech by the Islamic preacher Dr. Ahmad Yusuf Abu Halbiah. In that notorious speech, Abu Halbiah proclaimed, "The resurrection of the dead will not occur, until you battle with the Jews and kill them."

On August 6, 2000, in another official Palestinian Authority Television broadcast, a speech by the secretary general of the Movement for the Islamic Struggle, the speaker declared, "The end of the Zionist entity is a Koranic necessity; there is no place for [Israel] no matter how long it takes."

On August 11, 2000, this same Palestinian Authority Television station carried another speech by Dr. Ahmad Yusuf Abu Halbiah in which he announced, "O, our Arab brothers, O our Muslim brothers, don't leave the Palestinians alone in their war against the Jews." and "Let me take this opportunity to speak about the Jews, about their cunning ways, their heresy, their jealousy and their attempts to get you to lose your way."

On August 18, 2000, another speech by a Muslim religious preacher was aired by the Palestinian Authority Television in which he proclaimed:

Allah decreed that in our lives, we are to humiliate the Jews sooner or later. The Muslims and the Arabs must stand behind the sons of the nation of Palestine, for they are the vanguard against the enemies of Allah. And by Allah's life, the Jews are the enemies of Islam.

ISLAM IN THE SERVICE OF HATRED, WAR, AND BLOODSHED

Woe upon you, the murderer of the innocent. — Sharia, Islamic Holy Law

Islam forbids the killing of the innocent. However, the so-called Moslem spiritual leaders misuse Islam in order to justify their fanaticism against Jews and Christians, spreading hatred and vehement animosity amongst their followers.

The absurdity is that some of these leaders are within Israel's grasp or domain, yet nothing is done to stop their incitement or to arrest them.

Fighters of the jihad who sacrificed themselves are almost as honorable as the prophets. — Palestinian Authority official school reader, sixth grade

Q: How are the Jews described by these fanatic Moslem leaders?
A: The Jews are time and again described as the enemies of Islam. In his sermon at the Al-Aqsa mosque in Jerusalem on January 15, 1999, Sheikh Abu Sneinah declared, "Our struggle in Palestine is an ideological struggle between Islam and the enemies of Islam."

Q: How do these religious leaders consider suicide bombers, who murder many innocent bystanders at the time of their demise?

A: The chief mufti of Jerusalem, Sheikh Ikrama Sabri, is the most senior religious leader in the city. With regard to suicide bombers, he said that such bombings against Israelis are justified as "a response to the occupation."

Q: How does he view the United States?
A: In his sermon at the Al Aqsa mosque on September 12, 1997, which was broadcast on Palestinian Authority Radio, Sheikh Sabri said, "O Muslims, we must raise our voices against America, its ally Britain and all the infidel nations. . . . America is the chief of the terrorists. O Allah, destroy America, her agents and her allies. Cast them into their own traps, and cover the White House with black."

Q: What do they wish to happen to the United States?
A: The answer can be found in Sheikh Sabri's daily sermon from July 11, 1997. He said, "O Allah, destroy America, for she is ruled by Zionist Jews. . . . Allah will paint the White House black. . . . Allah shall take revenge on behalf of his prophet against the colonialist settlers who are sons of monkeys and pigs. . . . Forgive us, Mohammed, for the acts of these sons of monkeys and pigs who sought to harm your sanctity."

> *American diplomats and tourists were likewise often victims of the PLO. Like Ambassador Cleo A. Noel and his deputy, George Curtis Moore, in Khartoum or Leon Klinghoffer on the cruise ship Achille Lauro, they were randomly targeted but singled out for torture and death when kidnapped in the company of citizens of other lands. — Anti-Americanism is "a basic feature of Palestinian ideology."* — Noted French analyst Alain Gresh in Harris O. Schoenberg, *A Mandate for Terror.*[1]

> *There are two phases of our return: the first phase to the 1967 lines, and the second to the 1948 lines. . . . The third stage is the democratic State of Palestine. So we are fighting for these three stages. . . . In the past we said, no, on all of it, immediately, a democratic State of Palestine. Now we say no, this can be implemented in three stages. That's moderation.* — Farouk Al-Kadumi, PLO leader, *Newsweek*, March 14, 1977

Ehud Barak, former prime minister of Israel, wrote the following in the *New York Times* on April 14, 2002:

> *The aim of the Palestinian terror is not just to kill Israelis but also to break the will of Israeli society in order to dictate a political solution. Israel should never yield to this terror campaign. . . . We can win this struggle against terror. That struggle must take place on three levels: the war against terror, the struggle for the moral high ground of international legitimacy, and the efforts to keep unity and cohesion within Israeli society.*

Ridiculous! How can half a dozen splintered organizations partly ruled by criminals who quarrel among themselves about radical ideologies make such a claim? [that the PLO is the sole representative of the Palestinians]. What they call representation, or war of liberation, is nothing but terror. — The late King Hussein of Jordan, *Munchener Merkur*, Germany, October 28–29, 1978

From this day forward, any nation that continues to harbor or support terrorism will be regarded by the U.S. as a hostile regime. — U.S. President George W. Bush, *Jerusalem Post*, December 14, 2001

THE "HUDAYBIYYA" TREATY

A definite factor in getting a lie believed is the size of the lie. The broad mass of the people in the simplicity of their hearts, more easily fall victim to a big lie than to a small one. — Adolf Hitler

The Hudaybiyya Treaty was signed by the Prophet of Islam, Mohammed, with his enemies from the tribe of Kuraysh in the Arab Peninsula, which is Saudi Arabia today. When Mohammed signed the treaty, he was weak militarily. He knew that he could not win the battle against his enemies. Therefore, he agreed to sign a cease-fire treaty only as a ploy to gain time in order to increase his power. When he knew he was strong enough, he did not hesitate to violate the treaty by attacking the enemy and then winning the war. The Treaty of Hudaybiyya was named for the place in which the treaty was signed.

As early as Arafat's speech at the signing of the Declaration of Principles on September 13, 1993, there were indications that, for him, the agreement did not necessarily signify an end to the conflict. Arafat continued to appear publicly in his military uniform which symbolizes his status as a revolutionary commander. On numerous occasions, the PLO leader continued to use the language of jihad. The word jihad literally means "struggle," but in the specific, religiously colored, context of the Palestinian struggle, this is a clear reference to the violent option.

In a eulogy to a Palestinian official on June 15, 1995, and at the height of realization of the Oslo Agreement, Arafat paid homage, among others, to two women terrorists: Dalal al-Mughrabi and Abir Wahidi. In that same eulogy, he referred to the stone-throwing children as "the Palestinian Generals." He also swore to his audience that "the oath is firm to continue this difficult jihad, this long jihad, in the path of martyrs, the path of sacrifices."

Time and time again, Arafat has publicly repeated references to the Hudaybiyya Treaty, the treaty signed by the Prophet Mohammed with his Meccan enemies and which he violated once his forces were strong enough to conquer the city. Arafat first mentioned this treaty in his jihad speech in a Mosque in Johannesburg, South Africa. This speech was given shortly after the signing of the Oslo Agreement of September 1993 and was a direct violation of the treaty. To Muslim audiences, Arafat speaks in the familiar idiom of Islamic radicalism.

> Did the prophet, Allah's messenger, the last of the prophets, really accept a humiliation? No, and no again. He did not accept a humiliation. — Yassir Arafat, Palestinian Authority Television, August 21, 1995

Arafat's reference to the Hudaybiyya Treaty resurfaced in 1998 together with a warning that "all the options are open to the Palestinian people" (Orbit Television, April 18, 1998). Arafat's intentions for accepting the Oslo Agreement and the subsequent negotiations had its own rationale. The various commitments involved were viewed by him not as the building blocks of trust and cooperation but rather as temporary measures to be shed off when circumstances permitted.

To secular audiences, Arafat offers a possible argument for the temporary nature of his signed commitments by addressing them in the context of the "Strategy of Stages," which would lead up to the liberation of "Palestine." This was endorsed by the Palestinian National Council in 1974. Nabil Sha'at, a Palestinian leader, described this strategy in a speech in Nablus in January 1996. Again, this speech was delivered at a time when the negotiations with Israel were proceeding. He said the following:

> We decided to liberate our homeland step by step. . . . Should Israel continue — no problem. And so, we honor the

peace treaties and non-violence . . . if and when Israel says "enough" . . . in that case it is saying that we will return to violence. But this time, it will be with 30,000 armed Palestinian soldiers and in a land with elements of freedom. . . . If we reach a dead end, we will go back to our war and struggle like we did 40 years ago.

Another Palestinian leader, Muhammad Dahlan, head of preventive security in Gaza, warned that a return to the armed struggle, with the active participation of the Palestinian Authority forces, cannot be ruled out in view of the impasse in the process. — Interview in *Al Hayyat*, September 2, 1996

The mufti of Jerusalem is the highest religious functionary in the Palestinian hierarchy. The mufti Sheikh Ikrimah Sabri told the Palestinian newspaper *Al-Ayyam* on March 3, 1997, that Jerusalem cannot be retrieved through negotiations, and hence the only option is war.

Marwan Barghuti, fatah leader in the West Bank and a key in provoking the present crisis, warned as early as March 1997 that his men are inclined to resume the armed struggle. He applauded the Hamas bombing in Tel Aviv in which three women were killed. — *Al-Ayyam Val Hayyat, Al-Jadidah*, March 26 and 27, 1997

On November 15, 1998, speaking at a public rally, Arafat once again overtly threatened that "the Palestinian rifle is ready and we will aim it if they try to prevent us from praying in Jerusalem . . . the 'Generals of Stones' are ready." — Quoted in *Al Ayyam*, November 16, 1998

Nabil Sha'at explained Arafat's intentions when he said "all options are open" thusly:

No one believed him [Arafat] when he used to say it . . . [but] The choice is not at all between options of negotiation and fighting: you can have negotiations and fight at the same time. . . . the Palestinian people fight with weapons, with jihad, with intifada and suicide actions . . . and it is destined to always fight and negotiate at the same time. — ANN TV, London, October 7, 2000

The conclusion is very clear. Arafat and his colleagues have followed a strategy based upon deception, lies, and lack of trust. Arafat, instead of becoming a statesman who would lead his people, has proven that he has been and always will be a terrorist. The first victims of this strategy are the Palestinian people.

> *The establishment of an independent Palestinian state on the West Bank and in the Gaza Strip does not contradict our ultimate strategic aim, which is the establishment of a democratic state in the territory of Palestine, but rather is a step in that direction.* — PLO leader Abu Iyad, *Al-Safir*, Lebanon, January 25, 1988

PALESTINIAN AUTHORITY VIOLATION OF THE OSLO AGREEMENT

Israel signed the Oslo Agreement with the PLO in September 1993. The Israeli government was in euphoria. The government assured the Israeli people that the PLO would honor the agreement, that terror attacks would end, and that the Middle East had entered a new era of peace. Shimon Peres even wrote a book entitled *The New Middle East*, in which he envisioned and promised an era of peace with the Arabs. Peres befriended Yassir Arafat and trusted in his promises.

Reality proved, however, that Arafat cannot be trusted. The scores of violations of the Oslo Agreement on the part of the Palestinians proved that Arafat is not a man of his word. Here is just a partial list of such violations with regard to security.

1. Since the Oslo Agreement, Palestinian murderers of Israelis have escaped to Gaza. The PLO has refused to arrest these criminals and to hand them over to Israel for trial.

2. The PLO claimed that they were investigating these criminals, yet they refused to give Israel any details about these supposed investigations. In other instances, the Palestinian Authority held mock trials for the media. Within a few days, those convicted

were released by what has been termed the "revolving door" strategy.

3. No action has been taken against agitators in Gaza against Israel. The mosques of Gaza have become centers of anti-Israel propaganda, spreading hatred and hostility towards Israel.

4. In Jerusalem, the PLO has been acting as a state within a state. The PLO Palestinian Authority has been behaving like an independent state in clear violation of the Oslo Agreement.

5. The rifles and weapons of the PLO police have been used in terrorist acts against Israelis since October 1994. Moreover, the Palestinian police did not act at all against Palestinians in possession of illegal weapons. The Palestinian Authority has, instead, supplied weapons to other people in direct violation of the terms of the Oslo Agreement.

6. The Palestinian Authority has arrested and tortured Palestinians suspected of collaborating with Israel, once again a clear violation of the agreement.

7. The Palestinian Authority agreed to limit its police force to 9,000. Instead, they now number over 40,000.

8. The Palestinian police are using cars stolen from Israel. Gaza, Judea, and Samaria have turned into a safe haven for stolen Israeli property.

9. Thirteen Israelis were arrested and detained by the PLO police force. In other instances, PLO weapons were directed on Israelis. According to the Oslo Agreement, the PLO police agreed to only delay Israelis, not to investigate them, arrest them, or to use weapons against them.

10. In English, the Palestinian Authority calls itself the "National Palestinian Authority," while in Arabic it calls itself the "State of Palestine." Use of the terms "State of Palestine" and "national" are a very clear violation of the terms of the Oslo Agreement. In addition,

the Palestinian Authority uses the name "Palestine" on its stamps and on international driving licenses.

11. The Palestinian Authority published an ad in the Palestinian paper *Al Quds* in which it called upon the Palestinian Arabs in Judea and Samaria not to obey the Israeli law which has been in effect since June 5, 1967.

After the PLO terror attacks in Tel Aviv, Jerusalem, and the Sharon area, in which scores of innocent Israelis died, the Palestinian masses in Gaza went out into the streets to dance, cheer, and celebrate. The Palestinian police did not intervene, and in some cases were seen joining in the celebrations.

Bear in mind that all these violations were carried out while the late Yitzhak Rabin's government was in power. The situation has deteriorated dramatically since the uprising of September 2000. Israel wanted peace. Instead she unfortunately faced Yassir Arafat — the leader of gangs of murderers.

Selected "Jewels" from Palestinian Curriculum and Religous Sermons

One of the greatest crimes ever committed was to teach Palestinian children to hate, to kill, and to be killed. All across the world, children are taught science, literature, human rights, and tolerance toward others in their schools. Yassir Arafat, on the other hand, is systematically teaching and encouraging a new generation of murderers, criminals, and miserable fanatics in the Palestinian Authority school system. For this heinous crime alone, Arafat will be remembered in the history of the Middle East as an evil criminal deserving condemnation.

The following are a few select "jewels" found in part of the Palestinian school curriculum:

There is no alternative but Israel's destruction.

This book is dedicated to the fighters for the expulsion of the enemy from our land. — From the textbook entitled *Our Homeland Palestine*, sixth grade, published by the Palestinian Authority

The Jewish claim of Palestine is the biggest lie in world history.

Perhaps God brought the Jews to our land in order to destroy them just like what happened during their war against the Romans. — From the textbook entitled *Our Arabic Language*, fifth grade, published by the Palestinian Authority

If someone is tired [of the armed struggle] let him stay home and send me his children instead. — Yassir Arafat, PLO leader, 1995

When the enemies of Allah, the Jews, may Allah curse them, mutilate [the bodies], and chop off the organs — these organs will serve as evidence for our sons and brothers for whom paradise in the high heavens is a place of refuge. [Even when] a martyr's organs are being chopped off and he turns into torn organs that spread all over, in order to meet Allah, Mohammed, and his friends, it would not be [considered] a loss. — From a Friday television sermon, Palestinian Authority Television, October 2001

HAMAS: PRAISE OF SEPTEMBER 11, 2001, ATTACKS

Hamas Terrorist Carried Letter Praising 9/11 Aattacks in US — Headline in the *Jerusalem Post*, March 6, 2003

On March 5, 2003, the Hamas terrorist Mohammed Amran Kawasmeh from Hebron exploded himself on an Israeli bus killing 15 passengers. He carried a bag in which was found a letter in Arabic under the title, "One of the miracles of the holy Koran is given to Moslems, Jews, and Christians."

In that same letter, Kawasmeh praises the attacks on the World Trade Center and Washington, DC, on September 11, 2001. He based his praise on a verse from the Koran which reads, "To build a building based on God's belief is better than to build it on a hole which has no foundation and which is very close to hell" (Sura 11, verse 9). This chapter is comprised of 1,100 words which was the address on the World Trade Center buildings.

Kawasmeh justified the bombing of 15 innocent people — Jews and non-Jews alike — and his own suicide with other references to the miracles revealed in the Koran.

Kawasmeh's letter is only one example of the many others which have been published in the mass media by Islamic organizations such as Hamas, Islamic Jihad, Hizballah, Al-Qaeda, etc. These organizations and others describe the West in general and the United States in particular as the "Big Satan." America is described as evil and wicked and the Americans are referred to as the "enemies of Allah," "the enemies of Islam," and "the Moslems." Vehement hatred against the United States and American values is preached by Islamic religious figures and politicians in innumerable articles and speeches across almost the entire Arab and Islamic world.

On March 6, 2003 — the day after Kawasmeh's suicide bombing — the Palestinian newpaper *Al-Quds* published a story with photographs of Palestinian children holding a mock trial. President Bush was seen in the "defendant's" cage guarded by two "soldiers." The caption under the photo read: "Children acting as judges while another child wears a mask of President George Bush Jr. The judges found the American President guilty of crimes against humanity." The sign under the "judges" read: "High Court of the Palestinian Youth Parliament for the Trial of War Criminals."

MASS MURDERS ARE HEROIC SYMBOLS

Some wished to compare the American Revolution and many other wars of liberation of the past 200 years with indiscriminate terrorism. If there were instances during the American Revolution where innocent people suffered, there was no instance where the revolutionary leadership boasted of or condoned such crimes. There were no victims, on either side, of a deliberate policy of terror. — John Scali, U.S. ambassador to the United Nations, 1973–1975

For the Palestinians, the issue and the means are very simple: kill the Jews wherever you find them. Do not have mercy upon them. Kill them in the streets, on buses, in supermarkets, in coffee shops — everywhere and at all times. The more you kill, the better. Indiscriminate killing of men, women, and children — civilians as well as military personnel — is the name of the game, as long as they are Jews. If a few Arabs are among the victims, you are allowed to kill them as long as Jews also are murdered.

This is the hatred being spread by the Palestinian Authority through its media. It is geared for the Palestinian people and especially for the new generation of Palestinians. All this has been happening despite Arafat's commitment to solve any differences with Israel by political negotiations instead of force.

The week of March 12, 2003, marked the anniversary of a brutal Palestinian terrorist attack led by a Palestinian woman, Dalal Mughrabi. In that attack, a civilian Israeli bus was hijacked and the result was that 36 Israelis were murdered. Gail Rubin, an American nature photographer was killed as well when she was spotted taking pictures by the terrorists. The attack occurred on March 11, 1978, but has been cited in the Palestinian media as "one of the greatest successes of the struggle" (*Al-Ayyam*, March 9, 2000).

Dalal Mughrabi has since become a symbol for the Palestinians. Her memory is honored in the names of summer camps, schools, colleges, and in police and military courses. The terrorist attack is commemorated yearly in ceremonies throughout the Palestinian Authority and on television broadcasts.

The following article was published in the Palestinian Authority daily, *Al Hayyat Al Jadida*, on March 11, 2003. It was translated and printed out by the *Palestinian Media Watch Bulletin* on March 12, 2003. The article glorifies the terrorist act led by Dalal Mughrabi 25 years before:

> On the morning of March 11, 1978, a woman Palestinian fighter, Dalal Mughrabi, created a legend that would be taught for many years, when she and her Fedayeen unit infiltrated the Palestinian coastal plain near Tel Aviv [editor: the Palestinians routinely define all of Israel as "occupied Palestine"] causing tens of killed and injured, after taking Israeli passengers as hostages on a bus along the coastal highway. She and her unit opened fire at the military vehicles in the vicinity, resulting in hundreds of injuries among the occupying soldiers between the Zionist colonies in the suburbs and Tel Aviv. [Editor: Palestinians define all of Israel's cities as illegal "colonies."]
>
> The army, headed by [Ehud] Barak, and with the assistance of tanks and helicopters, pursued the bus until it was finally stopped near the colony of Herzliya. A real battle took place between Dalal and her unit and the occupation forces.

Photo depicting Moslem demonstrators shooting former U.S. President Bill Clinton in the head. (From Israeli Foreign Office pamphlet entitled "The PLO Non-Compliance: Record of Bad Faith," November 2000)

. . . Journalists' cameras captured the blind hatred that over-came Barak and his soldiers during the operation. . . .

Twenty-five years after this heroine's death as a shahi-da, many Palestinian women are following in her footsteps every day. Examples include Wafa Idris [first woman sui-cide bomber] and Ayyat al-Akhras [second woman suicide bomber], who performed acts of shahada, seeking during the blessed al-Aksa Intifada to protect the homeland. The sha-hada Dalal Mughrabi shall remain one of the symbols of the Palestinian national struggle.

In addition to military threats, in addition to economic threats, in addition to strategic threats, we must also learn to cope with ideological threats. — Tommy T.B. Koh, ambassador of Singapore

Endnotes

1 Harris O. Schoenberg, *A Mandate for Terror* (New York: Shapolsky Publishers, 1989).

PART V:

ARAFAT'S HISTORY OF TERROR AGAINST NON-JEWS

CHAPTER 9

INTIMIDATION

ARAFAT'S HISTORY OF ACTS AGAINST CHRISTIANS

At the end of March 2002, the Israeli Defense Forces began "Operation Defensive Shield." When the Israeli forces reached the city of Bethlehem, Palestinian Authority terrorists, many of them with bloodied hands, stormed the Church of the Nativity. For the duration of their presence in the church, they continually harassed the monks, nuns, and other church personnel, they desecrated the holy shrine and brazenly disregarded the call of the free world and the Vatican to leave the holy site.

To the world, Arafat likes to appear as the protector or defender of Christians and Christianity. Reality, however, has proven just the opposite. In the civil war in Lebanon, which erupted in the spring of 1975, thousands of Christians were either killed or wounded by Yassir Arafat's terrorists. The civil war in Lebanon proved that the Moslems will not accept Christian supremacy in Lebanon.

> *For nearly seven years, until the Israel army attacked and captured it last week, the town was inaccessible to its own people; the Palestine Liberation Organization made it a stronghold, using the churches as firing ranges and armories.*

A huge, new church, left unfinished by the fleeing Maronite Christians in 1976, is covered with spray-painted Palestinian nationalist slogans and plastered with posters. — David Shipler, *New York Times*, June 21, 1982

Throughout the siege of the Church of the Nativity, Yassir Arafat, who knew that his people were desecrating one of the holiest shrines of Christianity, blatantly refused to cooperate and did not order his people to leave. The Israeli forces which surrounded the church chose not to forcibly enter to capture the Palestinian terrorists. This decision was made out of Israel's concern that such a military action, however justified, might cause injury to the Christian hostages and might damage the church.

In the end, 12 Palestinian terrorists, who were known to be engaged in terrorist crimes, were exiled to European countries.

The Case of Bethlehem

Arafat had made a cynical attempt to conciliate Christian sympathy for his latest mini-war by choosing to locate his snipers not in one of the numerous Moslem villages surrounding Jerusalem, but in a Christian one, Beit Jalla, so that when Israeli troops fired back at the buildings which held the snipers they would be hitting Christian dwellings and their inhabitants. — Edward Alexander, *Outpost*, August 2001

Little is known to the Western and Christian world about the changes that have been occurring in Bethlehem since Arafat assumed control in 1995. Bethlehem has been "Islamized" by Arafat by his altering the municipal borders of the city and its twin towns, Beit Jallah and Beit Sahour.

In the past, these towns constituted the Christian enclave in Judea and Samaria. Arafat has purposely incorporated into the town three refugee camps: Dehaisheh, El-Ayda, and El-Azeh, thereby effectively altering the demography of the area. Thirty thousand Moslems have been added to the 65,000 residents within the municipal boundaries of Bethlehem. To further this policy of Islamization of Bethlehem, Arafat also added a few thousand Bedouins from the Ta'amrah tribe located east of Bethlehem. He also encouraged Moslem immigration from Hebron to Bethlehem and has induced Christian emigration from the city as well.

Q: Numerically, what is the result of Arafat's policy?
A: The Christian population in Bethlehem has been reduced from a 60 percent majority in 1990 to a 20 percent (23,000) minority in 2001. Today, more Beit Jallah Christians live in Belize, Central America, than in Beit Jallah itself.

Q: What can be said about the Christian population of Ramallah?
A: Similar changes have occurred in Ramallah, as well. The Christian population in Ramallah has been reduced to 20,000.

Q: Have Christians opposed these changes?
A: Yes. Christian leaders were well aware of what was likely to happen under Arafat's rule. They lobbied Israel against transferring Bethlehem to the Palestinian Authority from the signing of the Oslo Agreement in 1993 until the city was officially transferred in 1995. Elias Freij, the late Christian mayor of Bethlehem, warned that the city would become a town laden with churches, but with no Christians. He tried unsuccessfully to have Israel include Bethlehem within the boundaries of greater Jerusalem.

Q: What was the reaction of Christian leaders to the plans of Israel's former prime minister, Ehud Barak, to divide Jerusalem?
A: On July 17, 2000, leaders of the Armenian, Latin, and Greek-Orthodox churches sent a letter to U.S. President Clinton, to Ehud Barak, and to Arafat. They demanded to be consulted before any repartition of Jerusalem would be undertaken. Immediately after becoming public knowledge, Barak's proposal triggered a flood of requests for Israeli identification cards by the Arabs of East Jerusalem. They were well aware of the oppressive track record of the Palestinian Authority and wanted to ensure Israeli citizenship.

> *The wall of the church where the cross once hung is pockmarked by bullets. Below where the altar once stood lies a pile of greasy engine casings and spare parts. Oil stains spot the floor of the church, which evidently had been turned into a garage. In another part of town, the large St. Elias Church is in similar disarray. The Palestinians had apparently found a new use for this church as well; the pews inside have long since been removed and a volleyball net stretches across the interior between two pillars. — International*

Herald Tribune, July 7, 1982, describing Palestinian abuse of Christian churches in southern Lebanon

Q: What other steps did Arafat take to "de-Christianize" Bethlehem?
A: Arafat set out on a policy of religious cleansing of the city. First, he appointed a Moslem from Hebron as the governor of Bethlehem, Muhammed Ashad A-Jabari. Arafat then dismantled the city council, which had nine Christian and two Moslem members, and replaced them with a council equally divided between Christians and Moslems. He then proceeded to cleanse the entire top level of bureaucratic, security, and political officials of Christians. The area is now run by local Fatah Moslems along with Tanzim gunmen. All of them answer directly to Arafat.

Q: What has Arafat done to the Church of the Nativity and to other Christian strongholds ?
A: The Palestinian Authority has seized control of the Church of the Nativity. Arafat has tightened pressure on the Christian centers in Jerusalem. The Abraham's Oak Russian Holy Trinity Monastery in Hebron was seized by the Palestinian Authority on July 5, 1997, and the monks and nuns were violently evicted.

The history of the Jews and Christians in the Middle East is a very sad tale. According to Islam, Jews and Christians are considered Dhimmis — protected people. They are equal to each other, but can never be equal to Moslems. They may be tolerated in the Islamic world, but they can never be equal. Being non-Moslem means being inferior.

Q: What has happened to the curriculum in Christian schools?
A: The curriculum in Christian schools has been altered. Islamic studies have been added while Christian studies have been markedly reduced. During Christian services, Moslem sermons have been loudly magnified. Most famous is the Pope's sermon in Bethlehem in April 2000 which had to be postponed until a purposely loud Moslem sermon was completed.

Q: What has happened to Christian shrines under Arafat's "care"?
A: The Palestinian Authority has brazenly transformed a Greek Orthodox Church of the Nativity, into Arafat's official residence in Bethlehem. Christian cemeteries, monasteries, convents, and churches have been desecrated. Telephone lines have been cancelled,

Christian clerics and personnel are intimidated, and Christian shrines have been damaged or destroyed by rocks and stone throwers. Some of the land, including that of Christian worshipers, has been confiscated by the Palestinian Authority.

Q: What has happened to Christian businesses as a result of Arafat's terrorist policies?
A: Arafat's terrorists have intentionally set up positions next to, or in, Christian homes, hotels, churches — like St. Nicholas — and in the Greek Orthodox club in Beit Jallah. As a result, the military clash with Israel has harmed Christian businesses far more than it has those of the Moslems.

> *There has been congressional testimony on Arafat's oppression of Christians. According to former Senator Connie Mack (R-FL), "[The Palestinian Christian] was arrested and detained [by the PA] on charges of selling land to Jews. He denied the charge, since he owned no land. He was beaten and hung from the ceiling by his hands. After two weeks, he was transferred to a larger prison where he was held for eight months without trial. . . . These Christians conveyed to me a message of fear and desperation.* — Yoram Ettinger, former Israeli Consul General to Southwest USA, *Outpost*, January 2002

The Christian Arabs of Ramallah, Beit Jallah, and Beit Sahour and those in Bethlelem have been repeating the sad experiences of Christians in Lebanon during the years 1970–1982. They are considered a potential "fifth column" in the heartland of the Palestinian Authority. Their Western attire has been criticized and Christian women have been repeatedly intimidated by Palestinian Authority personnel. Rape of Christian women has been frequently reported in Beit Shour. To feed the flames of Islamic hostility toward Christians, Arafat has "imported" 20,000 terrorists from Sudan, Yemen, Iraq, Tunisia, Jordan, and Lebanon. Any Christian who dares to oppose the oppression of the Palestinian Authority is accused of collaborating with Israel and he faces execution.

> *Peace comes at the end of war, and is the word that describes the terms imposed by the winners on the losers. Once we've defeated the terror states, the PLO will become a minor*

player in the region and peace will be a lot easier. — Michael Ledeen, Zionist Information News Service, July/August 2002

ARAFAT: MURDERER OF AMERICAN DIPLOMATS

Open fire on the American enemy everywhere. Quake the earth under the feet of the invaders and the collaborators. — Abu Abbas, leader of the Popular Liberation Front, *Wall Street Journal*, August 31, 1990

In March 1973, "Black September" — the same group that had murdered the Israeli athletes at the Munich Olympics the year before — invaded a diplomatic reception held at the Saudi Arabian Embassy in Khartoum, Sudan. The terrorists demanded the release of Sirhan Sirhan, the assassin of Robert Kennedy, in exchange for the release of the group of diplomats being held hostage. Then U.S. President Richard Nixon refused to negotiate with the terrorists. In reaction, the terrorists murdered American Ambassador Cleo A. Noel Jr.; his deputy, George Curtis Moore; and Belgian Charge d'Affaires Guy Eid.

The story appeared in the *National Post* on January 16, 2002. In that article, Mr. George Jonas wrote the following:

> *On March 3 last year, I picked up a message on my service: "Mr. Jonas, my name is Jim Welsh," the flat American voice said. "I am curious about something regarding the Munich Olympic massacre that you wrote about many years ago. I worked in the Palestinian section of the National Security Agency [NSA], and I am curious whether you were aware of a particular specialist in clandestine affairs, but I did write a book about an Israeli counter-terrorist team set up to avenge the Munich massacre of 1972." On March 6, after making some inquiries, I phoned back Mr. Welsh. Mr. Welsh said that he knew details of the sad event.*

Q: *How did he know about the incident?*
A: Early in 1973, Mr. Welsh was involved in the interception of signals between Yassir Arafat in Beirut, Lebanon, and Khalil al-Wazir in the Khartoum, Sudan, office of Arafat's Fatah organization. According to Mr. Welsh, the two were discussing an

operation about to occur in Khartoum. In addition to logistics, the intercepts revealed the code name for the operation: *"Nahr al-Bard"* ("Cold River").

Q: Why did this early warning fail?
A: The warning was duly issued on February 28, 1973, based on the intercept. However, due to some mix-up between the NSA and the State Department, the warning was downgraded from "Flash" precedence to a communication of lesser urgency. The tragic results are now history. By the time it reached Khartoum on March 2, 1973, the three diplomats were already dead.

Mr. Jonas continued to reveal the story. He explained in his article that once Mr. Welsh decided to talk — 27 years after the event — few were willing to listen. He had no proof, and the mainstream media weren't interested. The same indifference marked the attitude of the congressional committees he approached. Initially, the matter might have been hushed up to conceal an organizational blunder — i.e., the failure to warn Ambassador Noel in time. Perhaps the intent was to protect the security of signal intercepts. However, by the spring of 2001, everyone across the board had too much invested in Yassir Arafat. The PLO leader was a Nobel Peace Prize laureate and Israel's "partner for peace," according to the Oslo Agreement of September 13, 1993. Arafat was a frequent guest in the White House under President Clinton, and few would risk rocking the boat over the murder of United States diplomats from the 1970s.

Mr. Welsh knew that tapes had been prepared of the intercepts and he attempted to discover their location in storage. He approached NSA, the State Department, and the CIA under the Freedom of Information Act, with no success. He questioned writers and journalists in hopes that they might have come across the material while researching other matters.

On the Internet, he questioned both the Intelligence Forum and the AFSA (American Foreign Service Association) Forum. The former is used as a bulletin board for retired agents and intelligence enthusiasts, and the latter is maintained for the AFSA.

Mr. Welsh posted the following question online on March 30, 2001: Has the AFSA ever called for an examination of the tapes of Yasser Arafat planning and directing the murders of Ambassador

Noel and Deputy Moore in Khartoum in 1973? If not, why has the AFSA not done so, inasmuch as evidence of these murders is in the possession of the U.S. government?

Q: Did anyone else raise questions on this subject?
A: In early 2001, a journalist — Joseph Farah — raised the subject on WorldNetDaily.com. However, the mainstream media continued with its silence.

Q: According to Mr. Jonas, what caused the change in climate?
A: The most important change occurred on September 11, 2001. Then, on December 12, 2001, Israel Prime Minister Ariel Sharon declared Arafat "irrelevant" to the peace process. The third catalyst for the change in climate occurred on January 3, 2002. That was when the cargo ship was boarded by Israeli commandos in the Red Sea. The intercepted freighter carried 50 tons of arms destined for the Palestinian Authority for attacks on Israel.

Q: How did the Wall Street Journal clarify the picture?
A: The *Wall Street Journal* ran an article on January 10, 2002, written by Mihai Pacepa, who did, in fact, confirm Mr. Welsh's story. Relying on far more facts than Mr. Welsh, Mr. Pacepa wrote, "James Welsh, a former intelligence analyst for the National Security Agency, has told a number of U.S. journalists that the NSA had secretly intercepted the radio communications between Yasser Arafat and Abu Jihad during the PLO operation against the Saudi embassy in Khartoum, including Arafat's order to kill Ambassador Noel."

Q: Did Arafat confess to this crime?
A: In May 1973, Arafat attended a private dinner with Nikolai Ceausescu, the late president of Rumania, in which Arafat overtly boasted about his operation in Khartoum. Ion Gheorghe Maurer, who had just retired as Rumanian prime minister, told Arafat, "Be careful. No matter how high up you are, you can still be convicted for killing and stealing." Arafat replied with a wink and smile, "Who me?. I never had anything to do with that operation."

Q: Who is Mihai Pacepa?
A: Until he defected to the West in 1978, Mr. Pacepa served as the chief of secret police. While serving as head of DIE (*Departmentual*

de Informatii Externe), Mr. Pacepa used to be one of Arafat's mission controllers while the PLO leader embraced the Kremlin. Therefore, Mr. Pacepa was able to observe the true Yassir Arafat and to quote his statements.

> *A prostitute never repents and a rock never melts.* — Palestinian saying

In 1988, an American citizen, Leon Klinghoffer, was murdered aboard the ship *Achille Lauro*. PLO terrorists took control of the ship lead by Abu Abbas. Mr. Klinghoffer was disabled and in a wheelchair. He dared to criticize the terrorists' behavior towards the other passengers. As a result, they shot Mr. Klinghoffer and threw his body overboard. When asked his reaction to the brutal murder, Abu Abbas said, "Maybe he was trying to swim for it" (*New York Times*, November 14, 1988). Abu Abbas is one of the leaders of the PLO and a close friend of Yassir Arafat.

The conclusion is very clear: Yassir Arafat is a murderer of thousands of people of different nationalities, including many Americans, countless Israelis, and even his own Palestinians.

> *We regard the U.S. Government as the controlling force of neo-colonialism, imperialism and racism.* — Yassir Arafat, PLO chairman, *South: The Third World Magazine*, London, January 1986

Benjamin Netanyahu, former prime minister of Israel, said the following when questioned once about world terror:

> *Terrorism is not the accidental killing of civilians that accompanies every war. It is not guerilla warfare in which irregular forces focus on military targets. Terrorism is the deliberate and systematic attack on civilians. . . . The terrorists target the innocent precisely because they are innocent. In assaulting them, he tells us that for him no atrocity is out of bounds, that he is prepared to pursue any means to achieve his goal, which is to frighten us into submission.* — From his speech to the United Nations as Israeli UN Ambassador

PART VI:

PALESTINIAN STATE: STRATEGIC AND MILITARY DANGERS

CHAPTER 10

ON THE
DEFENSIVE

PALESTINIAN STATE: A MORTAL DANGER TO ISRAEL

*The military struggle will not stop as a result of the Alge-
ria declaration. We will start with a little Palestinian state as
a first stage and, God willing, it would grow and get wider,
to east, west, north, and south. Three months ago I supported
the idea to liberate Palestine at once. I was stupid. Now I am
interested to liberate Palestine by stages. This is the art of Liberation.* — Abu Iyad, Arafat's deputy, *Al-Anba*, Kuwait,
December 18, 1988

Professor Louis Rene Beres, professor of international law at
Purdue University, expressed his opinion about a Palestinian state.
He said the following:

*Creation of a Palestinian state — as we have seen —
will greatly increase the chances of Arab attacks, not only
from the new state of Palestine [which would surely do very
little on its own], but from combinations with other Arab
states. This could even happen after Palestinian forces join
with Palestinian Arab residents of Jordan [where they constitute a majority] to overthrow King Abdullah and create a*

single super-Palestinian state [one that would extend all the way to Jordan's border with Iraq]. — *Jewish Press Magazine*, July 12, 2002

The establishment of a Palestinian Arab state west of the Jordan River would pose a severe threat to Israel's very existence. Moreover, it would undermine regional stability, directly threatening Jordan, and would endanger Western interests in the area. The following five points explain why:

1. A strategic threat to Israel — A Palestinian Arab state would be ruled by the PLO, the same PLO that has never relinquished its basic goal to destroy Israel. Such a state would not agree to its demilitarization, even should this be a pre-requisite to the establishment of the state.

Time and time again, the PLO has encouraged and turned a blind eye to attacks against Israel that originated in its territory. There is no indication that Israeli settlers wishing to remain in residence under Palestinian sovereignty would enjoy freedom and safety.

The establishment of a Palestinian state would serve as an inspirational base for an Israeli Arab separatist movement. It would continue to raise the banner of the "right of return" to Palestine.

Such a state would serve as a base for a strategic terrorist threat against Israel from, among others, small groups with surface-to-air missiles, able to paralyze Israeli civilian air traffic and cripple military activity. Its close proximity and topographical features would allow it to be used as a command, control, and communications station for hostile forces such as Arab states that are unreconciled to Israel's existence.

A Palestinian state would pose an ecological threat to Israel's scarce water supply which stems from the Jordan River headwaters in the north to the aquifers that go from the Israeli side of the armistice line into the West Bank and back into pre-1967 Israel.

2. A military threat to Israel — Even a totally pacifist PLO state would pose a military threat to Israel since neighboring Arab states such as Syria, Lebanon, Iran, and Arab terrorist organizations would seek to use its land as a springboard for a military attack against a weakened Israel. The PLO state would find it difficult to resist even if it desired to do so.

A more likely scenario would be a Palestinian state that would freely offer its territory as a forward base for an Arab wartime coalition on Israel's eastern front. In return, the PLO state would receive large Arab economic and military aid so sorely needed by the fledgling state. This would force Jordan to make similar offers to the Arab coalition so that it would not be marked a "traitor" to the Arab cause.

3. A PLO state would threaten Jordan — It is a fact that Jordan is the Arab state whose pro-Western ties have been the most stable in the history of American-Arab ties.

A Palestinian state would serve as a territorial base for Palestinians wanting to usurp the Hashemite Kingdom of Jordan. Such activities would, no doubt, cause unrest and dissention among the 65 percent majority of Palestinians living in Jordan, especially in major cities like Amman and Irbid in which there is a 75–85 percent Palestinian majority. The late King Hussein of Jordan fought and won against such a Palestinian uprising in 1970. Palestinians would seek autonomy inside Jordan or linkage with a Palestinian state on the West Bank.

The Israeli-Jordanian border is the longest in territory between an Arab state and Israel. This area could become a confrontation frontier between two enemies: the Palestinian state and the Hashemite Kingdom of Jordan.

The proximity of a Palestinian state on the West Bank and Gaza would facilitate PLO pressures on Jordan. This can be done through water sources, the flow of population between the two countries, through controlled access to Gaza seaports, etc. These issues have been defused over the years through mutual cooperation between Israel and Jordan.

4. America's regional and global interests would be threatened — A Palestinian state would ideologically and logistically be linked to its long-time ally, and other undemocratic regimes such as militantly Islamic Iran. A Palestinian state would increase the already existent threats to Western oil sources in Saudi Arabia and other conservative Gulf oil-rich states.

5. A PLO state would increase the likelihood of a comprehensive Arab-Israeli war — The establishment of a Palestinian state on land adjacent to Israel proper would undermine Israel's deterrent posture by making Israel more vulnerable to strategic surprise in a number of ways: a) by cutting the warning time of a surprise air attack from the east from 20 minutes to less than two minutes; b) by exposing Israel's arms depots to a surprise attack; c) by undermining the call-up of Israeli reservists by exposing call-up venues, transportation, and communication nodes to surprise attacks; and d) by exposing Israel's main population centers and cities to easy attack.

Such developments would force Israel into resuming a preemptive strike posture where even the beginning of a possible Arab threat would become a *casus belli*.

Today there is an increased availability of chemical and nuclear capabilities in Syria, Egypt, and Iraq. Iraq has already utilized chemical weapons against its own citizens. With this in mind, Israel might be forced into an unconventional preemptive strike, and the threat of unconventional warfare might turn into a full-scale reality.

> *What is there to talk about? If you agree to hold political negotiations with the PLO, you are essentially coming to terms with a third state between the Mediterranean and Jordan. Such a state will be a cancer in the heart of the Middle East.* — Yitzhak Rabin, Israeli Minister of Defense, September 1989

CAN ISRAEL SURVIVE A PALESTINIAN STATE?

> *Among the arms seized from the vessel* Karine-A *captured by the Israelis en route to Gaza from Iran was 3,000 pounds of C-4 explosives that would dramatically increase the killing power of future suicide bomb attacks, and Katyusha rockets with a range to threaten all Israeli population centers. This was no random purchase. The* Karine-A *demonstrates how vulnerable Israel would be if there were a sovereign Palestinian state to receive and accumulate weapons that could threaten both Israelis and the state of Israel. It also raises major questions about the whole concept of a demilitarized Palestinian state, side by side with Israel.* — Mortimer Zuckerman, editor-in-chief, *US News*, January 21, 2002

In 2002, U.S. President George W. Bush spoke about the vision and establishment of a Palestinian state in Judea, Samaria, and Gaza. The president spoke about two states living side by side — Israel and Palestine. Moreover, some honest people the world over believe that the solution to the Arab-Israeli conflict is based on the establishment of a Palestinian state in Judea, Samaria, and the Gaza Strip. They reason that once the Palestinians achieve such a state, they would accept Israel as a reality.

Israel is fully prepared to take risks to achieve peace. She proved this with the signing of the Oslo Agreement in September 1993 and by signing subsequent interim agreements. At the very moment Israel was about to make far-reaching concessions, Arafat reacted with the October 2000 intifada. The results have been staggering — more than 1,000 Israelis brutally murdered and thousands more maimed and injured. The creation of a Palestinian Arab state in Judea, Samaria, and the Gaza district would expose the state of Israel to mortal danger. No country can be expected to take a risk that, in effect, would jeopardize its very existence.

> Such a state would control strategic mountainous terrain on the West Bank overlooking the coastal plain. . . . This means the width of Israel's coastal plain (where two-thirds of the Jewish population lives) would, on average, shrink to about 14 miles. This would constitute a death sentence for Israel's main infrastructure. . . . — General Ariel Sharon, New York Times, March 5, 1990

Israel includes only about one-fifth of "Palestine." The other four-fifths form the Kingdom of Jordan. Thus, the Palestinian people are not a people without a land. Fewer in number than the Israelis, they hold four times more land than Israel.

> If the Palestinian Arabs can carry out such massacres when they do not have sovereignty, imagine how much worse it would be if they are given the powers of a sovereign state. Sovereignty does not necessarily put an end to terrorism. It only strengthens the existing pro-terrorist culture to wreak even more havoc. Iraq, Iran, and Syria are sovereign states; sovereignty has not turned them into civilized democracies. Wouldn't the world be better off if they did not have the powers

of soveriegnty? — Morton A. Klein, national president of ZOA, in a telegram to President Bush, June 18, 2002

ISRAEL'S DANGEROUS STRATEGIC DEPTH

[I have] never met an Arab leader that in private professed a desire for an independent Palestinian state. Publicly, they all espouse an independent Palestinian state — almost all of them — because that is what they committed themselves to do at Rabat [the 1974 Arab League summit conference]. But the private diplomatic tone of conversations is much more proper. . . . — Former U.S. President Jimmy Carter, 1979 press conference

Israeli withdrawal to the June 4, 1967, borders would place Israel under constant, severe danger to her very existence. It is impossible to speak about real peace and at the same time Israeli withdrawal to the June 4, 1967, borders in order to establish a Palestinian state in Judea and Samaria.

Tel Aviv, Israel's largest metropolitan area, with over a million inhabitants, was only 11 miles from the border. Netanya is even less — 9 miles from the border. The Ben-Gurion International Airport is only 14 miles from the border. Jerusalem, Israel's capital, was split in half by barbed wire. These borders were one of the factors that encouraged Arab aggression that led to the 1967 war.

A Palestinian state, with all the elements of a state and with the ambition to destroy Israel, would make it very difficult to protect the state of Israel with the borders of 1967 and the power of 1990. — General Matan Vilnay, commander of Israel's southern front, *Ma'Ariv,* February 26, 1990

Israeli Prime Minister Ariel Sharon put it thusly:

Under Resolution 242 . . . Israel withdrew from the Sinai Peninsula in accordance with the 1979 peace treaty with Egypt . . . and again in line with Resolution 242 Israel withdrew its military government over the Palestinian population so that by 1999, 98 percent of the Palestinian people in the West Bank and Gaza were under Palestinian rule. — New York Times, June 9, 2002

U.S. President Ronald Reagan said the following in 1977 about Israel's security being the main issue:

The real issue in the Middle East had to do with the Arab refusal to recognize that Israel has a right to exist as a nation. To give up the buffer zones Israel took in the Six-Day War could be to put a cannon on her front walk aimed at her front door by those who have said she must be destroyed.

It is said that in this era of rockets, borders are no longer important. Yet had the Yom Kippur War of 1973 been triggered from the borders existing prior to June 1967, it would not have been fought in the sands of Sinai and on the Golan Heights, but in the streets of Jerusalem and Tel Aviv instead.

The threat posed by the advancing Egyptian and Syrian forces was neutralized, to a large extent, by their distance from the heartland of Israel, which allowed the Israel Defense Forces the time necessary to call up its reserves, consolidate its forces, and prepare its counter-offensive.

People may mistakenly presume that in this era of sophisticated missiles that can reach very distant targets the value of borders is insignificant. This presumption is incorrect. Bombs and missiles can cause severe damage should they reach their target; however, they would not be the crucial factor if the country attacked — in this case, Israel — is willing and able to fight back. In order to defeat a country, you have to capture territory, and here lies the importance of strategic depth.

There is wide agreement among Israeli leaders and strategists, in both major political camps, that the Jordan River now represents Israel's "security border" to the east. It is a designation not very difficult to accept, considering that the distance from that ancient river to Israel's western border, the Mediterranean seaboard, is a scant 50 miles.

A PALESTINIAN STATE: WILL IT CONTRIBUTE TO REGIONAL STABILITY?

A Palestinian Arab state therefore would inevitably be a terrorist state. It would be the only time in history that a state would be established not to provide a better life for its

citizens, but to better pursue the destruction of another state.
— Morton A. Klein, national president of ZOA, in a telegram to President Bush, June 18, 2002

The great majority of the Israeli people consider the establishment of a Palestinian state as a mortal danger to Israel. Most Israelis believe that the national aspiration of the Palestinian people has been fulfilled in Jordan, which is an integral part of Palestine and a Palestinian state.

The PLO leaders in the past and today have declared at various times that the establishment of a state in Judea and Samaria is not the end of the struggle against Israel. They intend to continue the struggle until a Palestinian state is established on all the territory of Palestine.

Since the Oslo Agreement in September 1993, Arafat's behavior and that of his people has proved one simple clear fact: They do not honor their signatures. They have violated each agreement. Arafat's behavior is likened to the leader of a gang rather than to a head of state. Giving Arafat the chance to establish an independent Palestinian state would be a non-calculated risk.

Q: Should such a state be established, who would be in control?
A: A Palestinian state would be a PLO terrorist-controlled state.

Q: Why would such a state endanger Israel and others?
A: For the following reasons:

1. It would place Israel's major centers of population and the country's industrial infrastructure under perennial threat of the gun.

2. Israel's entire airspace could be fully controlled from these areas.

3. It would serve as a launching pad for attack by radical and uncompromising Arab states, and as a base for attack by the various terrorist factions operating independently of centralized, responsible government.

4. It would lack political and economic stability and thus would lead to general regional destabilization.

5. Demilitarization is not a viable expectation at this time.

6. It would inevitably become a radical satellite on Israel's doorstep.

Q: What conditions would such a state create?
A: Due to the short warning times available to Israeli decision-makers, if military control over Judea and Samaria were to be relinquished, Israel would have to respond preemptively even if only the probability of a threat is evident.

Q: Is there a danger that Israel would find herself cut in half?
A: Absolutely. For Israel, there would be very little room for error, no grey areas or time to reconsider. The possibility of Israel finding herself cut in half, with the bulk of its population and factories concentrated in a highly vulnerable 11-mile-wide strip, is a very real threat.

Q: What are the true intentions of the PLO?
A: Let the PLO speak for itself:

> *There are two [initial] phases to our return: the first phase to the 1967 lines, and the second to the 1948 lines . . . the third stage is the democratic state of Palestine. So we are fighting for these three states.* — Farouk Kaddoumi, head of the PLO Political Department, *Newsweek*, March 14, 1977

Q: How does the PLO view Jordan and Israel?
A: Once again the PLO answers this question. In the words of Zuheir Muhsin, head of the PLO Military Operations Department, in *Trouw*, a Netherlands daily, on March 31, 1977:

> *It is only for political reasons that we carefully stress our Palestinian identity, for it is in the national interest of the Arabs to encourage a separate Palestinian identity to counter Zionism. Yes, the existence of a separate Palestinian identity serves only tactical purpose. The founding of a Palestinian state is a new tool in the continuing battle against Israel. . . . Jordan is a state with defined borders. It cannot claim Haifa or Jaffa [cities in Israel proper], whereas I have a right to Haifa, Jaffa, Jerusalem, and Beersheba. After we have attained all our rights in the whole of Palestine, we must not*

postpone, even for a single moment, the reunification of Jordan and Palestine.

Q: *What about de-militarization of Judea and Samaria?*
A: Demilitarization is not the answer. It may work in a vast, nearly empty region like the Sinai peninsula. However, it will not work in a small, populated area bordering directly on Arab countries from which arms can be shipped in, surreptitiously or otherwise.

Q: *What is the policy of the United States?*
A: The traditional American policy, until the autumn of 2001, was the rejection of a Palestinian state in Judea, Samaria, and the Gaza Strip.

Q: *What is the American military view?*
A: A study of the defensive characteristics of the Judean-Samarian region was carried out by the United States Joint Chiefs of Staff in June 1967. The study concluded that Israel's minimum defense line should be drawn down the middle of Judea and Samaria.

Q: *What advantage would such demarcation provide?*
A: This line would widen the narrow portion of Israel and would provide additional terrain for the defense of Tel Aviv. The joint chiefs of staff noted that the hills of "West Jordan [northern Judea] overlook Israel's narrow midsection," and if held by Jordan, would present it with "a route for a thrust to the sea," enabling it to split Israel in half. The pre-1967 borders would not enable the containment of an enemy thrust, when the latter has the initiative and could utilize the sector of its choice for the direction of its attack.

> *Our activities will continue in Tel Aviv and elsewhere, until we achieve victory and hoist our flag over Jerusalem and the other cities in the occupied homeland.* — Yassir Arafat, Reuters, May 12, 1978

Q: *Will Israel withdraw to the June 4, 1967, lines (before the Six-Day War)?*
A: Israeli Prime Minister Ariel Sharon has provided the answer. He said the following: "Israel will not return to the vulnerable 1967 armistice lines, re-divide Jerusalem, or concede its right to

defensible borders under Resolution 242 . . ." (*New York Times*, June 9, 2002).

Q: What does the PLO think about Israel's right to exist?
A: Both Yassir Arafat and his chief advisor, Nabil Sha'at, have provided the answer to this question. Arafat said, "Jordan is ours, Palestine is ours, and we shall build our national entity on the whole of this land after having freed it of both the Zionist presence and the reactionary traitor's [i.e., Jordan's King Hussein] presence" ("A Letter to Jordanian Student Congress in Baghdad," as reported in the *Washington Post*, November 12, 1974).

Nabil Sha'at, Arafat's chief advisor said the following in the Kuwaiti paper *Al-Anba* on March 28, 1989: "I want to release a part of this Arab territory and this cannot be released by war. . . . Afterwards we would liberate all the rest."

Do the Palestinians Want a State?

. . . a report of the UN committee on the rights of the Palestinian people included important recommendations. The most salient of them is the one which refers to the establishment of a Palestinian state, which in fact means the negation of Israel's existence — an idea which is gaining new supporters every day. — Al-Gomhoriyya, Cairo, Egypt, June 27, 1976

The PLO vehemently opposes any political settlement regardless of boundaries or conditions, because its opposition is to the principle of a Jewish state in any size or shape. The PLO formulated this opposition to a political settlement in their National Covenant in its new version adopted by their congress in Cairo of July 1968 and reinforced with explicit resolutions.

Q: Do the Palestinians want a Palestinian state?
A: If they wanted a Palestinian state, why didn't they establish one in 1948, according to the United Nations Partition Plan of November 29, 1947?

Q: What did the Palestinian desire at that time?
A: The Palestinians in 1948 did not want to establish a Palestinian state. Instead, they wanted to prevent the establishment of a Jewish state, according to the Partition Plan.

Q: Did the Palestinians seek statehood between the years 1948 and 1967?
A: Not at all. Between the years 1948 and 1967, Judea and Samaria were under Jordanian control and the Gaza Strip was under Egyptian control. Not even one single Palestinian spoke of such a state in these territories.

Q: Isn't it true that the PLO, which was established in 1964, did want an independent Palestinian state?
A: Not at all. Like other Arabs, the PLO started its fight against Israel before 1967, when Judea, Samaria, and Gaza were in Arab hands.

Q: Did the PLO give clear expression to its rejection of such a Palestinian state and to the existence of Israel?
A: Yes. The following articles of the Palestinian National Covenant express this rejection:

> Article 15: The liberation of Palestine . . . aims at the elimination of Zionism in Palestine.
> Article 19: The partition of Palestine in 1947 and the establishment of the State of Israel are entirely illegal. . . .
> Article 21: The Arab Palestinian people . . . reject all solutions which are substitutes for the total liberation of Palestine. . . .

> *If we achieve part of our territory, we will not relinquish our dream to establish one democratic state on all of Palestine.* — Nabil Sha'at, Arafat advisor, *Al-Siyassa*, Kuwait, January 29, 1989

THE RIGHT OF RETURN: SEVERE DANGER TO ISRAEL

> *The Palestinian uprising will in no way end until the attainment of the legitimate rights of the Palestinian people, including the right of return.* — Yassir Arafat, Qatar News Agency, January 13, 1989

When Arafat states that the PLO acceptance of UN Security Council Resolution 242 is conditional upon the implementation of three conditions, one of which is the "right of return," it makes his statement meaningless and shows that Arafat continues to be committed to the destruction of Israel. No PLO demand exemplifies its aim for the liquidation of the state of Israel more than its repeated calls for the "right of return." The PLO views the "right of return" as a key element in its strategy to ultimately destroy Israel.

> *I want to go back to Lydda.* — George Habash, of the PLO, January 26, 1989

The "right of return," if it were to be implemented, would enable Palestinians to enter Israel, overwhelm it from within, and thereby bring about its dissolution. It is noteworthy that most PLO leaders do not come from the West Bank, but from towns and villages in the areas of Israel within the pre-1967 lines, which are more important to them than towns and villages like Nablus, Ramallah, and Jenin in the West Bank.

Q: Will the Palestinians be satisfied with an independent Palestinian state in Judea and Samaria?
A: "Impossible, impossible, impossible, impossible. Bush, Gorbachev, Thatcher, all should know that this will not be the solution. They think it will be a solution. But those people living in Shatila and Rashidiyeh [two camps in Lebanon] will not regard it as a solution. What about the Palestinians living in Lebanon, Syria, and Kuwait? What about them? You know, five years from now there will be another revolution against Israel" (George Habash, *Independent*, London, January 26, 1989).

Q: Do other Palestinians say the same?
A: "Our return to Palestine and our victory will be possible only with Allah's help and with our return to Paluja, Jaffa, and Haifa" (Rafik Al-Natshe, PLO representative in Saudi Arabia, on Radio Riyadh, January 1, 1989).

Q: Who is really responsible for the Arab refugee problem?
A: The answer is clear, according to Sir John Bagot Glubb, British commander of the Arab Legion. He said: "I can recollect no precedent in history on the part of those in power. The Arab governments were largely responsible for the ruin of the Palestinian Arabs."

According to the Jordanian daily *Ad Difa'a*, on September 6, 1954:

> *The Arab governments told us: "Get out so that we can get in!" So we got out, but they did not get in.*

Emile Ghoury, secretary, Palestine Arab Higher Committee, said the following in the *Beirut Telegraph* on September 6, 1948: "The fact that there are these refugees is the direct consequence of the act of the Arab States in opposing partition and the Jewish State."

Q: What is Leila Khaled's opinion? She was secretary general of the PLO General Union of Palestinian Women.
A: In the *Middle East Monthly* of London, January 1989, she said the following: "Our first objective is to return to Nablus, and then move on to Tel Aviv. The day that we achieve independence will signify the defeat of Israel as a state."

> *The leaders of the Arab states, when they cry about the poor fate of the Palestinians, remind me of the child who killed his father, then cried for pity because he is an orphan.*
> — An Arab in a refugee camp

Q: Why does Israel consider the "right of return" unacceptable?
A: Since Israel is neither responsible for the creation of the refugee problem nor for its perpetuation, it cannot take upon itself responsibility for this problem. It is a fact that from 1948 until the Six Day War in 1967, Gaza was under Egyptian authority and the West Bank was controlled by Jordan. For Israel to declare responsibility for Palestinian refugees, it would have far-reaching implications:

1. It would legitimize the Palestinian demand for a "right of return" to areas that are part of the state of Israel. Millions of Palestinians would arrive in Israel.

2. It would be used by the refugees as a basis for advancing claims against Israel for compensation for property claimed to have been lost.

3. It would facilitate claims by the refugees' "host countries" for compensation from Israel for the cost of "hosting" these refugees, when these same countries are, in fact, primarily responsible for creating and maintaining the problem.

The establishment of an independent Palestinian state on the West Bank and in the Gaza Strip does not contradict our ultimate strategic aim, which is the establishment of a democratic state in the territory of Palestine, but rather a step in that direction. — PLO leader Abu Iyad, *Al Safir*, Lebanon, January 25, 1988

The element of return is mentioned quite often in Palestinian literature. There are various and different stories about the homeland, which is described as a house without which a Palestinian cannot live.

A Jordanian-Palestinian poet wrote the following:

> Oh world, I will never forget my land.
> My land is my life, my soul.
> I know all its parts.
> I know my Homeland liberated.
> I am willing to sacrifice for the sake of my
>   Homeland's land.
> I am willing to sacrifice for its soil.
> I am homesick, I have nostalgia for Palestine.
> Oh children, and the next generation.
> You are the hope.
> Sing with us in order that we will not forget Haifa,
> Jaffa, Jerusalem, Palestine. . . .

No nation, regardless of past rights and wrongs, could contemplate taking in a fifth column of such a size. And fifth column it would be — people nurtured for 10 years [now 22] in hatred of Israel and totally dedicated to its destruction. The readmission of the refugees would be equivalent to the admission to the U.S. of nearly 71,000,000 sworn enemies of the nation. — *New York Times*, May 14, 1967

Q: What precedents in history can be cited concerning refugees?
A: There are numerous examples to be cited. In conflicts between neighboring societies, refugee problems emerge. For example:

- There were 14 million refugees between India and Pakistan when those countries became independent.

- There were 6¼ million German refugees from the areas annexed to Poland at the end of World War II, and 3 million German refugees from Czechoslovakia.

- 800,000 North Vietnamese fled to South Vietnam.

- More than one million refugees from North Korea settled in South Korea after 1952.

- Altogether, since World War II, more than 40 million persons have become refugees all over the world.

Nowhere in the world has a refugee problem, created by a conflict, been solved by the return of the refugees to their original place of residence. Nowhere in the world — except among the Arabs — has a society refused to absorb refugees of its own culture.

The perpetuation of the refugee problem by the Arab Governments exploits the refugees as instruments for keeping the Israeli-Arab conflict alive.

Dr. Nabil Sha'ath, who headed the PLO negotiating team with Israel before and after the signing of the Oslo Agreement in September 1993, said the following in an interview in the Arab daily *Al Hayat* on September 28, 1993:

> *800,000 Palestinians among those who left after 1967 will come back in the transitional period, which is five years. Those who left in 1948 will come back after the declaration of the Palestinian independent state.*

The Palestinians never hid their true intentions about the return of the Palestinian refugees to what they claim to be their homes, which, in reality, do not exist.

> *We, the refugees, who have brothers and friends among the Arabs of Israel, have the right to address the members of the Arab League Council and declare: We left our land on the strength of false promises by crooked leaders in the Arab States. They promised us that our absence would not last more than two weeks, a kind of promenade, at the end of which we would return.* — From the Jordanian daily *Falastin*, May 30, 1955

Operation Defensive Shield, March 2002

Between October 2000 and the end of March 2002, over five hundred Israelis were killed by Palestinian terrorists, and thousands more were maimed and wounded. Arafat made a conscious decision to begin the intifada with the aim of forcing Israel to withdraw from Judea, Samaria, and the Gaza Strip. Today, the majority of Israelis are convinced that Arafat is not interested in a Palestinian state alongside Israel, but instead wants his state in place of Israel.

On March 27, 2002, Passover eve, a terrorist succeeded to gain entry into the Park Hotel in Netanya, a seaside resort city in Israel. He exploded himself and caused the death of 29 men, women, and children, all gathered to celebrate the holiday. Many more were injured. The following day, the Israeli government decided to start what would be called "Operation Defensive Shield."

Q: What were the defined goals of this operation?
A: The goal was three-fold: a) to eliminate the infrastructure of Palestinian terrorism in Judea and Samaira, b) to destabilize and undermine the Palestinian Authority in Judea and Samaira, and c) to isolate and de-legitimize Yassir Arafat as head of the Palestinian Authority. It was believed that Israel would not have to forcefully evict Arafat from the area, but that his own people would replace him or that he would voluntarily resign or leave.

During Operation Defensive Shield, the Israeli Defense Forces captured a wealth of documents which leave no doubt as to the role played by Arafat and the Palestinian Authority in the systematic and ongoing financing of terrorist infrastructures and activists. These groups included the Fatah Tanzim and Al-Aqsa Brigades. The documents prove that large sums of money were transferred on a monthly basis in order to finance terrorist infrastructures. All this was going on while civilian infrastructures of the Palestinian Authority, which depend on financial grants of the Arab world and the European Union, were collapsing causing the enhanced suffering of the Palestinian people from poverty and distress.

Q: How much does the aid amount to from the European Union?
A: The European Union transfers a sum of approximately 10 million euros each month to the Palestinian Authority. Along with

the financial aid from Arab countries, the Palestinian Authority can exist and it can pay monthly salaries.

Q: How are the funds used in reality?
A: The documents in Israel's hands today prove that instead of channeling the funds to the needs of its citizens and for the maintenance of the administration and public order, the Palestinian Authority uses a good portion of the money in order to finance terrorist activities.

Q: How did the Palestinian Authority cover up this illegal activity?
A: To cover up this illegal activity, the Palestinian Authority transmitted false reports to the supervising funds regarding the exaggerated quantity of employees, or would maneuver the currency rate and "overcharges" approximately 20 percent of the exchange value.

Q: Can a specific example be cited?
A: Yes. One document seized by the Israel Defense Forces during "Operation Defensive Shield" was written to the head of the Palestinian General Intelligence in the West Bank, Tawfiq Tirawi. It referred to members of the Fatah Tanzim, and was written by the head of the Palestinian General Intelligence in the city of Tulkarm. The author of the letter notes the ongoing contact, close ties, and coordination between the terrorists and the General Intelligence and describes the terrorist attack as a "successful high-quality attack." This was the attack in a wedding hall in Hadera on January 16, 2002, where 6 Israelis were murdered and 25 others were wounded.

Another document that was seized during the Israeli operation revealed that Chairman Arafat had authorized the allocation of $800 for the Tanzim terrorists mentioned in the previous document as well as for other operatives.

These documents, along with many others, prove beyond a doubt the close ties maintained between the Fatah Tanzim and senior Palestinian Authority officials in the security apparatus and in the leadership of the Palestinian Authority. This is reflected in funding and other support for Fatah Tanzim terrorist attacks against innocent civilians.

Q: *What is the purpose of the financial assistance of the Palestinian Authority?*
A: This financial assistance is the fuel which sustains the terror infrastructure of the Fatah/Tanzim and Al-Aqsa Brigades. Without this funding, they would find difficulty in operating effectively and continuously.

Q: *Why is Arafat involved personally?*
A: Arafat maintains a personal involvement in the financial funding as a weapon by which to enforce his control over the men in the "field." Some of the funds which are transferred to the "field" for the perpetration of terrorist attacks find their way into the pockets of individuals.

Do you know that:

- Terror activities in the territories are part and parcel of the Palestinian Authority and constitute support and backing for this strategy?

- The Fatah/Tanzim terror infrastructure in the territories is involved in terror operations within Israel proper?

- The infrastructures of the Fatah, the Tanzim, and the Al-Aqsa Brigades are all controlled and financed by Arafat?

- Arafat is personally directing and funding terror? Proof is in the documents seized by the Israel Defense Forces with Arafat's signature.

- Marwan Barghuti, head of the Fatah/Tanzim in the West Bank, directed the terror infrastructure in Tulkarm and he encouraged his activists to escalate their terror activities? Barghuti was captured by the Israeli Defense Forces during "Operation Defensive Shield."

- Financial support for the terror infrastructure affects the daily life of the Palestinian populace? Instead of being directed to the betterment of the welfare of the Palestinian people, the funds are directed to terror elements.

The Palestinian Liberation Organization
The Palestinian National Authority
The President's Bureau

To the Fighting President
Brother Abu Amar, may the Lord protect you,
Greetings,

I hereby request you to allocate financial aid in the sum of $2500 for the following brethren:

1. Ra'ed el Karmi *(note: Former commander of the Tanzim in Tulkarm)*.
2. Ziad Muhammad Da'as *(note: Commander of a group in the Fatah/Tanzim Tulkarm that masterminded the attack on the Bat-Mitzvah party in Hadera)*.
3. Amar Qadan *(note: a senior activist of Presidential Security/Force 17 in Ramallah, involved in the activities of its operational cell)*.

Thank you,

Your son, Hussein al Sheikh
(note: senior Fatah activist in the West Bank)

(Note: in Yasser Arafat's handwriting:

Treasury/Ramallah
Allocate $600 to each of them.
Yasser Arafat *(signature)*
(19/9/2001)

A translated memo requesting terrorism funding,
from a Fatah terrorist to Arrafat.

The following sum up the main points in just two of the documents seized by the Israel Defense Forces in March 2002.

A signed order from Arafat, allocating stipends for terrorists.

One document is an order of Arafat to the Palestinian Authority "Finance Ministry" dated September 2001 (eight days after the Bin-Laden attacks in the United States) to grant $2,500 to three terrorists. Two of them are senior activists of the Fatah infrastructure in Tulkarm — Ra'ed Al-Karmi and Ziad Da'as. The former headed the group responsible for the attack in the wedding hall in Hadera. The order is given on an official letter of the Presidential Bureau in the Palestinian Authority.

A second document was another direct order of Arafat dated January 2002 in which he ordered the allocation of $350 to each of the Fatah activists listed in the document. The names are those members in the Fatah/Tanzim Tulkarm district involved in ten different terrorist attacks in Israel.

> *There are six things which the Lord hates, no seven; a proud look, lying tongue and hands that shed innocent blood, a heart that devised wicked thoughts, feet that are swift in running in mischief, a false witness that breathes us lies and one that sows discord among brethren.* — Proverbs 6:15–19

INTERNATIONAL GUARANTEES VIS-À-VIS SECURE BORDERS

Many good people the world over want to see Israel withdraw to the vulnerable cease-fire lines of June 4, 1967, for the sake of peace. These same people claim naively that in an era of peace, the need for secure borders is not crucial. Moreover, the United Nations would send its peace-keeping forces to the borders between Israel and her neighbors. These UN forces would thereby become a kind of buffer zone between Israel and her neighbors and, as such, an international guarantee to maintain peace.

What is the value of international guarantees? In his memoirs, the late Abba Eban, the former minister of foreign affairs of Israel during the 1967 war, wrote the following:

> *History is not encouraging either as regards guarantees in general or guarantees to Israel in particular. . . . For example, in March 1957, the government of France undertook to stand by us in the event of a new blockade of the Tiran Straits or at least support us in our rights to defend ourselves. France declared this not only in speeches, but in an exchange of notes on the highest governmental level. In 1967, I went to see President de Gaulle and said, "France is not showing any understanding of our right of self-defense. What has changed between 1957 and 1967?" I shall never forget his reply. "You are asking, monsieur, what has changed? The date has changed! Then is not now." He then uttered the motto that I have never forgotten: "Guarantees are not absolute. The weights of a guarantee are a function of time."*

No wonder Israel has had a very bad experience with international third-party guarantees. United Nations or Big Power guarantees are no substitute for defensible borders. The lessons of history, as they affected, for instance, Czechoslovakia in 1938, Israel's own bitter experience with UN and Big Power guarantees, the shifts in international relations, and the possibility of contradictory analysis of intelligence data rule out guarantees as a reliable guard against aggression.

Promises of demilitarization have always turned out to be empty ones. Hitler was not impeded by the demilitarization of the Rhineland, because he knew that no one would go to war over the movement of German troops on German soil. Likewise, the United States sold Patton tanks to Jordan in the 1960s on the condition that they not be deployed in Judea and Samaria, yet they appeared in the hills around Jerusalem a week before the Six Day War of 1967.

The Straits of Tiran were blocked by Egypt in 1951 to Israeli ships and any foreign ships sailing to or from Eilat. This was contrary to the age-old custom of international law, which became a written rule of international law in the Geneva Convention.

In May 1950, the United States, Great Britain, and France issued the Repartite Declaration pledging to control the qualitative and quantitative flow of armaments to the Middle East so as to prevent any future imbalance in the region. The declaration in no way tempered Arab aggressive designs against Israel. From 1949 to 1956 Israel suffered countless incursions and acts of sabotage from across the armistice lines. In September 1955, Czechoslovakia and Egypt concluded a massive arms deal. This deal was a major cause of the 1956 Sinai War.

On May 16, 1967, President Gamal A. Nasser of Egypt demanded the withdrawal of the United Nation forces from the Sinai Desert. The United Nations agreed. This was a direct breach of the 1957 arrangement in which it was agreed that the UN forces could not be withdrawn arbitrarily.

On May 22, 1967, Nasser declared the Straits of Tiran closed for Israeli ships. The act was contrary to international law (the 1958 Geneva Convention was signed by all nations; it included a special "Tiran clause") and to the agreement of 1957. According to international law, an act of blockade is an act of war.

After the Six Day War, the Egyptians began a war of attrition along the Suez Canal. In order to put an end to the war of attrition, the United States pressured Israel to accept a cease-fire in August 1970. In exchange, Egypt agreed not to place missiles closer than 20 miles west of the Suez Canal. The agreement included assurances "that the U.S. would use all its influence to maintain the cease-fire."

A few days later, Israeli intelligence reported that hundreds of Egyptian SA-2 and SA-3 missile batteries were being rushed to the canal. Despite having forced Israel to accept the cease-fire, the United States refused first to acknowledge and then to act against Egypt's brazen violations of the agreement. These violations contributed directly to the heavy loss of Israeli life in the 1973 Yom Kippur War.

PART VII:

JEWISH RIGHTS
VIS-À-VIS
PALESTINIAN
RIGHTS

CHAPTER 11

CROWDED NEIGHBORHOOD

THE LAND OF ISRAEL BELONGS TO THE PEOPLE OF ISRAEL

After being forcibly exiled from its Land, the people kept faith with it throughout its dispersion, and never ceased to pray and hope for its return to it and for the restoration in it of its political freedom. — Declaration of the Establishment of the State of Israel, May 14, 1948

There are not many nations in the history of the world which can claim such deep-rooted attachment to their land over the centuries like the Jewish people. The Jews were expelled from the land of Israel by the Romans 2,000 years ago. Yet despite their expulsion and dispersion around the world, their loyalty and attachment to the land of their forefathers — the land of Israel — remained steadfast. Throughout history, Jews have continued to come from all corners of the globe to visit the land, to live in it, and then to die in it. Others have resided on the land, but none ever claimed that the land was theirs or that Jerusalem was their capital.

- Do you know that the name "Jerusalem" is mentioned 628 times in the Bible?

If I forget thee, oh Jerusalem, let my right hand forget its cunning, let my tongue cleave to the roof of my mouth. — Psalm 137:5–7

- Do you know that, according to Islam, Jerusalem is only third in its holiness after Mecca and Medina? For the Jews, Jerusalem is the holiest city and is the very soul of the Jewish people.

Pray for the peace of Jerusalem. They who love thee should prosper, peace be with thy walls and prosperity within your palaces. — Psalm 122:6–7

- Do you know that Palestine is both banks of the Jordan River?

- Do you know that the East Bank is a Palestinian state and is today called Jordan?

- Do you know that Emir Abdullah, former ruler of Jordan and the late great-grandfather of Jordan's present king, Abdullah, wanted to call his state Palestine? Only under British pressure did he agree to name it Jordan.

- Do you know that the Palestinian State — Jordan — is about 77 percent of mandatory Palestine?

THE WORLD COMMUNITY SAID THE LAND BELONGS TO THE JEWISH PEOPLE

The establishment in Palestine of a national home for the Jewish people in recognition of the historical connection of the Jewish people with Palestine and to the grounds for reconstituting their national home in that country. — Preamble to the British Mandate for Palestine, given to England by the League of Nations (1920)

On November 2, 1917, the then British foreign minister granted the historical document known as the Balfour Declaration to the Jewish people. This declaration recognized the rights of the Jewish people to the land of Israel. The Balfour Declaration was accepted and adopted by the world community at the League of

Nations and then became an integral part of the British mandate over Palestine.

- Do you know that the Balfour Declaration recognized the rights of the Jewish people to Palestine? The declaration reads:

    His Majesty's Government views with favour the establishment in Palestine of a national home for the Jewish people, and will use their best endeavours to facilitate the achievement of this object. (November 2, 1917)

- Do you know that the term "Arab" is not mentioned at all in the declaration?

- Do you know that while for the Jews the declaration speaks of national rights, for non-Jews it speaks of civil and religious rights alone?

- Do you know that after the First World War the League of Nations adopted the Balfour Declaration and asked Great Britain to agree to have the mandate on Palestine in order to fulfill the Balfour Declaration?

    As the mountains are round about Jerusalem, so the Lord is round about his people from henceforth and forever. — Psalm 125:1–2

- Do you know that Palestine, which was promised to the Jews, was merely a very small portion of the area that was taken from the Ottoman Turks and given to the Arabs?

- Do you know that the aspirations of the Arab national movement were fulfilled in Cairo, Baghdad, Damascus, Riyadh, etc.?

- Do you know there are 21 Arab states and only one tiny Israel?

- Do you know that Israel's area totals 8,299 square miles while the 21 Arab states total 5,300,000 square miles? The Arab states are 640 times the size of Israel with Judea, Samaria, and the Gaza Strip.

- Do you know that the Arab world in combined territory is twice as big as the United States?

- Do you know that the term "Palestinian" applies not only to Palestinian Arabs, but to Palestinian Jews as well?

- Do you know that after the First World War, the Palestinian Arabs declared that Palestine is Southern Syria — *"Surya Algianubiya"*?

- Do you know that in 1922 Britain gave 77 percent of Palestine to Emir Abdullah to establish the Emirate of Jordan?

- Do you know that the rights of self-determination in Palestine apply to Jews and Arabs? Both nations have attained it — the Jews in Israel and the Palestinian Arabs in Jordan. Jordan and Israel are mandatory Palestine.

- Do you know that the Emirate of Jordan gained its independence in 1946 and became the Palestinian state of Transjordan?

The Land of Israel is intertwined far more intimately into the religious and historical memories of the Jewish people; for their connection with the country . . . has been continuous from the second millennium BCE up to modern times — and their religious literature is more intimately connected with its history, its climate and soil. The land, therefore, has provided an emotional center which has endured through the whole of their period of 'exile' and has led to constant returns or attempted returns culminating in our own day in the Zionist Movement. — Dr. James Parkes, British historian and theologian, *Whose Land?*

- Do you know that Judea, Samaria, and Gaza are only 2,200 square miles or 5,720 square kilometers?

- Do you know that Jordan's King Hussein, Yassir Arafat, and all the PLO leaders have declared time and again that Jordan is Palestine and that Palestine is Jordan?

I was glad when they said to me, let us go into the house of the Lord. When our feet stood within the gate of Jerusalem. O, Jerusalem built as a city that is compact together. — Psalm 122:1–3

- Do you know that in 1950 the independent Palestinian state of Transjordan became known as the Hashemite Kingdom of Jordan and that it consists of about 77 percent of mandatory Palestine?

- Do you know that the majority of citizens in Jordan are Palestinians?

[Judaism is] tied to the history of a single people and the geographic actuality of a single land. — Dr. James Parkes, British historian and theologian, *Whose Land?*

Q: What are the roots of the name "Falastin"?
A: The term "Falastin" was related to the Philistines, one of a series of conquerors of part of the Land of Israel. The Romans revived the memory of the Philistines by referring to parts of the Land of Israel as "Palestina." This was a deliberate attempt on the part of the Romans to obliterate any sign of Jewish attachment to a homeland. Following the Ottoman-Muslim occupation in 1517, Falastin was the name given to parts of the country. It was late in the 19th century that the whole western side of the country was referred to as Falastin.

This right was recognized in the Balfour Declaration of November 2, 1917, and reaffirmed in the Mandate of the League of Nations, which, in particular, gave international sanction to the historic connection between the Jewish people and the Land of Israel and to the right of the Jewish people to rebuild its national home. — Declaration of the Establishment of the State of Israel, May 14, 1948

Ze'ev Jabotinsky, the Zionist Revisionist leader, appeared before the British Royal Committee in 1937. The committee was sent to investigate and to evaluate the situation in Palestine. Ze'ev Jabotinsky told the committee the following:

> Yes, we do want a state; every nation on earth, every normal nation, beginning with the smallest and humblest who do not claim any merit, any role in humanity's development, they all have a state of their own. That's the normal condition for a people. — *The Zionist Idea*, New York, 1970

Former U.S. President Ronald Reagan said the following:

> What we hold in common are the bonds of trust and friendship — qualities that in our eyes make Israel a great nation. No people have fought longer, struggled harder, or sacrificed more than yours in order to survive, to grow, and to live in freedom.

> Grass withers, flowers wilt, but the word of our God remains forever. Go up on a high mountain, you who bear good tidings of Zion. Lift up your voice forcefully . . . lift it up, be not afraid, you who Hear good tidings of Jerusalem. Tell the cities of Judah: Your God is here. — Isaiah 40:8–9

God spoke to Abraham at Shechem and told him, "It is to your descendants I give this land" (Genesis 12:7).

- Do you know that the Jews mention Jerusalem in Jewish celebrations? The well-known act of breaking a glass as part of the ceremony of Jewish weddings is the way in which to remember Jerusalem.

- Do you know that the Jewish religion combines universal values and a particular relationship to the Jewish people and the Jewish homeland — the land of Israel?

- Do you know that on Tisha B'av — the ninth day of the month of Av — the destruction of the temple is mourned?

- Do you know that the burial prayer says: "May the Lord comfort you among all those that mourn for Zion and Jerusalem"?

You [the Jews] have prayed for Jerusalem for 2,000 years, and you shall have it. — Winston Churchill, *Times,* London, May 5, 1983

- Do you know that the Jews express their commitment to Jerusalem in prayer? Three times a day the religious Jew says: "Have mercy, O Lord, and return to Jerusalem, Thy city." On Passover he says: "Next year in Jerusalem." After each meal he says: "Build Jerusalem the Holy City, speedily in our days." and during a wedding: "May Zion (Jerusalem) rejoice as her children are restored to her in joy."

- Do you know that Hebrew and Jewish literature in exile is imbued with a longing for the land of Israel symbolized by Jerusalem? An example is expressed by the great poet Yehuda Halevi, who wrote: "Would that I have wings that I could wend my way to Thee, O Jerusalem." Only the Jews, although in exile, maintained a special relationship to the land of Israel, seeing it as their national home and not as a province in an empire. The Arabs saw it as a province of Syria.

Jerusalem Is the Capital of Israel: Not from Camp David but from King David

Following the Six Day War of June 1967, the Israeli Knesset passed the Law and Administration Ordinance (Amendment No. 11) immediately upon entering the territories. Contained in this ordinance are the following words: "The law, jurisdiction, and administration of the State of Israel shall extend to any area of Eretz Yisrael designated by the government by order." Under this provision, the government issued an order dated June 28, 1967, which applied the law, jurisdiction, and administration of Israel to East Jerusalem, establishing it as an integral part of the state of Israel.

When the Lord brings his people home, what joy for Jacob, what happiness for Israel. — Isaiah 44:23

United Nations Resolution 194:
What Does It Say and Mean?

The traditional Arab claim, since 1948, has been that Israel rejected United Nations Resolution 194. According to the Arabs, the resolution calls for the return of Palestinian refugees to their homes. All Palestinian spokesmen from Yassir Arafat down insist that a permanent settlement must be based on Resolution 194. Moreover, the Palestinians claim that the resolution provides international backing for the refugees' "right of return" to Israel.

Q: What is the main point of Resolution 194?
A: For the most part, the resolution deals with seeking a diplomatic solution to the conflict with Israel. This includes setting up an international conciliation commission to mediate between the sides involved.

Q: What does the resolution say with regard to the refugees?
A: The refugees are mentioned only in Article 11 of the resolution. It reads:

> . . . that the refugees wishing to return to their homes and live at peace with their neighbors should be permitted to do so at the earliest practicable date, and that compensation should be paid for the property of those choosing not to return and for loss of or damage to property which, under principles of international law or in equity, should be made good by the governments or authorities responsible.

Q: What is missing from the resolution?
A: Resolution 194 never mentions the word "Israel." It does not blame Israel for creating the refugee problem, nor does it hold Israel responsible for solving the problem.

Q: What other points are mentioned in Resolution 194?
A: The resolution instructs the conciliation commission to "facilitate the repatriation, resettlement, and economic and social rehabilitation of the refugees and the payment of compensation."

Q; What is the power of such a resolution?
A: Unlike resolutions of the Security Council, those written by the General Assembly, like Resolution 194, are non-binding.

Essentially, they are only suggestions. The resolution does not specify the nationality of the refugees. Moreover, it does not use terms like "rights" or "right of return."

The resolution does speak of refugees who wish "to live at peace with their neighbors," but it was the Arabs that began the war.

It is a fact that had the Arabs accepted the United Nations Partition Plan of November 29, 1947, there would not have been any refugee problem. The Arab aggression against Israel resulted in the Arab refugee problem.

Q: What is the traditional Israeli position toward the Palestinian refugees?
A: Since Israel did not create the problem, Israel has insisted that she would not accept "legal or moral responsibility" for solving the problem. Moreover, Resolution 194 does not assign any such responsibility to Israel.

Q: Has Israel agreed to accept part of the refugees back?
A: Yes. At the time, David Ben-Gurion — Israel's first prime minister — agreed to absorb 100,000 refugees in Israel at the end of the War of Independence. This concession was made at the Lausanne Conference in 1949. The condition was that Israel be allowed to settle the returnees wherever it wanted and, specifically, "far from contact with potential enemies."

The Arabs' answer to this concession was total rejection. The Arab delegates refused to accept Israel's right to limit the number of returnees.

SECURITY COUNCIL RESOLUTION 242: WHAT DOES IT SAY AND MEAN?

We are not the ones to say where other nations should draw lines between them that will assure each the greatest security. It is clear, however, that a return to the situation of June 4, 1967, will not bring peace. — U.S. President Lyndon B. Johnson, September 10, 1968

The United Nations Security Council Resolution 242 of November 22, 1967, is the legal foundation of any forthcoming negotiations to achieve peace between Israel and her neighbors.

What Does It Say?	What Does It Mean?
"Termination of all claims or state of belligerency. . . ."	The Arab states must end the state of war initiated and maintained by them since 1948.
". . . respect for and acknowledgment of the sovereignty, territorial integrity, and political independence of every state in the area. . . ."	The Arab states must recognize Israel's right to exist.
". . . [every state's] right to live in peace within secure and recognized boundaries free from threats or acts of force."	Israel is entitled to clearly defensible borders. This is not a favor, but rather a right guaranteed by international law.
"Withdrawal of Israeli armed forces from territories occupied in the recent conflict."	Israel should withdraw from some, not all, of the territories captured in the 1967 Six Day War.
"A just settlement of the 'refugee problem.'"	The resolution did not say "Arab refugee" and that was not incidental. Both Jewish refugees, who were kicked out of their Arab homeland and settled in Israel, and Palestinian Arab refugees, have the same rights.

It is a fact that Israel has already withdrawn from the whole Sinai desert as a part of the Camp David Accords. The Sinai desert is 91 percent of the territory captured in Israel's 1967 war of defense. Since the signing of the Oslo Agreement in September 1993, Israel has withdrawn from parts of Judea and Samaria as well for the sake of peace with the Palestinians.

Israel has proven its willingness to take calculated risks for peace. Israel will never agree to withdraw to the June 4, 1967, lines. These were the lines that encouraged the Arabs to wage war against her. The Arabs' claim that UN Resolution 242 calls for complete Israeli withdrawal contradicts the content and spirit of Resolution 242.

Arthur J. Goldberg, who was the U.S. ambassador to the United Nations in 1967, was one of the authors of UN Resolution 242. With regard to the interpretation of the resolution he said the following: "It calls for respect and acknowledgment of the sovereignty of every state in the area. Since Israel never denied the sovereignty of its neighboring countries, this language obviously requires those countries to acknowledge Israel's sovereignty. The notable omissions in regard to withdrawal are the words 'the' or 'all' and 'the June 4, 1967 lines' . . . the resolution speaks of withdrawal from occupied territories, without defining the extent of withdrawal' " ("The meaning of 242," June 10, 1977).

Another co-author of Resolution 242 was the British ambassador to the United Nations, Lord Caradon. He said the following about Resolution 242:

> *We didn't say there should be a withdrawal to the '67 line; we did not put the "the" in, we did not say all the territories, deliberately. . . . We all knew — the boundaries of '67 were not drawn as permanent frontiers, they were a cease-fire line of a couple of decades earlier. . . . We did not say that the '67 boundaries must be forever. — MacNeil/Lehrer Report*, March 30, 1978

Professor Eugene V. Rostow, who was U.S. undersecretary of state for political affairs (1966–1969) said the following about the resolution:

> *Security Council Resolutions 242 . . . rest on two principles. Israel may administer the territory until its Arab neighbors make peace; and when peace is made, Israel should withdraw to "secure and recognized borders," which need not be the same as the armistice demarcation lines of 1949. — "The Truth about 242,"* November 5, 1990

In August 2001, Rostow elaborated on his points concerning Resolution 242. He said the following in an article published in the *Jewish Political Chronicle*:

> *Resolution 242, which as undersecretary of state for political affairs between 1966 and 1969 I helped produce, calls on the parties to make peace and allows Israel to administer the territories it occupied in 1967 until "a just and lasting peace in the Middle East" is achieved. When such a peace is made, Israel is required to withdraw its armed forces "from territories" it occupied during the Six-Day War — not from "the" territories nor from "all" territories, but from some of the territories, which included the Sinai Desert, the West Bank, the Golan Heights, East Jerusalem, and the Gaza Strip.*
>
> *Five and one-half months of vehement public diplomacy in 1967 made it perfectly clear what the missing definite article in Resolution 242 means. Ingeniously drafted resolutions calling for withdrawals from "all" the territories were defeated in the Security Council and the General Assembly. Speaker after speaker made it explicit that Israel was not to be forced back to the "fragile" and "vulnerable" armistice demarcation lines, but should retire once peace was made to what Resolution 242 called "secure and recognized" boundaries, agreed to by the parties. In negotiating such agreements, the parties should take into account, among other factors, security considerations, access to the international waterways of the region, and, of course, their respective legal claims.* — Eugene W. Rostow, professor of international law, *Jewish Political Chronicle*, August 2001

ISRAEL: NEVER AN ARAB LAND

> *I really wish the Jews again in Judea an independent nation for, as I believe, the most enlightened men of it have participated in the amelioration of the philosophy of the age.* — Former U.S. President John Adams, 1818

One of the myths related to the Arab-Israeli conflict is that Israel and the whole of mandatory Palestine before it, was stolen from the Arabs as a result of imperialist machinations and settled by alien Jews.

The fact is that until the defeat of the Ottoman Turkish Empire during World War I, there was no geopolitical entity called Palestine, no Arab nation lived on this soil, and no national claim was ever made to the territory by any group other than the Jews.

Between the expulsion of the Jews by Rome in 70–132 C.E. and the defeat of the Ottoman Empire in 1918, Palestine was occupied by 14 conquerors over 13 centuries. The following table shows the approximate historical periods of the various rulers of Palestine:

Israel rule (biblical period)	1350 B.C.E. to 586 B.C.E.
Babylonian conquest	587 B.C.E. to 538 B.C.E.
Israel autonomy (under Persian and Greco-Assyrian suzerainty)	538 B.C.E. to 168 B.C.E.
Revolt of the Maccabees	168 B.C.E. to 143 B.C.E.
Rule of the Hasmoneans and their successors	143 B.C.E. to 70 C.E.
Jewish autonomy (under Roman and Byzantine suzerainty)	70 C.E. to 637 C.E.
Rule of Arab Caliphates:	637 C.E. to 1072 C.E.
Mecca	637 C.E. to 661 C.E.
Umayyides	661 C.E. to 750 C.E.
Abbasides	750 C.E. to 870 C.E.
Fatimides	969 C.E. to 1071 C.E.
Seljuks' rule	1072 C.E. to 1096 C.E.
Crusaders' rule	1099 C.E. to 1291 C.E.
Ayyubis	1175 C.E. to 1291 C.E.
Mamelukes' rule	1291 C.E. to 1516 C.E.
Ottomans' (Turks') rule	1516 C.E. to 1918 C.E.
British Mandate	1918 C.E. to 1948 C.E.

Go through Zion, walk around her, counting her towers, admiring her walls, reviewing her palaces. Then tell the next generation that God is here . . . for ever and ever. — Psalm 48:12–14

I made my covenant with them to give them the Land of Canaan, the land they lived in as strangers, and I have heard the groaning of the sons of Israel . . . and have remembered

my covenant . . . with my arm outstretched and my strokes of power I will deliver you . . . bringing you to the land I swore to Abraham, Isaac, and Jacob. I the Lord will do this.
— Exodus 6:5–8

WHAT THE CONFLICT IS ALL ABOUT

. . . Jews strove in every successive generation to re-establish themselves in their ancient homeland. In recent years they returned in their masses. . . . — Declaration of the Establishment of the State of Israel, May 14, 1948

The Arab-Israeli conflict was neither about what is called Arab refugees nor about Arab-occupied territories. The Arabs refused to accept Israel in their midst long before the Arab refugee problem was created and when Israel was outside the "Arab occupied territories." The Arabs' refusal to accept Israel as a sovereign state is the reason for all the trouble and bloodshed, with the subsequent death and injury of many tens of thousands — Jew and Arab alike.

The Arabs did not hide their intentions to destroy Israel.

The conflict with the Zionist enemy goes beyond the struggle of the countries whose territories were occupied in 1967 and involves the entire Arab nation in view of the military, political, economic, and cultural danger which the Zionist enemy represents to the entire Arab nation, its fundamental nationalist interests, its civilization and destiny. — Declaration of the Baghdad Conference, November 1978

The Arab Palestinian refusal to face reality, and to behave accordingly, has caused hatred, enmity, and various destructive wars. Moreover, it caused severe damage to the Palestinian Arabs.

We, the Palestinians, lost the possible because we always demanded the impossible. — Muhammad Abu Shilbaya, Palestinian journalist, 1975

The leaders of the Jewish National Home between the First and Second World Wars made different and various attempts to reach a kind of compromise with the Palestinian Arabs. However, all the efforts failed. The Palestinian Arabs, under the notorious Mufti Haj Muhammed Amin al-Husseini, refused to compromise.

We extend our hand to all neighboring states and their peoples in an offer of peace and good neighborliness and appeal to them to establish bonds of cooperation and mutual help with the sovereign Jewish people settled in its own land. The state of Israel is prepared to do its share in a common effort for the advancement of the entire Middle East. — Declaration of the Establishment of the State of Israel, May 14, 1948

Immediately after the First World War, it appeared that the Palestinian Arabs' undisputed leader tended to recognize the Jewish rights to Palestine. In a letter that Emir Faisal wrote to Felix Frankfurter on March 3, 1919, Faisal said, "The Jewish movement is nationalist and not imperialist, our movement is nationalist and not imperialist and there is room in Syria for us both." (Palestine was known as Southern Syria.)

The honest words of Emir Faisal with regard to the Jews' right to Palestine were immediately rejected by the other Palestinian leaders. After World War I, the Palestinian radicals, who rejected any compromise, became the speakers for the Palestinian Arabs.

Palestine which, desolate for centuries, is now renewing its youth and vitality through enthusiasm, hard work, and self sacrifice of the Jewish pioneers who toil there in a spirit of peace and social justice. — U.S. President Herbert Hoover

Despite the fact that 77 percent of Palestine (Jordan) promised to the Jews was given to the Arabs, the Palestinian Arabs of the West Bank of Jordan resisted the establishment of the Jewish national home in Palestine (the remaining 23 percent).

In Genesis 29:35 it is written that Leah bore four sons to Jacob (whose name was to be changed to Israel): "And she conceived again, and bore a son. And she said, 'Now I will praise the Lord': Therefore she called his name Judah. . . ." The Hebrew root of "praise" and "Judah" is the same. The name Judah, Judea, or Yehuda in Hebrew comes from the same linguistic root as the word *odeh*, which means "I will praise." The word *todah*, meaning "thank you," has the same root. Thus, the root of the name of the land of Judea, and its people, Judeans, means something close to "praise" or "thanks," and relates to the birth of Jacob and Leah's fourth son.

> *It is impossible for one who has studied at all the services of the Hebrew people to avoid the faith that they will one day be restored to their historic national home and there enter on a new yet greater phase of their contribution to the advance of humanity.* — U.S. President Warren Harding, 1921–1923

- Do you know that the Palestinian Arab opposition to the Jewish national home caused the death and injury of many thousands of Jews and Arabs in Palestine?

- Do you know that the Palestinian Arabs rioted against the Jews in Palestine in the years: 1920, 1921, 1929, 1933, 1936–1939, and 1948? The Arabs demanded the end of Jewish immigration to Palestine, to stop the sale of land to the Jews, and the establishment of an Arab Palestinian state.

- Do you know that in the riots of 1936–1939 Palestinian Arabs killed more Palestinian Arabs than Jews?

> *For God will save Zion and rebuild the towns of Judah (Judea); they will be lived in, owned, and handed down to his servants' descendants.* — Psalm 69:35

God spoke to Abraham at Hebron:

> *Look all around from where you stand, toward the north and the south, toward the east and the west. All the land you see I will give to you and your descendants forever.* — Genesis 13:14–17

PART VIII:

SETTLEMENTS IN JUDEA, SAMARIA, AND GAZA STRIP — OBSTACLE TO PEACE OR NOT?

CHAPTER 12

"SETTLEMENTS": PA PROPAGANDA

A few years ago on a trip to Israel, General Sharon took me on a helicopter flight over the West Bank. And what a trip that was. What struck me . . . is the tiny distance between enemy lines and Israel's population centers. The general said that before the Six-Day War, Israel was only nine miles wide at its narrowest point. In Texas, some of our driveways are longer than that. — U.S. President George W. Bush in a campaign speech prior to his election

The Israeli position on the Jewish settlements in Judea, Samaria, and the Gaza Strip is the following: As long as the future status of these territories is subject to negotiations, Israeli historic and legal claim to these territories is no less valid than that of the Palestinians.

It is a fact that Jewish settlement in Judea, Samaria, and Gaza has existed since time immemorial and was expressly recognized as legitimate in the Mandate for Palestine adopted in 1922 by the League of Nations. The mandate provided for the establishment of a Jewish state in the Jewish people's ancient homeland. Article 6 of the mandate reads:

The administration of Palestine . . . should facilitate Jewish immigration under suitable conditions and shall encourage, in cooperation with the Jewish Agency referred to in Article 4, close settlement by Jews on the land, including state lands not required for public use.

We have to bear in mind that the settlements in the territories were not there prior to the 1967 war. The settlements were established after the Six Day War in June 1967, which was a war of defense against joint Arab aggression. U.S. Secretary of Defense Donald Rumsfeld put it thusly:

> *My feeling about the so-called occupied territories is that there was a war. Israel urged neighboring countries not to get involved in it once it started. They all jumped in, and they lost a lot of real estate to Israel because Israel prevailed in that conflict. In the intervening period, they've made some settlements in various parts of the so-called occupied area, which was the result of a war, which they won.* — As quoted by former Congressman and Cabinet member. Jack Kemp, *Washington Times*, August 25, 2002

SETTLEMENTS PROMOTE PEACE

The Arabs and their supporters in their never-ending battle of propaganda against Israel succeeded to convince many the world over that Israel is an occupying power. Moreover, that the settlements in the territories are an obstacle to peace and there can never be peace as long as Jewish settlements in these territories are not removed.

Unfortunately, Israel's dull public relations has never seriously related to these twisted and incorrect views. Reality is quite the opposite. Settlements in Judea, Samaria, and the Gaza Strip not only are not an obstacle to peace, but promote peace.

The following are a number of points to prove this thesis:

1. Between the Mediterranean Sea and the Jordan River there are, and always will be, Israeli Jews, Palestinian Arabs, and other minorities.

2. In Israel, there are about 1.2 million Palestinian Arabs and other non-Jewish communities, all of whom

enjoy full Israeli citizenship. They reside in Haifa, Jerusalem, Jaffa, Lydda, Nazareth, in the Galilee, and in the Negev, as well as in other parts of Israel.

3. Today, in Judea, Samaria, and Gaza, there are over 200,000 Israeli Jews. Why are 1.2 million Palestinian Arabs allowed to live in Israel (pre-1967 lines), while 200,000 Jews are *not* allowed to live in Judea, Samaria, and Gaza? Why is it unacceptable for Jews to live in Ariel, ElQana, Immanuel, Itamar, Hebron, Neve Dekalim, etc. — Israeli settlements in Judea, Samaria, and Gaza?

4. In some future agreement, the Jewish residents of the territories will be able to vote for the Israeli Knesset, if they maintain Israeli citizenship, or they can vote for the Palestinian Authority rule and institutions, should they prefer Palestinian citizenship. Israeli Arabs would have the same options: if they maintain Israeli citizenship, they can vote for the Knesset, as they do today, or they can choose Palestinian citizenship and vote for the Palestinian rule. Both Jews and Arabs would be granted the freedom to choose.

   It is important to emphasize here that the Israeli Arabs, especially their elected representatives and leaders, must understand that they cannot support the positions of their brethren in the Palestinian Authority while simultaneously insisting to maintain Israeli citizenship with their representative members of the Knesset. Whoever chooses to support the Palestinian Authority over Israel would relinquish his Israeli identity card and would become a Palestinian citizen under the Palestinian Authority rule.

5. When the Oslo Agreement was signed in September 1993, the Jewish settlements already existed in Judea, Samaria, and Gaza. They were built on state land and Palestinian Arabs were not kicked out of their homes. The Palestinian Authority cannot claim today that Israel changed the status quo in these territories.

6. The world forges ahead as it becomes a global village. European nations have moved into the age of the euro — their new currency. European citizens can travel from state to state without a visa. The political borders have lost their importance in favor of economic welfare for all. In light of this positive precedent, there is no reason why Israeli Jews cannot visit Palestinian Authority cities and villages and vice versa. Each will vote for his own institutions. The relationship between both peoples will be based on mutual recognition, good will, and the common goal of economic welfare.

7. The demand to forcibly remove people from their homes — Jews or Arabs — is dangerous and unrealistic besides being cruel and inhumane. Most Israelis oppose this option. No government in Israel can evacuate tens of thousands of families from their homes in the settlements. Most of these settlers are very idealistic and strongly rooted in their homes. A forced evacuation would lead to civil war in Israel. Jews fighting Jews would be the beginning of the end of the state. Israel's former prime minister, Ehud Barak, expressed his consent to move most of the settlements for the sake of peace. This, besides being unrealistic, would have proven to be impossible. The Israeli people expressed their opposition to Barak's views by removing him from power in the last elections.

8. Bear in mind that in Jordan today, which is 77 percent of mandatory Palestine, Jews are forbidden to live. It was forbidden by Jordanian law. Is it just or even logical that Jews will not be able to live everywhere on the remaining 23 percent? This is all the territory from the West Bank of the Jordan River to the Mediterranean Sea.

9. The Arab world in territory is 640 times the size of Israel. Is it just to tell Israelis that they are limited where they can live even on their mere 1/6 percent of territory?

To sum up, Jews and Palestinian Arabs will continue to live between the River Jordan and the Mediterranean Sea. This is the reality, and acceptance of this fact will benefit all sides. Whoever says that the settlements are an obstacle to peace is strengthening the misconception among the Palestinian Arabs in Judea, Samaria, and Gaza who believe that the Jews must be removed from these areas.

Yassir Arafat, in an interview with the Israeli daily *Ma'Ariv* said that if the settlers were ready to live under Palestinian supervision, he would be ready to grant them citizenship. By Israeli law, Israelis can hold dual citizenship. Therefore, there is nothing preventing the settlers from remaining in their homes and to continue voting for the Israeli Knesset.

WORLD MEDIA: DOUBLE STANDARD

There are many wars in the Middle East. Yet while journalists are diligently neutral about bearing arms in these conflicts, many reporters and editors inadvertently participate in a war of words and unconsciously influence readers, viewers, and listeners.

After Israel successfully defended itself during the Six Day War in 1967 — when hostile Arab nations vowed to "drive the Jews into the sea" but wound up losing the war and territories, too — news stories originating in those territories became datelined "Occupied West Bank" or "Israeli-Occupied Gaza."

The psychological effects of this selective terminology are powerful. The implication of the language is clear, reminiscent of World War II when "occupied" territories or nations were under the boots of invading Axis armies. Occupiers are outsiders, invaders who have no business being there.

Never mind that when Israel captured Gaza and the West Bank, it acted in self-defense and was clearly not the aggressor. And never mind that the West Bank was part of Israel more than 1,000 years before the birth of Islam, and that Jews lived there until Jordanian troops violently exiled them in 1948.

It is crucial to note here the double standard applied against Israel by most media. Consider: The land known as the West Bank — called Judea and Samaria by the Jews who inhabited it for so many centuries before Arabs arrived on the scene — was illegally seized by Jordan through military force in 1948. Only two countries in the entire world, Pakistan and England, subsequently recognized Jordan's sovereignty there.

Between 1948 and 1967, did any print or broadcast media dateline stories originating there as being from "Jordanian-occupied West Bank"?

Before Israel captured the Gaza Strip in 1967, it was occupied by Egypt, even though the residents of Gaza are not Egyptian and Gaza is separated from Egypt by the Sinai Desert. When Egypt occupied Gaza, did any medium dateline a story with "Egyptian-occupied Gaza"?

Consider Afghanistan, Poland, Hungary, Czechoslovakia, and so many other countries invaded by the Soviet Union and forcefully occupied by Soviet troops. Did you ever see a story datelined "Soviet-occupied Poland" or "Soviet-occupied Afghanistan"?

Consider calling the West Bank by its biblical name, Judea and Samaria. Or consider using neutral terms such as the "disputed territories" or "the West Bank and Gaza," and avoiding using prejudicial phrases such as "occupied territories."

Words and images are powerful forces, capable of righting wrongs or inflicting evil. Israel has been wronged in the past by the use of semantically loaded negative phrases.

> *The land of Israel is intertwined far more intimately into the religious and historical memories of the Jewish people; for their connection with the country . . . has been continuous from the second millennium b.c.e. up to modern times — and their religious literature is more intimately connected with its history, its climate, and its soil. The land, therefore, has provided an emotional center which has endured through the whole of their period of "exile" and has led to constant returns or attempted returns culminating in our own day in the Zionist movement.* — Dr. James Parkes, British historian and theologian, *Whose Land?*

JUDEA AND SAMARIA: ACCORDING TO INTERNATIONAL LAW

By withdrawing from Sinai and parts of Judea and Samaria, Israel has already retreated from about 90 percent of the territories captured in the war of defense in June 1967. Security Council

Resolution 242 from November 22, 1967, emphasizes three main points:

1. Withdrawal of Israeli and armed forces from territories occupied in the recent conflict

2. Termination of all claims or states of belligerency and respect for and acknowledgement of the sovereignty: territorial integrity and political independence of every state in the area and their right to live in peace within secure and recognized boundaries free from threats or acts of force

3. Achieving a just settlement of the refugee problem

The resolution intentionally uses the phrase "withdrawal from territories." It does not stipulate "all" or "the" when referring to the territories. This means that Israel should not be expected to return to the dangerous and ridiculous borders of June 4, 1967. Israel is expected to withdraw to what the resolution calls "secure and recognized borders."

In addition, the resolution speaks about "settlement of the refugee problem," namely Palestinian as well as Jews from Arab lands. The number of Jews from Arab countries who settled in Israel after the establishment of the state in 1948 is equal to the number of Palestinians who left Israel at the same time. There was, in reality, an exchange of population.

There is. I think, an open question as to who has legal right to the West Bank. — Cyrus Vance, former U.S. secretary of state at a Washington press conference, July 28, 1977

The West Bank clearly was not and is not the sovereign territory of Jordan, from whom Israel took it in a war of self-defense in 1967. The West Bank is an integral part of the Palestine mandate within which a Jewish national home was to be created. In this sense, the territory must be considered today to be unallocated territory. — William O'Brien, *Washington Star*, November 26, 1978

And he bought the hill Samaria from Shemer for two talents of silver and built on the hills, and called the name of

the city which he built after the name of Shemer, owner of the
hill Samaria. — 1 Kings 16:24

Israel's former ambassador to the United Nations, Professor Yehuda Blum, has explained the legal basis for Israel's attitude thusly: a) Jordan and Egypt illegally occupied the areas in question as a result of a war of aggression waged against Israel in 1948, and therefore did not acquire any right of sovereignty over these areas; b) Israel acted in self-defense; and c) since no state can produce a legal claim to these areas that is equal to that of Israel, this relative superiority of claim may be sufficient, under international law, to make Israel's possession of these areas virtually indistinguishable from that of an absolute sovereign.

However, in practical terms, and despite these legal considerations, Israel established a military government in Judea, Samaria, and Gaza which functioned in accordance with all internationally accepted rules. With the signing of the Oslo Agreement on September 13, 1993, Israel withdrew from eight Palestinian cities and villages. Today, over 95 percent of the Palestinians are under the jurisdiction of the Palestinian Authority.

> *The only possible geographic, demographic, and political definition of Palestine is that of the [League of Nations] mandate, which included what are now Israel and Jordan as well as the West Bank and the Gaza Strip. The term "Palestine" applies to all the peoples who live or have a right to live in the territory* — *Jews, Christians, and Moslems alike. Thus, the West Bank and the Gaza Strip are not "Arab" territories in the legal sense, but territories of the mandate which have been recognized as belonging to Israel or to Jordan.* — Dr. Eugene V. Rostow, professor of law and public affairs, Yale University, under-secretary of state (1966–69), *Yale Studies in World Public Order*, vol. 5, 1979

International law requires the peaceful settlement of disputes through negotiations. A country cannot perpetually violate this precept and at the same time make claims against the other party to such a dispute. Moreover, international law does not require a state to retain the status of an occupying power indefinitely, in order to accommodate the destructive policies of the state which formerly governed the disputed territory. This is especially so if the territory had changed hands as a result of a war of aggression initiated by the state which is unwilling to negotiate peace.

> *Where the prior holder of territory had seized that territory unlawfully, the state which subsequently takes that territory in the lawful exercise of self-defense, has, against that prior holder, better title.* — United Nations International Law Commission, *American Journal of International Law*, 1970

- Do you know that except for 18 years (between 1949 and 1967), when Judea and Samaria were under Jordanian control, these areas were always an integral part of the land of Israel?

- Do you know that cities such as Jericho, Hebron, Bethel, Shechem, and Bethlehem in Judea and Samaria are a part of Jewish history and are as famous as Jerusalem, Jaffa, etc.?

- Do you know that Samaria became the capital of the northern kingdom — Israel — and Jerusalem was the capital of the southern kingdom — Judah or Judea?

- Do you know that the sons of Jacob, one of our patriarchs, herded his flocks near the city of Shechem?

- Do you know that Judea and Samaria never belonged to Jordan? They were designated to be the second Palestinian state by the United Nations Partition Plan and were captured by the Jordanian army in a war of aggression against Israel.

- Do you know that Jordan's occupation of Judea and Samaria nullified the Partition Plan?

- Do you know that Jordanian occupation of Judea and Samaria and its annexation of these territories in 1950 were rejected by the international community? (Only England and Pakistan recognized the annexation.)

- Do you know that even the Arab League rejected Jordan's annexation of Judea and Samaria?

- Do you know that this territory's ultimate status remains to be determined?

- Do you know that Jordan, in blatant violation of the 1949 Israel-Jordan agreement and the United Nations charter, launched an attack on Israel in June 1967?

- Do you know that in a legal counterattack, Israeli forces kicked out the Jordanian forces from Judea and Samaria in the Six Day War of 1967?

- Do you know that the armistice lines that divided Judea and Samaria from the rest of Israel between the years 1949 and 1967 were never meant to be permanent borders?

- Do you know that Judea and Samaria are only about 30 to 35 miles wide and little more than 2,000 square miles in total area?

. . . as between Israel, acting defensively in 1948 and 1967, on the one hand, and her Arab neighbors, acting aggressively in 1948 and 1967, on the other, Israel has better title in the territory of what was Palestine, including the whole of Jerusalem, than do Jordan and Egypt. . . . — Stephen Schwebel, former legal advisor to the U.S. State Department, *American Journal of International Law*, May 1970

In a letter to the *New York Times* from September 15, 1983, Dr. Eugene Rostow, former U.S. undersecretary of state, wrote the following: "Israel's claims to the territory are at least as good as those of Jordan, since Jordan held the territory for 19 years after a war of aggression, whereas Israel took the area in the course of a war of self-defense, so far as Jordan was concerned."

- Do you know that the Sinai desert is more than ten times the size of Judea and Samaria? Sinai is desert land, almost uninhabited, thereby enabling Israel to mobilize her forces in case Egypt decides to go to war against Israel in the future.

- Do you know that although the Israelites wandered through the Sinai desert for 40 years, Sinai was never considered part of the land of Israel?

- Do you know that Judea and Samaria are an integral part of Israel's history?

- Do you know that Judea and Samaria are the bottleneck of Israel? Arab control over these areas can pose mortal danger to Israel's very existence.

Jewish settlements on the West Bank is an issue today only because the existence of Israel is an issue. . . . The issue of Jewish settlements in the West Bank today is simply one thin layer that emanates from and partially conceals the core of the conflict, namely, the non-recognition by the Arab states of Israel's right to exist. — Fred Gottheil, University of Illinois, to U.S. House of Representatives Committee on International Relations, September 12, 1977

- Do you know that before the 1967 war, the coastal strip, in which 75 percent of Israel's population and industry are located, was not wider than 9 to 15 miles?

- Do you know that Judea and Samaria served as a base for Jordanian aggression against Israel in 1948 and again in 1967?

- Do you know that whoever controls the mountainous area in Judea and Samaria also has control over the coastal strip?

- Do you know that Israel fulfilled the contents and spirit of United Nations Resolution 242 by giving up the entire Sinai Peninsula to the Eygptians? Sinai is the great bulk of the areas captured in Israel's defensive war of 1967. Therefore, Israel has already given up most of the territories.

The heated question of Israel's settlements in the West Bank during the occupation period should be viewed in this perspective. The British Mandate recognized the right of the Jewish people to "close settlement" in the whole of the mandated territory. It was provided that local conditions might require Great Britain to "postpone" or "withhold" Jewish settlement in what is now Jordan. This was done in 1922. But the Jewish right of settlement in Palestine west of the Jordan River, that is, in Israel, the West Bank, Jerusalem, and the Gaza Strip was made unassailable. That right has never been terminated and cannot be terminated except by a recognized peace between Israel and its neighbors.

And perhaps not even then, in view of Article 80 of the U.N. Charter, "the Palestine article," which provides that "nothing in the Charter shall be construed . . . to alter in any manner the rights whatsoever of any states or any peoples or the terms of exciting international instruments. . . . " — Eugene W. Rostow, professor of international law, *Jewish Political Chronicle*, August 2001

SETTLEMENTS IN JUDEA, SAMARIA, AND THE GAZA STRIP: NUMBERS AND MEANING

The charge by the [Carter] administration at the time those settlements first started that they were illegal is false. . . . All people — Moslems, Jews, and Christians — are entitled to live on the West Bank. — U.S. President Ronald Reagan press conference, October 1980

Q: How many settlements are there in Judea, Samaria, and the Gaza Strip?
A: Since 1967, over 145 Jewish settlements have been established in Judea, Samaria, and Gaza.

Q: What is their population?
A: The population numbered approximately 200,000 at the end of 2000. This number constitutes only 5 percent of the total population of Judea, Samaria, and Gaza.

Q: Why did Israel establish these settlements?
A: After the 1967 war, the Israeli government began to establish settlements in order to strengthen her security. Populating these areas was a reaffirmation of Jewish rights to live in all parts of the land of Israel. This view is accepted mainly by religious and nationalistic parties in Israel, as well as by some segments of the Labor Party.

Q: What is the difference in views between the Likud and Labor Parties in this respect?
A: The Labor Party stands for confining Jewish settlements to only those areas expected to remain in Israel's hands after the conclusion of a peace treaty with the Arab states. Some in the Likud bloc, and most of its religious allies, stand for the unqualified right of the Jews to live anywhere in these territories.

> *You will plant vineyards once more on the mountains of Samaria.* — Jeremiah 31:5

Q: Why can't Israel stop the settlements?
A: William Safire supplies the answer to this question in an article in the *New York Times* of May 24, 1979. He wrote:

> *Sovereignty — who owns the land — is the key. Jordan claims it, the PLO claims it, and Israel, through its continued settlement policy, asserts its own claim. The moment Israel gives up its right to settle, it gives up that claim to sovereignty. If Israel were to admit it is not at least part owner, an independent Palestinian state would be born which — in this decade, at least — would be an intolerable threat to Israel's security.*

> *There will be no confiscation or requisitioning of any*
> *private land whatsoever. Any expansion of the settlements*
> *or allocation of land to them will be done from state-owned*
> *land, after strict and detailed scrutiny by the attorney general.*
> — Decision adopted by government of Israel to expand
> seven existing settlements, October 14, 1979

Q: What is the meaning of 130 settlements in these territories?
A: Some people are of the opinion that the rapid increase of Jewish settlements in the territories has created an irreversible situation; namely, there is no way now in which any Israeli government would give up all the territories even if it would wish to do so. Others have made it clear that the final borders will be determined in negotiations between Israel and her neighbors, rather than by the location of Jewish settlements in the territories.

Q: How many new immigrants have settled in Judea and Samaria?
A: Their number is small. "Well, in my opinion this is a side issue," said the late Egyptian president Sadat, in reference to the Jewish settlements, on ABC-TV, August 4, 1977.

Q: Will the Jewish settlements pose an obstacle to peace in the future?
A: Not at all. Whenever people live together, in this case Jews and Arabs, they come to know and understand one another. This can only increase the chances for peace between them. On the western side of Palestine — from the Jordan River to the Mediterranean Sea — Jews and Arabs live together almost everywhere, including Judea and Samaria.

Q: Will Israel, in the long run, annex these territories?
A: No. Israel is committed to the Camp David Accords and the Oslo Agreements, which call for the establishment of a Palestinian entity in Judea, Samaria, and Gaza.

Q: Would the Palestinian Arabs vote for the Israeli Parliament?
A: No. The Palestinian Arabs are Palestinian citizens and they would exercise their right to vote for the Palestinian Authority. The Jewish settlers are Israeli citizens and they would, therefore, vote for the Israeli Parliament.

> *The relationship between the settlements and the prin-*
> *ciple of self-determination cannot be discussed in isolation,*

because the settlements are but a single factor involved in negotiating peace. — Alfred Atherton, U.S. asst. secretary of state before a House committee, Washington, DC, October 1977

Q: Can these territories be anything other than an autonomy?
A: Yes, if the parties involved would agree on a status different from autonomy.

Israel has an unassailable legal right to establish settlements in the West Bank. The West Bank is part of the British mandate in Palestine which included Israel and Jordan as well as certain other territories not yet generally recognized as belonging to either country. While Jewish settlement east of the Jordan River was suspended in 1922, such settlements remained legal in the West Bank. — Eugene V. Rostow of Yale University, *New York Times*, September 13, 1983

There have always been Jewish settlements on the West Bank. Hebron, a city with many ancient historical ties with Israel, had a prospering Jewish community until most of them were slaughtered during the Arab riots of 1929–1936; the rest fled. — Abbot Leo Rudloff, former head of Benedictine monastery on Mount Zion, Jerusalem, *New York Times.* July 17, 1979

In any event, however, the rules of conduct laid down in the Geneva Convention contain no restrictions on the freedom of persons to take up residence in the area involved. It bars forcible transfers, not voluntary acts of individuals or groups. Moreover, not a single Arab resident of Judea and Samaria has been evicted as a result of the establishment of Jewish settlements.

Let me make one point clear: The settlements will not decide the final borders between Israel and its neighbors. The borders will be decided upon in negotiations between Israel and its neighbors. — Moshe Dayan, late foreign minister of Israel, United Nations General Assembly, October 10, 1977

Q: What can be said of the claim that the settlements are an obstacle to peace?

A: According to the late Chaim Herzog, then Israeli ambassador to the United Nations, in an address before the General Assembly, October 26, 1977:

> *For 19 years from 1948 to 1967 we were not establishing settlements in Judea, Samaria, Gaza, Sinai, and the Golan, because we were not there. There was no such 'obstacle' from 1948 to 1967. Did the Arabs talk about peace or negotiate peace?*

> *There is no basis in international law or historic practice for United Nations Secretary-General Kofi Annan's assertion that Israel's occupation of the West Bank is "illegal." Israel's 1967 borders are armistice lines from 1948, when Arab nations, rather than accept Palestinian statehood provided by UN resolutions and accepted by Israel, attempted to destroy Israel.* — George Will, *Star-Ledger*

ISRAEL AND ARAB STATES IN NUMBERS

- The size of the Arab states, if we include Iran, is 5.3 million square miles.

- That's almost double the size of the United States.

- The size of the Arab states is larger than all Europe by one-third.

- The size of Israel is 8,299 square miles, which is about the same size as the state of New Jersey — one of the smallest states in the United States.

- The Jewish population in Israel is about 5.1 million. The Arab population in the Arab states is over 200 million.

- Israel is 640 times smaller than the Arab world.

- Demonstrating its will for peace, Israel transferred the Sinai desert to Egypt and was willing to give most of Judea and Samaria to the Palestinians.

- The Sinai desert alone is three times larger than Israel.

- The Arabs make up 3 percent of the human race, hold 10 percent of the vote in the United Nations and have a virtual hold over 30 percent more, control 15 percent of the earth's land surface and 60 percent of the world's oil resources.

We will escalate the armed struggle so that only rifles and gasoline bombs determine the course of the talks. — From a pamphlet distributed by Fatah — largest PLO faction under Yassir Arafat, 1994

Two Bluffs: Settlements and Occupied Territories

The only area in the world known totally as "occupied territory" is the approximate 2,000 square miles of the West Bank and the Gaza Strip. Moreover, it is well accepted that Jewish "settlements" are an obstacle to peace. The Arabs, in their propaganda campaign, have succeeded to mislead almost all the people all the time.

In fact, the West Bank and Gaza are not "occupied territory." According to international law, "occupied territory" is land taken in a war of aggression from its sovereign and legal owner. This is certainly not the case with the West Bank and Gaza. Both were taken in a war of aggression by Jordan and Egypt, respectively, in 1948.

Jordan and Egypt, therefore, were holding these territories illegally. "The international community never recognized the annexation of the West Bank and the Gaza Strip by Jordan and Egypt. Even the Arab League never recognized the illegal annexation.

Unlike Jordan and Egypt, Israel captured these territories in 1967 in a war of defense from their illegal occupiers: Jordan and Egypt. As a result, Israel has a better right to these territories than Jordan, Egypt, or the Palestinians.

As for the Palestinians, they lost their right to the land when they refused to accept the Partition Plan of November 29, 1947. Instead, they joined the Arab armies in their futile wars against Israel since 1948.

The West Bank and Gaza Strip are, therefore, not "occupied territory," but "disputed territory." The final status of these territories should be determined in the negotiations between Israel and the Palestinians.

The Israeli government, meanwhile, signed the Oslo Agreement in September 1993 and has withdrawn from parts of Judea and Samaria.

With regard to the Jewish "settlements" in these territories, it is commonly said that such settlements are an obstacle to peace. The only obstacle to peace is the repeated Arab refusal to accept Israel as a sovereign state in the Middle East.

Why can Jews and Arabs live in Jaffa, Haifa (northern Israel), and Be'er Sheva (southern Israel), and in Israel prior to the 1967 war, yet they cannot live together in Hebron, Bethlehem, and Jericho in the land of their forefathers? When Jews and Arabs live together, this can only promote peace, not become an obstacle to peace.

Why can Jews live in Jericho, New York, in Bethlehem, Pennsylvania, and in Hebron, Ohio, yet they cannot live in these cities in the land of their forefathers? Why should Jews be forbidden to live in Hebron where Judaism started and where our father Abraham lived, died, and is buried? Why should any city in the world be *Judenrien* (empty of Jews)? To claim that Jews and Arabs cannot live together everywhere from the Jordan River to the Mediterranean Sea would mean that Arab-Jewish coexistence is indeed impossible. Such a claim is far more an obstacle to peace.

Peace is not based solely upon a document that someone holds in his hand. Peace is based on mutual cooperation, respect, trust, and relationships which come from living together and learning to know one another.

The only way to achieve a genuine and real peace is when Jews and Arabs live together everywhere on the land of Israel — from the Jordan River to the Mediterranean Sea.

Yes, the settlements are an obstacle, but not to peace. They are an obstacle to an Arafat-dominated terror state in the future and an obstacle to any new Arab military surprise attack against Israel.

As such, the settlements promote peace, reduce the chances for war in the future, and they promote Arab-Jewish coexistence. In reality, settlements promote peace rather than obstruct peace.

Part IX:

Constructive Thinking about the Golan Heights

CHAPTER 13

THE
HIGH GROUND

THE GOLAN HEIGHTS: WRONG CONCEPTS,
NEW CONCEPTS, AND CREATIVE THINKING

Historically, there have never been secure or recognized boundaries in the area. Neither the armistice lines of 1949 nor the cease-fire lines of 1967 have answered that description . . . such boundaries have yet to be agreed upon. An agreement on that point is an absolute essential to a just and lasting peace. . . . — Arthur Goldberg, U.S. ambassador to the United Nations, November 15, 1967

Q: What are the current concepts in Israel concerning the Golan Heights and Lebanon?
A: In Israel, there are three misconceptions, especially among the left-wing elements. They are:

1. If there is no peace with Syria, Israel will reach a stalemate. Such a stalemate would inevitably lead to war with Syria and perhaps with other Arab states. The involvement of Iran in southern Lebanon can only escalate the situation.

2. The second misconception was, for years, to connect directly the Syrian dilemma with the situation on the southern Lebanese border. Namely, if there is no solution to the Golan Heights issue, there can be no solution to the southern Lebanon problem.

   Meanwhile, reality proved that Israel is still on the Golan Heights, yet out of Lebanon altogether. What will happen on the Lebanese border in the future, one can only guess.

3. The third misconception in Israel assumes that peace with Syria would mean peace with all the Arab states and perhaps a final end to the Arab-Israeli conflict.

Q: Why is the first concept wrong? (Give up the Golan Heights or war with Syria is inevitable.)

A: 1. Syria has never fought against Israel alone in the past. In 1948, Syria joined the other Arab states. In 1967, Syria fought alongside Jordan and Egypt. In 1973, Syria joined Egypt with the support of other Arab states.

2. Although Assad and the Syrian regime is radical, unlike Saddam Hussein of Iraq, the Syrians are not foolish. They never took non-calculated risks in the past and it is unlikely they would do so in the future.

3. The Syrians are fully aware that Syria has no chance to win a war against Israel. Why?

   a. Syria does not enjoy the support of what was the former Communist Bloc.

   b. Syria knows that sophisticated weapons cost huge amounts of money that Syria simply does not have.

   c. Syria knows that in a war that she would initiate, she would not enjoy military support of neighboring Arab states such as Jordan and Egypt. Both countries have peace treaties with Israel.

      Therefore, Syria may pay "lip service," but nothing concrete to support or initiate any military confrontation against Israel.

d. If Syria loses a war against Israel, Assad may subsequently lose his regime. The young president belongs to the small *Alawite* minority in Syria. The Sunnite majority would look for any opportunity to topple his regime.

e. Assad knows very well, just like his father before him knew, that on the Golan, Israel has the advantage of being up while his forces are below. Strategically and militarily, this is a huge advantage over Syria.

Q: What are the risks facing Israel should she give up the Golan Heights?
A: Giving up the Golan would amount to taking a non-calculated risk on Israel's part. What would Israel do if, after having withdrawn from the Golan and signing a peace treaty with Syria, a coup d'etat would break out in Syria and a new leader like Saddam Hussein of Iraq would take power? Would Israel send her troops to recapture the Golan Heights, thereby endangering the lives of thousands of her soldiers once again?

Q: What is the difference between the Sinai desert and the Golan Heights?
A: If a coup occurs in Egypt and a new radical regime provokes Israel, Israel would still have time to mobilize her forces. Between Israel and Egypt there is about a 200-mile buffer zone. In the case of Syria, the military surprise would be complete. The distance between Damascus, the Syrian capital, and the Golan is only 30–35 miles.

Q: What is the conclusion?
A: The conclusion is very clear:
1. Assad has no military option, especially when Israel enjoys the strategic advantage over Syria. The concept — that if Israel does not withdraw from the Golan a war will break out — is wrong. Since 1973, the border with Syria has remained very quiet. Assad, just as his father before him, knows quite well why he should maintain this quiet.

2. Syria is a very poor country with very high unemployment and rampant corruption. The last thing Assad needs now is to start war with Israel. Moreover, a little known fact is that the Golan comprises only 1/2 percent (0.5%) of the total Syrian territory.

Q: Why was the second concept wrong? (If there is no peace with Syria, Israeli soldiers will continue to fall in southern Lebanon.)
A: Israel completely withdrew from Lebanon in June 2000. At that time, Israel warned the Lebanese government that if Katyusha rockets fell upon Israel, Israel would retaliate severely and immediately, destroying the power stations that supply electricity to Beirut, the Lebanese capital. Lebanon would be in darkness for months or years to come. Furthermore, if Katyusha rockets fall upon Israel, thousands of rockets would fall upon southern Lebanon in turn. The result would mean hundreds of thousands of Lebanese would flood Beirut and create upheaval in the country.

When the Lebanese saw that Israel would not tolerate any aggression and would react harshly and swiftly to any provocation, they would find the way to stop the Hizbullah terrorists in southern Lebanon. In the meantime, the Hizbullah has been declared a terrorist organization by the United States in the aftermath of the September 11, 2001, attacks.

The conclusion is very clear: There was no connection between the Golan Heights and southern Lebanon. By connecting the Golan with southern Lebanon, Israel was, unwittingly, giving Assad a military and political weapon to use against her. Israel left Lebanon, according to UN Security Council Resolution 425, and at the same time warned the Syrians and the Lebanese about the harsh consequences of any provocation against Israel.

Q: Why is the third concept wrong? (Peace with Syria would mean peace with the Arab states.)
A: The Arab states are not one unit. They each have different interests and different state policies. In 1990, Iraq invaded Kuwait. Between 1981 and 1989, there was a bitter war fought between Iran and Iraq in which hundreds of thousands of Arabs and Moslems died. Since 1948, many wars have been fought between the Arab states.

In light of all this, no one can guarantee that all the Arab states would be willing to sign a peace treaty with Israel, when and if a peace treaty is signed between Israel and Syria.

> *I must tell you quite frankly, and this is very unfortunate, that we are accustomed to this conflict among ourselves in the Arab world. It is not now or the last year or so; it is since history. And we shall always be having these conflicts and difficulties until the end of the world.* — Anwar Al-Sadat, the late former president of Egypt, ABC interview, October 4, 1976

Q: *What does Israeli public opinion say about the Golan?*
A: There are three main views in Israel concerning the Golan. They are:

1. There are those in Israel who say Israel should do nothing. They claim that the Golan Heights is an integral part of Israel. It was formally annexed by the Knesset in 1981 during the late Menachem Begin's term as prime minister. Syria is weak militarily and cannot regain the Golan by force. Sooner or later the Syrians will come to the conclusion that they will have to sign a peace treaty with Israel, just like Jordan, Egypt, and other Arab states in the future.

2. There is a second group in Israel that believes by giving up the Golan Heights to Syria, Israel may achieve a comprehensive peace with Syria, Lebanon, and the Arab world.

3. The third group believes that Israel should give up only a part of the Golan in exchange for peace with Syria.

THE SOLUTION IS ECONOMIC, NOT TERRITORIAL

Q: *What is the economic solution to the Golan Heights?*
A: In my opinion, the solution to the conflict with Syria is not territorial, but economic. With the Syrians, Israel should talk "business." The Golan Heights should be turned into the "Silicon Valley of the Middle East." It could become a huge project employing tens

of thousands of workers: Israelis, Syrians, Jordanians, Palestinians, and many others. Thousands of professionals: engineers, scientists, technicians, and others would be employed in this project.

Q: What would Syria gain from this economic solution?
A: Syria, a very poor country, can benefit from this project. Syria can gain billions of dollars annually from the Golan Heights project, and Israel and the other participants in the project would benefit as well.

Q: Who would back this project financially?
A: The possibilities are many: the United States, the World Bank, rich Arab oil states, the European Union, Israel, private investors, etc.

Q: What would be the role of the settlements of the Golan Heights in this project?
A: The base and infrastructure, upon which this project would be founded, are the existing Israeli settlements and the Druze communities on the Golan Heights today. Not even one single person — Jew, Arab, or Druze — need be removed from his home. To physically remove, uproot, or transfer people from their homes does not spell peace, but just the opposite.

Q: Who would maintain sovereignty over the Golan?
A: The sovereignty over the Golan Heights can be a joint Israeli-Syrian sovereignty, with or without the umbrella support of the United Nations. Other options can be discussed, including the proposal that the sovereignty issue would be discussed in one hundred years from now by our great-grandchildren. Hong Kong is the historical precedent to this idea.

Henry Kissinger, a former U.S. secretary of state, used to say that a good compromise is one that satisfies or dissatisfies all sides equally. This proposal may meet this criterion.

The ultimate goal is that Israel's security be assured and maintained. The Golan Heights will become a source of welfare to Arabs and Jews alike, instead of a threat to Israel.

Syria Used the Golan as a Base for Aggression

Opponents to this proposal may say that the Syrians will reject it. My reaction to this is:

1. We never proposed it before as an option.

2. It will be difficult for the Syrians to accept less than the return of the entire Golan, as promised to them by the late Rabin's government and then by Ehud Barak's government.

3. So what?

Q: What should be done if Syria rejects this economic option?
A: If the Syrians reject this proposal, Israel should exercise patience and explain to them time and again that the benefits from this proposal are worth it.

We have to bear in mind that Syria was the last Arab country to accept UN Resolution 242 of November 22, 1967, and 338 of October 22, 1973.

Syria was the last to accept the cease-fire agreement after the Yom Kippur War in 1973 as well.

Assad — the father — was a very slow thinker, yet he also knew to change his mind when needed. Moreover, when the other side is firm and determined in its position, it may take one year, five years, or even ten, but, sooner or later, the Syrians will come to the conclusion that the best solution is the economic solution and not uprooting people from their homes.

Q: What is the danger to Israel's water supply in case Israel should withdraw from the Golan?
A: The Golan Heights is the source of one-third of Israel's water supply. Israel suffers today already from a serious shortage of water. Why should Israel give Syria the option of cutting her supply of water by completely withdrawing from the Golan?

Q: Does Israel have to withdraw from all of the Golan Heights, according to UN Security Council Resolution 242?
A: The Golan Heights was captured in a war of defense in 1967. The resolution of November 22, 1967, does not speak about Israeli withdrawal from "all" or "the" Arab territories. It is clear that the cease-fire lines of June 4, 1967, were not "secure and recognized borders," to use the language of Resolution 242. By having already withdrawn from the entire Sinai part of Judea and Samaria, Israel has already given up 92 percent of the territory captured in the war

of defense in 1967. Israel has already fulfilled her part of Resolution 242.

Q: What did the British and American ambassadors to the United Nations think about Resolution 242?
A: Lord Caradon, who was the British ambassador to the United Nations in 1967, together with his American counterpart, the late Professor Arthur Goldberg, wrote Resolution 242. Lord Caradon was very familiar with all the discussions concerning the resolution. He said, in the *Beirut Daily Star* on June 12, 1974, "It would have been wrong to demand that Israel return to its positions of June 4, 1967, because those positions were undesirable and artificial. After all, they were just the places where the soldiers of each side happened to be on the day the fighting stopped in 1948. They were just armistice lines. That's why we didn't demand that the Israelis return to them, and I think we were right not to."

Q: Did the Syrians change their mind in the past about disputed territories?
A: Yes. The Syrians are known to have changed their minds when necessary. We have a historical precedent to prove this. In 1938, the Turkish army entered the area of Alexandretta, which was part of Syria, and captured it. The annexation of Alexandretta to Turkey caused an outcry in Syria against Turkey and France. Demonstrations were held demanding the return of the district to Syria. After gaining independence, Syria established diplomatic relations with Turkey. This implied accepting her borders, but, in reality, Syria, to this day, has never recognized Turkish sovereignty over the area. From time to time the issue is raised and Syrian maps still show Alexandretta as part of Syrian territory. The issue remains unresolved to this day.

Q: What is the difference between the Turks and the Israelis?
A: The Turks know how to speak the language that the Syrians understand. The Turks remain threatening and tough with regard to Syria. Israeli leaders are different. Some have said openly that the Golan Heights is an integral part of Syria. Others speak about the fantasy of the "New Middle East." Others speak of a territorial compromise.

Q: Is the threat from the north more serious or less serious than it was before the withdrawal from southern Lebanon?

A: "The potential that exists today in Lebanon is far more grave than it was in the period when we were in the security zone (an Israeli-controlled strip on the Lebanese side of the border). Hizballah, together with the Syrians and the Iranians, has created a strategic threat to the north of the country, which consists of a combination of rockets of various types and various ranges that are threatening Israeli population centers in the north" (Moshe Ya'alon, Israel Chief of Staff, in an interview with Steven Plaut, *Outpost*, September 2002).

> *The U.S will support the position that an overall settlement with Syria in the framework of a peace agreement must assure Israel's security from attack from the Golan Heights. The U.S. further supports the position that a just and lasting peace, which remains our objective, must be acceptable to both sides. The U.S. has not developed a final position on the borders. Should it do so it will give great weight to Israel's position that any peace agreement with Syria must be predicated on Israel remaining on the Golan Heights. My view in this regard was stated in our conversation of September 13, 1974.* — U.S. President Gerald Ford in a letter to the late Israeli Prime Minister Yitzhak Rabin, September 1, 1975

Q: Is Bashar Assad, president of Syria, really more adventurous than his father was?

A: "As the Arabs wrestled with the problem between agreements and the armed struggle, Hafez Assad sat on the fence with both his legs and both his hands in the direction of a settlement. Bashar Assad is sitting on the same fence with both his legs and both his hands on the side of the armed struggle. There is a dramatic difference between the father and his son." — Moshe Ya'alon, Israel chief of staff in an interview with Steven Plaut, *Outpost*, September 2002

The Golan Heights:

- Is Israel's defense line

- Until 1967 was used by Syria to attack Israel

- Controls 30 percent of Israel's water resources

- Has 33 Israeli communities and 18, 000 residents

- Is part of Israel by law

- Is Israel's prime agricultural producer

- Has 2,100,000 visitors annually

SYRIA ON THE GOLAN: HISTORY OF HATRED AND BELLIGERENCE

Blessed be the Lord, my rock, who trains my hands for war and my fingers for battle. — Psalm 144:1–2

Israeli troops captured the Golan Heights during the 1967 Six Day War after bitter fighting. For years, Israeli settlements had suffered from Syrian shelling, which caused many casualties and heavy damages. Israel knew that the only way to release her settlements from the Syrian threat was to capture the Golan Heights.

Syria's loss of the Golan Heights occurred when Hafez al-Assad, the late Syrian president (and father of Bashar al-Assad, Syria's president today), served as minister of defense. As a result, Assad believed that since he was the one to lose the Golan Heights, he had the moral obligation to recapture it from the Israelis. Many of Assad's rivals and enemies frequently mocked him with this expression: *"Assad fi Lubnan waarnab fi al Giulan."* Rhyming in Arabic, this expression means: "You, Assad [Assad means lion in Arabic], are a lion in Lebanon, yet a rabbit on the Golan."

Blow, O wind of the jihad, uproot the children of Zion in the storm and destroy them. — Radio Damascus, May 22, 1981

Q: What marked Syria's control of the Golan Heights for 19 years?
A: From 1948 to 1967, the Golan Heights was exploited by Syria to disrupt civilian life in northeastern Israel by shelling the villages of the Hula Valley and sniping at fishermen on the Sea of Galilee.

Q: Who called for peace during this period?
A: Throughout these 19 years, Israel repeatedly called upon the Syrian leadership, as on the other neighboring Arab states, to turn

the fragile armistice signed in 1949 into a permanent peace settlement. All of these calls were either flatly rejected or ignored altogether.

Q: What exactly was Syria's reaction to the Israeli calls for peace?
A: The Syrian attacks on the Israeli farms and villages continued unabated, The situation reached a point, in June 1967, where Israel was left with no choice but to strike back. Under withering Syrian fire, the Israeli troops scaled the 3,000-foot escarpment of the Golan on June 9, 1967, and engaged the entrenched Syrian forces atop the Heights. After two days of intensive battles, the Golan was in Israeli hands.

Q: What did Israel do after the war?
A: Israel immediately sent signals to all the Arab states that it would be prepared to make substantial withdrawals on all fronts, within the framework of peace negotiations.

Q: What was the reaction of the Arab states?
A: The unanimous Arab answer, given at the notorious Khartoum Summit on September 1, 1967, was the same as before: "No peace with Israel, no recognition of Israel, no negotiations with Israel." This line was to be reiterated by Syrian leaders, with great vigor and persistence, in the years that followed. In October 1973, Syria joined Egypt in a massive surprise attack on Israel — an attack which was beaten back after heavy initial casualties. In November 1977, Egypt announced its readiness to negotiate peace with Israel. The direct talks that ensued led to the conclusion of the Camp David Agreements of September 1978 and to the signing of the Israel-Egypt peace treaty of March 1979. Syria rejected the peace treaty.

Q: What was Syria's reaction then?
A: Syria not only refrained from joining the peace process, but placed itself at the forefront of an all-out Arab campaign designed to stymie that process.

There is no rule of international law which requires a lawful military occupant, in this situation, to wait forever before putting the control and government of the territory on a permanent basis. Many international lawyers have wondered,

indeed, at the long-suffering patience which led Israel to wait as long as she did before establishing that permanent basis.
— Julius Stone, California Hastings College of Law

Q: What was Israel's reaction to Syria's hostility?
A: On December 14, 1981, the Knesset applied the law, jurisdiction, and administration of Israel to the Golan Heights — a move that, by normal criteria of international behavior, was long overdue.

Q: Was the Knesset law proper?
A: Absolutely. Modern history is full of examples of nations altering their borders as a result of victory in war, not to mention wars which they did not initiate. Usually, such changes are ratified in the peace treaties that normally follow these wars.

Q: Does Syria have rights on the Golan?
A: Syria's abnormal behavior over the years — its inveterate belligerence and its longstanding political designs against Israel — bestows no right upon it to maintain a permanent stranglehold on the possibility of normal life in an area that is vital to Israel's security.

> *Before 1967 the Syrian gunners were up on the plateau; their guns could deal death up to a range of 20 miles. No fishing was then possible on the Sea of Galilee, farmers had armor plating on their tractors, and children slept in shelters at night.* — John Bulloch, Middle East correspondent, *Daily Telegraph*, June 1, 1973

Q: The Israeli Golan Heights Law, passed on December 14, 1981, extends Israeli civilian law and administration to the residents of the Golan. This is instead of the military rule that had been in effect on the Golan since 1967. Is this in line with Security Council Resolution 242?
A: Security Council Resolution 242 stressed the need for "secure and recognized boundaries." The former armistice demarcation lines between Israel and Syria were in no sense boundaries, and they certainly were neither secure nor recognized. Ambassador Arthur Goldberg told the Security Council on November 15, 1967, "Historically there have never been secure or recognized

boundaries in the area. Neither the armistice lines of 1949 nor the cease-fire lines of 1967 have answered that description. . . . Now such boundaries have yet to be agreed upon."

> *The Syrian regime is directly involved in the production and marketing of drugs, which are grown and produced in the Beka'a Valley in Lebanon. Publications of the U.S. Enforcement Drugs Agency note that 20 percent of the heroin distributed in the U.S. originates from this area. Therefore, negotiating a contractual peace with Syria demands the utmost caution.* — Golan Heights Committee pamphlet, "The Golan Heights: Important Facts"

The Golan was the biblical home of the tribe of Manasseh. During the Hellenistic period, the Maccabeans protected the numerous Jewish towns and villages in the Golan from marauders. In the revolt against the Romans, Flavius Josephus commanded the defense of northern Israel from the town of Gamla on the Golan.

Gamla was built in 81 B.C.E. by the Hasmonean king, Alexander Yannai. It served as the capital of the Golan for almost 150 years. It was constructed on an outcrop of rock on a steep slope.

In the days of the great revolt against Rome in 66 C.E., Gamla rose up in revolt and heroically staved off two major attacks and a month-long siege. The people of Gamla defended their city until they were forced to the edge of the cliff. The Romans killed 4,000 Jews and another 5,000 were killed fleeing down the slope. Only two women survived.

Josephus recounts the events in detail in his book, *The Wars of the Jews.* Archaeological excavations have revealed a number of unique bronze coins. On one side is a chalice, similar to that found on the shekel coins stamped in Jerusalem. The other side is inscribed in ancient Hebrew with these words: "To the redemption of Jerusalem the holy." These findings and many others attest to the heroic links of Gamla in the north and the campaign to save Jerusalem. Gamla fell in 67 C.E. The Golan was liberated in the Six Day War in 1967.

The history of Jewish habitation on the Golan Heights continued through Byzantine times, until the end of the 11th century. Jewish farming attempts resumed there in the 1880s and continued for some 40 years. In 1967, the Jewish presence on the plateau was reestablished with the founding of a network of farming villages, many on the sites of ancient Jewish towns.

> *The people of Syria are Allah's lash in His land. He wreaks His vengeance through them against whomsoever He wishes among His slaves. It is unthinkable that those who are double faced among them should prosper over the faithful. They will certainly die out of grief and desperation.* — The Islamic holy hadith

Q: *What was the percentage of the Golan Heights of Syria?*
A: The Golan Heights is only 0.5 percent of Syria's 71,498 square miles.

> *A few months before the 1967 war, I was visiting Galilee, and at regular intervals the Russian-built forts on the Golan Heights used to lob shells into the villages, often claiming civilian casualties. Any future pattern for a settlement must clearly put a stop to that kind of offensive action.* — Sir Alec Douglas-Hume, former prime minister of England, *Daily Mail*, April 22, 1974

Q: *What is the size of the Golan Heights?*
A: The Golan is a small plateau 45 miles long, less than 16 miles wide, and totaling only about 450 square miles. The strategic importance of the Golan Heights is out of all proportion to its size. The altitude of the heights ranges from nearly 2,000 to about 3,000 feet above sea level. The Golan overlooks and controls the Sea of Galilee and the Hula Valley.

Q: *Who resides on the Golan?*
A: The population of the region consists of Druze living in four villages, some Alawite Moslems in one village, and Jews living in one town. The main source of income of Golan residents is agriculture. There is also some light industry.

Q: *Is the Golan an integral part of Syria?*
A: Most of the Golan was originally included in the territory of British mandatory Palestine after World War I. However, as a part of a division of colonial spheres of influence in San Remo in 1923, the British transferred it to France, which then had the mandate over Syria.

Q: *What was the Golan considered to be prior to the 1967 war?*
A: Prior to the 1967 war, Syria regarded the area as strictly a military zone and had gravely neglected civilian needs. Most homes had no running water or electricity. School attendance was sporadic at best. Seventy percent of the workers were unskilled. Wages were low, welfare services non-existent, and agriculture primitive.

> *Syria will speak to Israel in the language of iron and fire.*
> — Radio Damascus, December 22, 1980

Q: *What has happened on the Golan since 1967?*
A: 1. Since June 1967, Israel has either connected the Golan villages to its electricity grid or equipped them with modern generators, and has piped in running water.

2. Education is now free and compulsory till the end of the ninth grade. New schools have been built, with books and supplies provided free of charge.

3. Israeli social welfare and national insurance benefits — including medical insurance, three-month paid maternity leave, and old-age pensions — have been extended to the region.

4. Agriculture and construction have flourished, health care improved, and living standards in general have risen dramatically.

5. Religious freedom has replaced the Syrian restrictions on gatherings at Druze shrines and the Druze are now free to conduct their own religious and personal affairs.

On May 31, 1974, Israel and Syria signed a disengagement agreement. Israel agreed to evacuate part of the Golan Heights and security arrangements were put into effect. At that time, Syria confirmed that "this agreement . . . is a step toward a just and durable peace on the basis of Security Council Resolution 338 dated October 22, 1973." In reality, Syria was reluctant to continue the peace process. After repeated declarations by high-ranking Syrian officials that Syria would never make peace with Israel, the Israeli

Parliament passed the Golan Heights Law on December 14 1981, extending Israeli law and administration to the residents of the Golan Heights.

Prime Minister Ariel Sharon expressed his opinion about the strategic importance of the Golan Heights. He said the following in the *Wall Street Journal* on March 27, 2000:

> *Joint deterrence. Israel must retain control of the commanding grounds of the Golan Heights, even after peace with Syria. In fact, there must be a clear link between its final border with Syria and an overall move toward normalization, security, and reconciliation with Israel's entire eastern front (Syria, Iraq, Saudi Arabia, and Jordan).*

It is untenable for Israel to undertake the risk of withdrawal just as threats from Iraq and Iran intensify. Large Iraqi forces fought on the Golan in the 1973 war, while Iran remains a key strategic partner of Syria.

The Golan Heights: Best Guarantee for Secure Borders

With the presence of the Israeli Defense Forces on the Golan Heights, Israel maintains tactical and strategic parity with the Syrian army.

Tactical parity is maintained as a result of the topographical outlay which creates defensible borders. The Yarmuch and Rokad Rivers in the southern portion of the Golan Heights form a natural barrier which is impassable for armored vehicles. It is difficult, as well, for infantry divisions to pass. As a result, Israel maintains a few outposts manned by a relatively small number of troops at this point of the border. To the east and north, the Mt. a-Saki and Mt. Hermon mountain ranges and hills permit a Syrian breakthrough only from a limited number of passes, Therefore, it would be easy to identify any Syrian military build-up and to respond swiftly and accordingly.

No less in importance is the strategic parity created by the presence of the Israeli Defense Forces only 60 kilometers from Syria's capital, Damascus. This alone is a constant deterrent to Syrian aggression.

Any territorial compromise on the Golan Heights would endanger the security of Israel achieved in 1967.

- Do you know that Syria has always been the most intransigent of Israel's enemies? As far back as 1947, the Syrian army attacked Jewish farming villages in the Hula Valley. In May 1948, Syria was among the Arab countries that invaded the newly established state, and Syrian guns on the Golan wrought havoc on the agricultural communities below.

- Do you know that after the war of 1948, Syria was the last of the four countries bordering Israel to sign an armistice? Soon after, it flagrantly violated that agreement when the Syrian army took Al-Hama, in the demilitarized zone, in 1951, as well as by its continued attacks on Israeli civilian life in the valley. Moreover, Syria insisted that cease-fire lines are not permanent borders.

- Do you know that between 1948 and 1967, frequent Syrian artillery shelling from the Golan Heights made life in Israel's Hula Valley villages virtually unbearable? A full generation of children grew up in shelters, under the shadow of the Syrian guns.

- Do you know that beginning in 1964, Syria tried to cut off Israel's principle source of water by attempting to divert the headwaters of the Jordan River, which flow into the Sea of Galilee?

I have personally followed and supported Israel's heroic struggle for survival ever since the founding of the state of Israel 34 years ago. In the pre-1967 borders Israel was barely 10 miles wide at its narrowest point. The bulk of Israel's population lived within artillery range of hostile Arab guns. I am not about to ask Israel to live that way again. — Former U.S. President Ronald Reagan, *Washington Post*, September 2, 1982

- Do you know that Syria was also one of the main sponsors of the PLO terrorist organization, to which it provided political backing, financial support, military equipment, training facilities, and logistics support?

- Do you know that Syria has even established its own terrorist faction within the PLO, *As-Saika*, which is under the direct control of the Syrian army?

- Do you know that Syria was the last Arab confrontation state to accept Resolution 242?

On behalf of all the Arab delegations . . . we now confirm, as we have stated in the past, our non-recognition of the state of Israel. . . . That denial of recognition to that state should be reaffirmed time and time again. — George Tomeh, Syrian representative to the United Nations General Assembly, July 17, 1967

Q: What was the Golan Heights before 1967?
A: Prior to the June 1967 War, the Golan Heights was one of the most massively fortified regions in the world. The terrain was covered by extensive minefields and by three solid lines of heavily armed concrete bunkers connected by trenches. The ascent from the Israeli side was steep and difficult, and anyone attempting it was exposed to heavy Syrian fire from the mountaintops.

Q: When was the Golan captured?
A: On June 9, 1967, Israel launched the counter-attack that finally put an end to the Syrian menace atop the Heights.

Q: What were Syria's true intentions?
A: Among the Syrian Army documents captured there were maps detailing an operational plan for the conquest of northern Israel, up to Haifa. Clear evidence was also found that Soviet military advisers had been stationed in forward positions on the Heights.

. . . even if the PLO recognizes Israel, Syria will not be able to recognize it. — Hafez al-Assad, the late Syrian president, *Al Ra'i Al-amm*, Kuwait, December 13, 1981

Q: What was the size of Syrian military power in 1973?
A: By the outbreak of the 1973 Yom Kippur War, Syria had increased its tank inventory nearly eightfold, to 2,000. Its air force numbered

almost 400 combat aircraft. It had 5 armored and mechanized divisions, 34 surface-to-air missile batteries, and 1,200 artillery pieces.

Q: What was the meaning of Israeli presence on the Golan?
A: It was only Israeli control of the Heights, at the outset of that surprise invasion of 1973, which prevented the Syrians from penetrating deep into Israeli territory and wreaking untold havoc and casualties on Israel's civilian population.

Q: Why is Israel unable to give up the Golan Heights?
A: The fact that some of Israel's main water sources, such as the Banyas River, originate on the Golan Heights is a crucial geophysical factor.

> *No nation is eager for peace more than the Israeli nation and no nation is more ready to sacrifice for survival.*
> — Chaim Herzog, Israeli President

The Golan Heights: Source of Water Supply

It is a fact that the Golan controls 30 percent of all of Israel's water resources. The Sea of Galilee is the source of the National Water Carrier, and provides a third of Israel's water needs. It is fed by the Jordan River and other streams flowing mainly from the Golan Heights.

The Jordan River has three sources:

1. The Hatzbani — which flows from Lebanon (under Syrian control).

2. The Banyas — which flows from the Golan. Any withdrawal from the Golan would place this source under Syrian control.

3. The Dan — which originates near the pre-1967 border.

It is clear, therefore, than any withdrawal from the Golan Heights would endanger Israel's water sources.

Endnotes
1   Harris O. Schoenberg, *A Mandate for Terror* (New York: Shapolsky Publishers, 1989).

THE "ROADMAP": 18 PROBLEMS

American Christian leader Pat Robertson has criticized U.S. President George W. Bush over the roadmap, saying the plan to create a Palestinian state "will be the beginning of the end of the state of Israel as we know it."

Speaking on the Christian Broadcasting Network, which reaches millions of homes across the United States, Robertson said, "I think that the president of the United States is imperiling the nation of Israel. Not only is he going against the clear mandate of the Bible, which is very important, but he's also setting up a situation where Israel will no longer have secure borders."

Describing plans for Israel to give up land to the Palestinians as "insanity," he cited the biblical Book of Joel, which speaks very harshly about "those who divided My land," a reference to the Promised Land.

Robertson added that Israel will be unable to defend itself against "a flood of Palestinians who will be coming in" as a result of the implementation of the roadmap, and said there is no guarantee that the Palestinians will halt terrorism against the Jewish state.

As the founder of the Christian Coalition and a former Republican presidential candidate, Robertson is considered to be one of the most influential Christian leaders in the United States. — Jerusalem Post, June 2, 2003

I. The Main Points of the "Roadmap"

Stage "A" — Until the end of May 2003: A cease-fire, normalization, and building Palestinian institutions

- A declaration, from both sides, on a cease-fire and an end to incitement.

- The Palestinians would end terror attacks and would take preventive measures with regard to future terror attacks. Palestinian forces would undergo reorganization. Israel agrees not to take steps that would undermine the trust between both sides.

- After improvement of security, the Israel Defense Forces would withdraw to the lines that existed prior to the uprising.

- The Palestinian Authority would appoint a prime minister with authority and operative power.

- Israel would reopen the Palestinian institutions that were closed in Jerusalem.

- Israel would remove illegal hilltop communities and would freeze all construction in the settlements.

Stage "B" — Until the end of 2003: The transitional period

- Elections would be held in the Palestinian Authority and an international conference would be convened.

- A Palestinian state with temporary borders would be established.

- The Arab states would renew their relations with Israel to the level prior to the uprising.

- An additional Israeli withdrawal and perhaps the removal of some settlements.

- The international "quartet" — the United States, the United Nations, the European Union, and Russia — will endorse acceptance of the Palestinian state in the United Nations.

- Security cooperation between Israel and the Palestinians would continue.

Stage "C" — 2004–2005: The permanent solution and an end to the conflict

- A second international conference would convene to confirm the permanent solution.

- The parties would end the occupation that began in 1967, they will agree about a solution to the refugee problem, Jerusalem, and would fulfill the vision of two states: Israel and Palestine.

- The Arab states will agree to have diplomatic relations with Israel.

Benjamin Netanyahu, former Israeli prime minister, wrote the following to all members of the Likud Party Central Committee (Sharon and Netanyahu's party):

We will demand to drop the right of return, no dismembering of [Jewish] settlements, not to touch the unity of Jerusalem, to destroy the terrorist organizations, and in any case we will have in our hands sovereign authorities in Judea, Samaria and Gaza, such as to control the passages and the air space and we will insist that the Palestinian Authority be fully demilitarized. — June 2, 2003

The following are the 18 problems created by the "roadmap" thereby dereasing drastically the chances of its success:

1. To stop the incitement against Israel

For over a century the Palestinians have continually spread hatred and have killed innocent Israelis. This atmosphere of hostility and animosity cannot be altered and removed within a short period. To educate the Palestinian Arabs to relinquish their hatred and to begin behaving like a normal, civilized people will take many years. Education for peace and tolerance is a mission of many years.

2. The creation of a Palestinian state

Who will guarantee that such a state, once established, will not pose a mortal danger to Israel? Through the years, Israel and the world have come to know the true face of Yassir Arafat and most of his colleagues. Why should Israel be expected to trust the words of Arafat, who, time and again, has violated all his signed agreements with Israel?

3. International conferences

The "roadmap" calls for two international conferences. The first was to be in 2003 following elections in the Palestinian Authority. The goal of the conference was "initiating negotiations leading to declaration of a Palestinian State with temporary borders."

Scheduled for 2004, the second international conference intends to give final approval to a Palestinian state with temporary borders and to initiate talks for a permanent agreement.

Israel has had bad experiences with international conferences. Unlike the Americans, who may be honest brokers, most of the other parties have proven in the past, time and again, that they are biased and almost always favor the Arabs. International conferences and their decisions will be rejected by Israel. After all, the United Nations once equated Zionism to racism by vote.

4. To reward terrorists is morally wrong

Arafat and his colleagues have proved that there is no value to their commitments. They started the uprising of September 2000. The tragic results have been thousands of casualties among Israelis as well as Palestinians. Why should Yassir be rewarded by granting him a Palestinian state?

By its insistence on establishing a Palestinian state, the "roadmap" would be proving that terror does indeed pay off, by the fact that Arafat began the bloodshed and achieved a state.

5. Disregarding the Israeli reservations

There is no mention in the "roadmap" of all the Israeli reservations, such as: demilitarization of the Palestinian state, Israeli control of air space, the control of territorial passages, etc.

6. The Jewish character of the state of Israel

There is no mention in the "roadmap" of the Jewish character of the state of Israel. On the other hand, Israel is required to accept an ethnic Palestinian state without Jews. This means, therefore, there will be a purely Arab Palestinian state alongside the binational state of Israel. Then the world will be expected to deal with the Jewish "problem" in Palestine, rather than the Arab Palestinian one in Israel.

7. The right of return

Israel considers the Palestinian right of return a mortal danger. The "roadmap" mentions the Saudi initiative which speaks about the solution of the refugee problem, according to United Nations Resolution 194 (see section about Resolution 194 in this book).

If the Palestinians insist on demanding the right of return, that would mean the total failure of the whole process.

8. A return to the risky borders of June 4, 1967

Israel can, by no means, return to the very dangerous lines of June 4, 1967. The late Abba Eban, former foreign minister of Israel, coined those lines as "Auschwitz borders." Israel cannot defend herself from these lines. Moreover, the Arabs have no right to demand Israel's return to these lines since they started the war from these lines and subsequently lost them.

9. Jerusalem

The "roadmap" gives equal rights to both sides with regard to Jerusalem. This means dividing, once again, the capital of Israel. It also insists that Israel reopen the closed Palestinian institutions in Jerusalem. This will be rejected by Israel. Jerusalem is the capital of Israel and it is indivisible.

10. Bypassing Israel's Judgment

The quartet is the instrument by which the sovereign Palestinian state is to be established. The quartet, with its representatives from the United States, the United Nations, the European Union, and Russia, is to have supreme decision making control. It will:

a. decide when conditions are right for progress. In other words, this foreign body will decide when to recognize a Palestinian state. This ultimately bypasses Israeli's precondition that all progress be determinant on Israel's judgement. This would take into account factors such as the cessation of terror, the collection of illegal armaments, the end of incitement, etc. In short, Israel's decision-making control is severely limited, if existant at all.

b. initiate an international observer force to examine Israeli-Palestinian progress. It is a fact that Israel has not undertaken major military actions against the provocations of the Palestinian Authority since the outset of the uprising. This was done in order to prevent the implementation of an international observer force in Judea, Samaria, and Gaza.

c. guarantee that both sides to the conflict implement all obligations simultaneously. This is in direct contradiction to Israel's requirement that any Israeli implementation would occur only after full implementation by the Palestinians.

11. To freeze settlements

According to the "roadmap," Israel must freeze all settlement activity, including any natural growth of existing communities. It also requires that priority must be given to a freeze in areas which may threaten contiguously populated Palestinian regions, including areas around Jerusalem. This means that Israel must demand that her people stop getting married, that they stop raising children, and perhaps they should stop breathing altogether. This demand is simply unrealistic.

12. Terror vis-à-vis settlements

The "roadmap" equates the Palestinian obligation to end terror to Israel's obligation concerning settlement activity. With the signing of the Oslo Agreement in September 1993, Yassir Arafat agreed to and promised that any political differences with Israel would be resolved by direct negotiations rather than by terror. Israel should not pay twice for the same promise that has been violated innumerable times. Terror has nothing whatsoever to do with settlements.

13. No direct negotiations

For many years, Arabs have tried to avoid direct negotiations with Israel preferring an imposed solution. According to the "roadmap," the quartet will be directly involved in all negotiations between the two sides. This demand thereby negates a cardinal Israeli rule which insists upon direct negotiations between the sides.

Moreover, the quartet is to be involved in all facets of a Palestinian transition to statehood, including: financial, legal, administrative, and security issues.

14. Uprooting settlements

The "roadmap" demands that as the declaration of a Palestinian state draws near, Israel must allow maximum geographic contiguity. This includes further measures on Israel's part with regard to settlements. This infers the uprooting of settlements that interrupt Palestinian territorial contiguity.

The transfer of people from their homes — Jews or Arabs alike — is not a solution. Whoever truly believes in peace should let Jews and Arabs live side by side in Judea, Samaria, and Gaza just as Palestinian Israeli Arabs live today in Haifa, Jaffa, Lod, and other Israeli cities (see secton "Settlements promote peace").

15. The Saudi initiative

The Saudi initiative was adopted at the Beirut Arab League Summit in March 2002. It was renamed the "Arab Peace Initiative" and it calls for

> . . . full Israeli withdrawal from all the territories occupied since 1967, including the Syrian Golan Heights to the June 4, 1967 lines, achievement of a just solution to the Palestinian refugee problem to be agreed upon in accordance with UN General Assembly Resolution 194 — refugees wishing to return to their homes and live at peace with their neighbors should be permitted to do so at the earliest practicable date — and the acceptance of the establishment of a sovereign independent Palestinian state on the Palestinian territories occupied since June 4, 1967, in the West Bank and Gaza Strip, with East Jerusalem as its capital.

It is clear that if the Saudi initiative be accepted, it will be the main obstacle to achieving peace with the Palestinians. Israel rejects all the conditions mentioned in the initiative — mainly, withdrawal to the ridiculous and vulnerable lines prior to the Six Day War of June 1967, acceptance of the Palestinian refugees, and dividing Jerusalem and thereby establishing East Jerusalem as the capital of the Palestinian state.

16. Leaving the main issues to the final talks

The main issues are:

a. Jerusalem
b. Palestinian refugees

c. the settlements

d. the final and permanent borders of Israel and the Palestinian state

With regard to these issues, the gap between the parties is huge and almost unbridgeable. Israel should not make any concessions before the Palestinians understand that Israel has her limits. Israel will not agree to make concessions at the outset of negotiations only to find herself "stuck" with the heavy issues at the end.

17. Mutuality

Israel is a democratic sovereign state with legal, effective, and elected institutions. The Palestinian Authority is a terrorist authority. There is no mutuality. Israel has always and will always respect its commitments. Arafat and his colleagues have proved, time and again, that they cannot be trusted. The "roadmap" approaches both sides as equal partners. This is wrong and unfair.

18. Free and open elections

The "roadmap" speaks about free and open elections amongst the Palestinians. However, it fails to mention what should be done if the Hamas and Islamic Jihad terrorist groups win the elections. The Europeans, as well as the Americans, do not know the Arab psyche, mentality, and way of thinking. They may be wrong if they judge the Arabs by their Western standards. Arabs are not Westerners. However well intended, the Americans and Europeans may give Israel the wrong advice and, if accepted, Israel may find herself in grave trouble. Israel, and only Israel, knows what is best for her and her people. Israel must be free to make decisions void of pressure. After all, Israel has never and will never ask others to send troops to defend her.

In light of all these obstacles, can any objective observer be sure as to the outcome? I doubt it.

For Zion's sake I will not be silent and for Jerusalem's sake I will not rest. — Isaiah 62:1

CONCLUSION

In May 1981, Israel bombed and destroyed the Iraqi French-made nuclear reactor called "Osirak." Israel was condemned by the United Nations Security Council for its "aggression" against "peaceful" Iraq. Moreover, the Security Council resolution, supported by the United States, called upon Israel to pay compensation for the damage it caused Iraq.

On August 2, 1990, Saddam Hussein, the Iraqi dictator, invaded and occupied neighboring Kuwait. The international community was shocked and taken by surprise. The United Nations Security Council demanded complete Iraqi withdrawal from Kuwait, yet Saddam Hussein refused. As a result, the United States, joined by a coalition of other nations, sent about half a million troops to the Arab peninsula in order to oust the Iraqi invading army from Kuwait. The coalition forces won the war against Hussein and the Iraqi forces withdrew suffering a severe blow and a crushing defeat.

Imagine the worst horror scenario that would have threatened the coalition troops in 1990–91, had Israel not had the foresight to destroy the Iraqi nuclear reactor nine years before. Perhaps Israel saved the lives of hundreds of thousands.

In the aftermath of the September 11, 2001, tragedy, which resulted in the death of thousands of Americans in one day, the world in general and the United States in particular woke up to a horrifying and shocking reality. The subsequent terror attacks that occurred in different parts of the world before and after the 9/11 attacks have made it clear to the world at large that fanatic Islam is the source of terror and destruction and that it must be stopped.

The leaders of this form of fanatic Islam are dictators and murderers. The list includes: Osama Bin-Laden; Yassir Arafat, leader of the PLO; Ali Haminai of Iran; Bashar Assad of Syria; Hassan Nasrallah, the fanatic leader of the Hizballah in Lebanon; as well as many others. Moreover, there are thousands of Islamic "spiritual" leaders all over the world, who, day and night, preach hatred, warfare, the shedding of blood, and suicide bombing in order to kill and maim anyone not a Moslem. According to these notorious religious leaders, a non-Moslem is an enemy of Islam and an infidel.

For many years, Israel, who suffered time and again from Palestinian Islamic terror, found it difficult to convince others about the impending dangers. The events of September 11, 2001, irrevocably changed the atmosphere. Since 9/11, more and more people the world over have come to realize the threat and danger of fanatic Islamic terror. Such terror can target any person anywhere across the globe.

One can only imagine the havoc these fanatic terrorists can wreak upon the world should they succeed to put their hands on nuclear weapons. These zealous Moslems, using the name of Islam in vain and screaming "Allahu Akbar" ("God is great"), would not hesitate for a second to use weapons of mass destruction to kill millions of innocent people in the world. The unfathomable belief that by doing so they will enjoy the light of Paradise, convinces them to carry out such heinous acts. The message to the world is clear: whoever is capable of killing thousands of innocent people in the United States will not hesitate to murder millions more.

Fortunately, the United States, the only remaining superpower in the world, decided to act in order to face these global threats, to destroy the infrastructure of these terrorist networks and their bases and to act against countries that harbor or support these terrorists.

As in the past, there are other countries which, for the sake of their own selfish interests, may oppose the goal of the United States to defeat world terrorism. Yet even these countries will know, sooner or later, that they may find themselves the victims of their short-sighted policies. There should not and cannot be any negotiations with terrorists. The only language understood by such terrorists is the language of power. These terrorists must be destroyed before they kill other innocent people. It is no surprise, therefore, that Saudi Arabia, the country from which 15 of the 19 terrorists of the 9/11 attacks originate, was the victim of terrorist attacks as well. The lesson is clear: whoever harbors, supports, or allows these fanatic Moslems to prosper within its borders, may find itself the victim of such attacks.

Israel is the only democracy in the Middle East and is the staunchest ally of the United States. Israel has sought peace with her neighbors since her establishment in 1948. The events following the signing of the Oslo Agreement in 1993 have proven that Arafat and his colleagues do not want peace with Israel. Instead, they want Israel piece by piece. They claim in their propaganda that Israel is being provocative. In reality, Israel's being is provocative.

The ultimate victory of Western civilization over fanatic Islam, the removal of Islamic dictators, terrorists, fanatic preachers and others, may prove to be a ray of hope for the free world. Such hope would provide a better future for the world in general and for Israel and her struggle for peace in particular.

A great sage once said, "Even should a sharp sword be directed against the neck of a person, he or she should not lose hope, because the salvation of the Almighty is like the blink of an eye."

Bibliography

Answers to Frequently Asked Questions. Israeli Ministry of Foreign Affairs, April 2001.

Ben-Gad, Yitschak. *Politics, Lies and Videotape: 3000 Questions and Answers on the Mideast Crisis.* New York: Shapolsky Publishers, 1991.

Emerson, Steven. *American Jihad: The Terrorists Living Among Us.* New York: Free Press, 2002.

The Future of the Israeli Settlements in Final Status Negotiations. Jerusalem: Final Status Publications Series, 1997.

The Golan Heights Important Facts. Golan Residents Committee, 1997.

Hizballah. Israeli Ministry of Education, 2002.

The Involvement of Arafat, Palestinian Authority Senior Officials and Apparatuses in Terrorism Against Israel, Corruption and Crime. Prime Minister's Office Publication. Spring 2002.

Israel News. Kansas City, KS: National Unity Coalition for Israel.

Israeli dailies: *Ma'ariv, Ha'aretz, Yediot Acharonot, Jerusalem Post.*

The *Jewish Political Chronicle.* Great Neck, NY.

Kaufman, Dr. Jerome S. Editorial. Zionist Information News Service, August 2002.

Marcus, Dr. Itamar. Palestinian Media Watch.

The Middle East Peace Process. Israeli Foreign Office Publication.

The National Unity Coalition for Israel Publications. Kansas City, KS.

The *New York Times*

Outpost. Monthly publication. Americans for a Safe Israel.

Palestinian Authority and PLO Non-Compliance — A Record of Bad Faith. Israeli Foreign Office Publication. November 2000.

Roumani, Dr. Maurice. *The Case of Jews from Arab Countries: A Neglected Issue.* Tel Aviv, 1983.

Z.O.A., Zionist Organization of America publications.